UNCANNY X-MEN

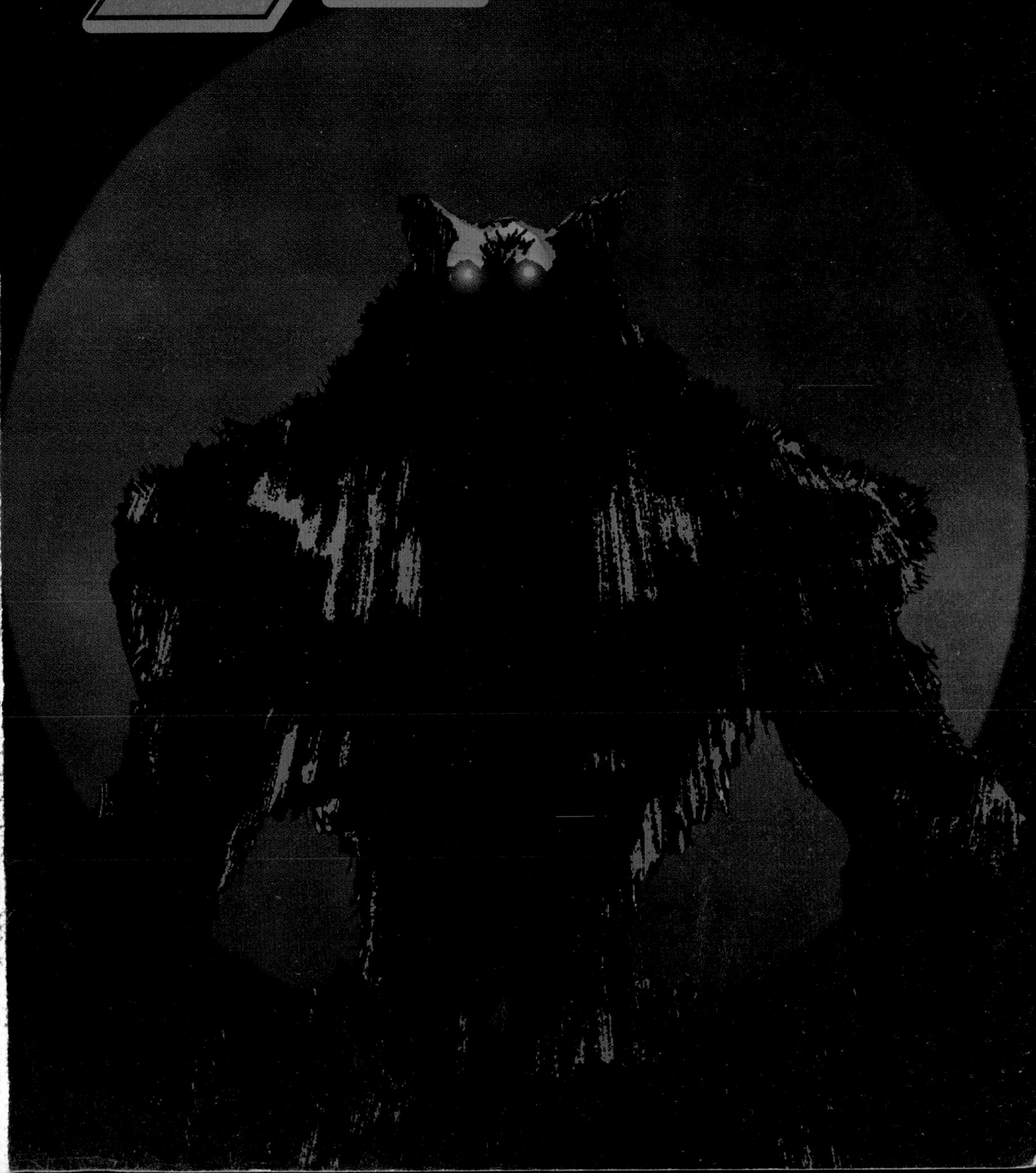

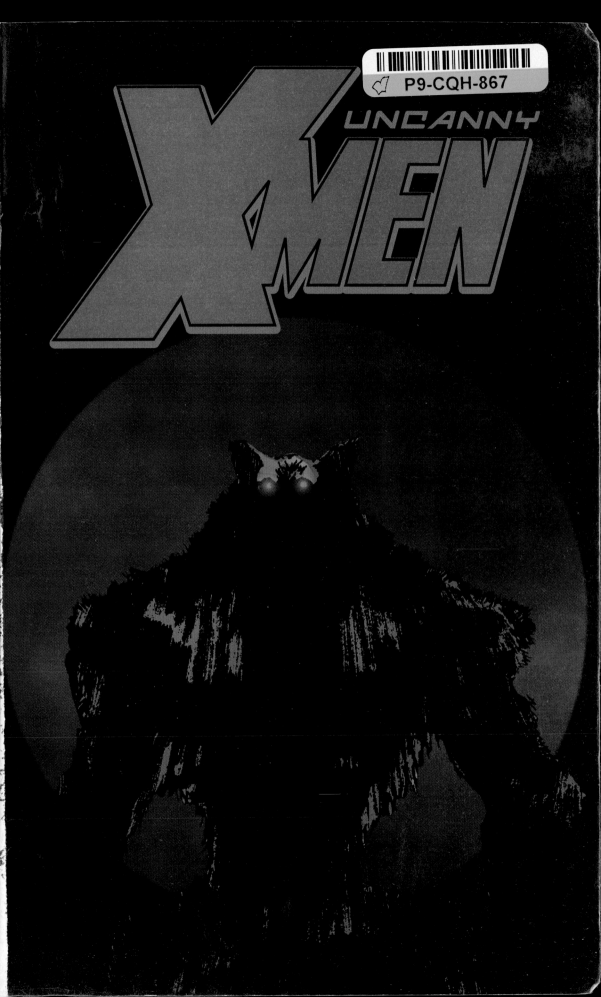

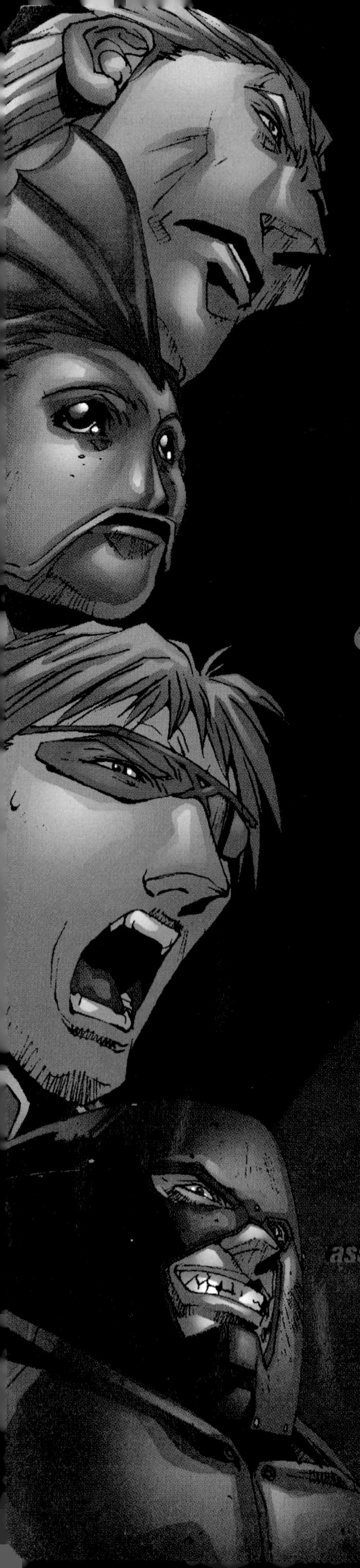

story **CHUCK AUSTEN**
art **KIA ASAMIYA**

colors **JD SMITH**
letters **PAUL TUTRONE**
assistant editors **MIKE RAICHT & NOVA REN SUMA**
editor **MIKE MARTS**

colletions editor **JEFF YOUNGQUIST**
assistant editor **JENNIFER GRÜNWALD**
book designer **JEOF VITA**

editor in chief **JOE QUESADA**
puslisher **DAN BUCKLEY**
special thanks to
C.B. CEBULSKI and **AKI YANAGI**

UNCANNY
X-MEN
DOMINANT SPECIES

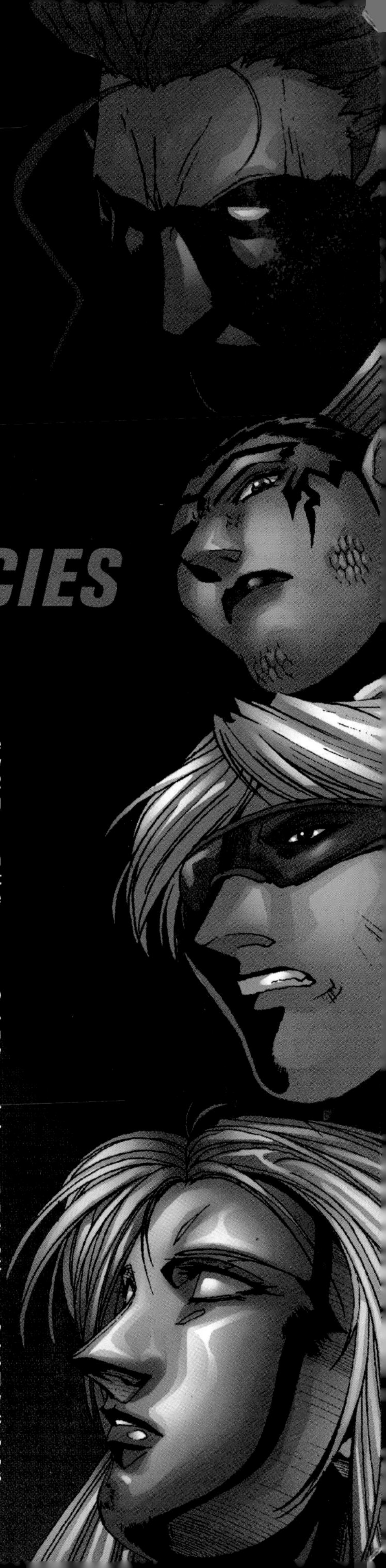

PREVIOUSLY IN UNCANNY X-MEN

The X-Men, a group of heroes with strange mutant powers, are forever sworn to protect a world that hates and fears them. They have been called together by their mentor, PROFESSOR CHARLES XAVIER, to fight the neverending battle of promoting unity between humans and mutantkind.

Their headquarters, the Xavier Institute for Higher Learning in upstate New York, was once Professor Xavier's family estate, but is now a school organized to teach mutants of all ages how to use their powers responsibly.

Recently, there have been some new additions to Xavier's …

NORTHSTAR, a former member of the Canadian super-group Alpha Flight, was recruited by Professor X to teach at the school. But no sooner did Northstar accept Xavier's offer to join the X-Men than he was immediately injured, landing himself in the infirmary under the care of the new school nurse, Annie Ghazikhanian.

ANNIE, who endured a long, unrequited crush on one of her comatose patients, ended up following that patient to the Xavier Institute when he turned out to be the long-lost X-Man HAVOK.

STACY X was a prostitute at a mutant brothel called the X-Ranch long before she came to Xavier's and began joining the X-Men on missions. She's been having a hard time of late fitting in at the school. Her advances toward ARCHANGEL have been rebuffed, and on a recent mission, her snake-like skin began shedding out of control.

But the most surprising newcomer of all is the JUGGERNAUT, Professor Xavier's step-brother and—until recently—sworn enemy. As the Juggernaut, Cain Marko has tried to kill Xavier on numerous occasions. It was only lately, when his powers were weakened and his will to live nearly destroyed, that Cain began to turn over a new leaf. In a moment of life-or-death under the waters of the Atlantic Ocean, one of Xavier's new students, a young boy named SAMMY, swam underwater to save Cain from an untimely end. Shockingly, Professor X ended up inviting his step-brother to make Xavier's his temporary home …

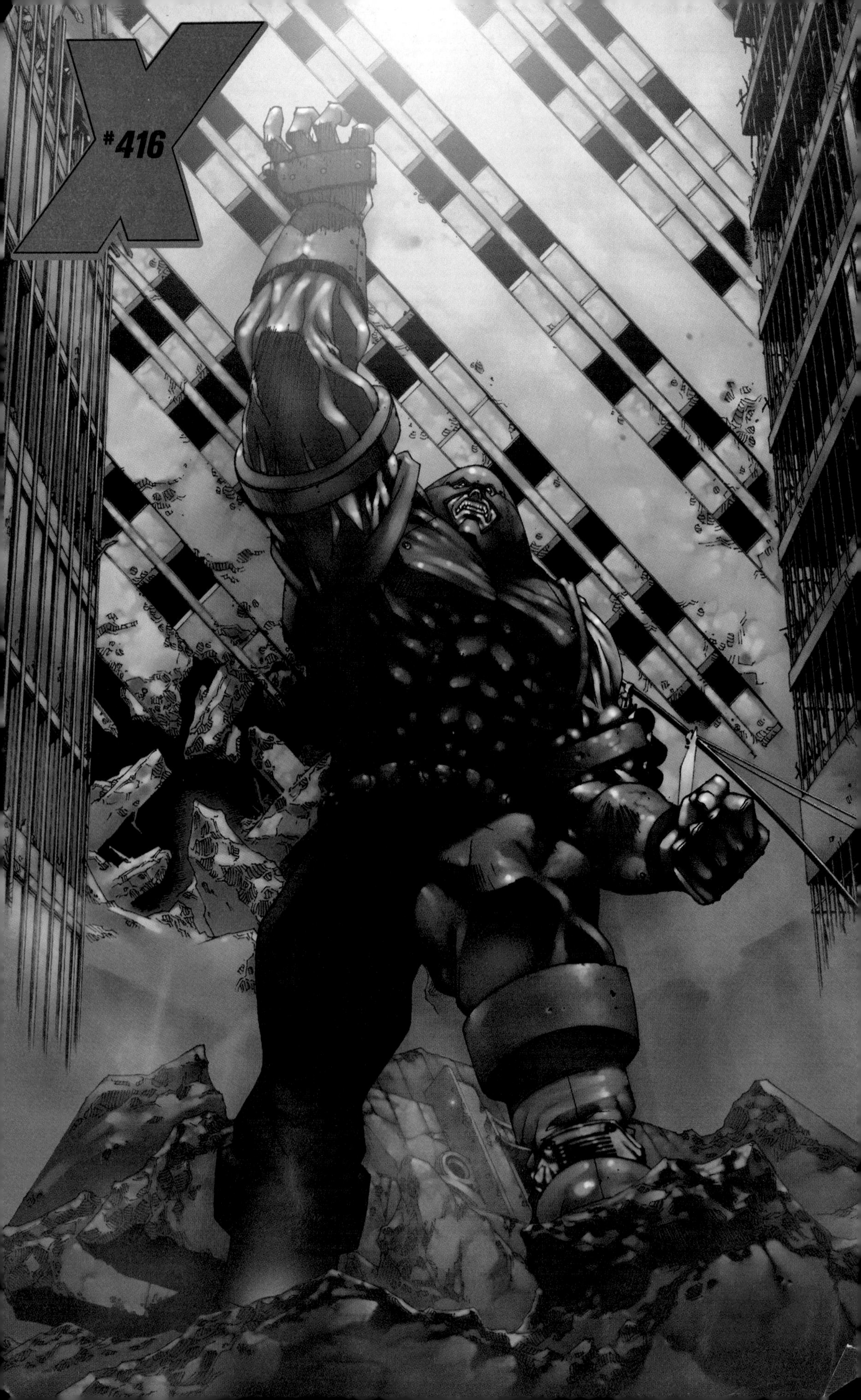
X
#416

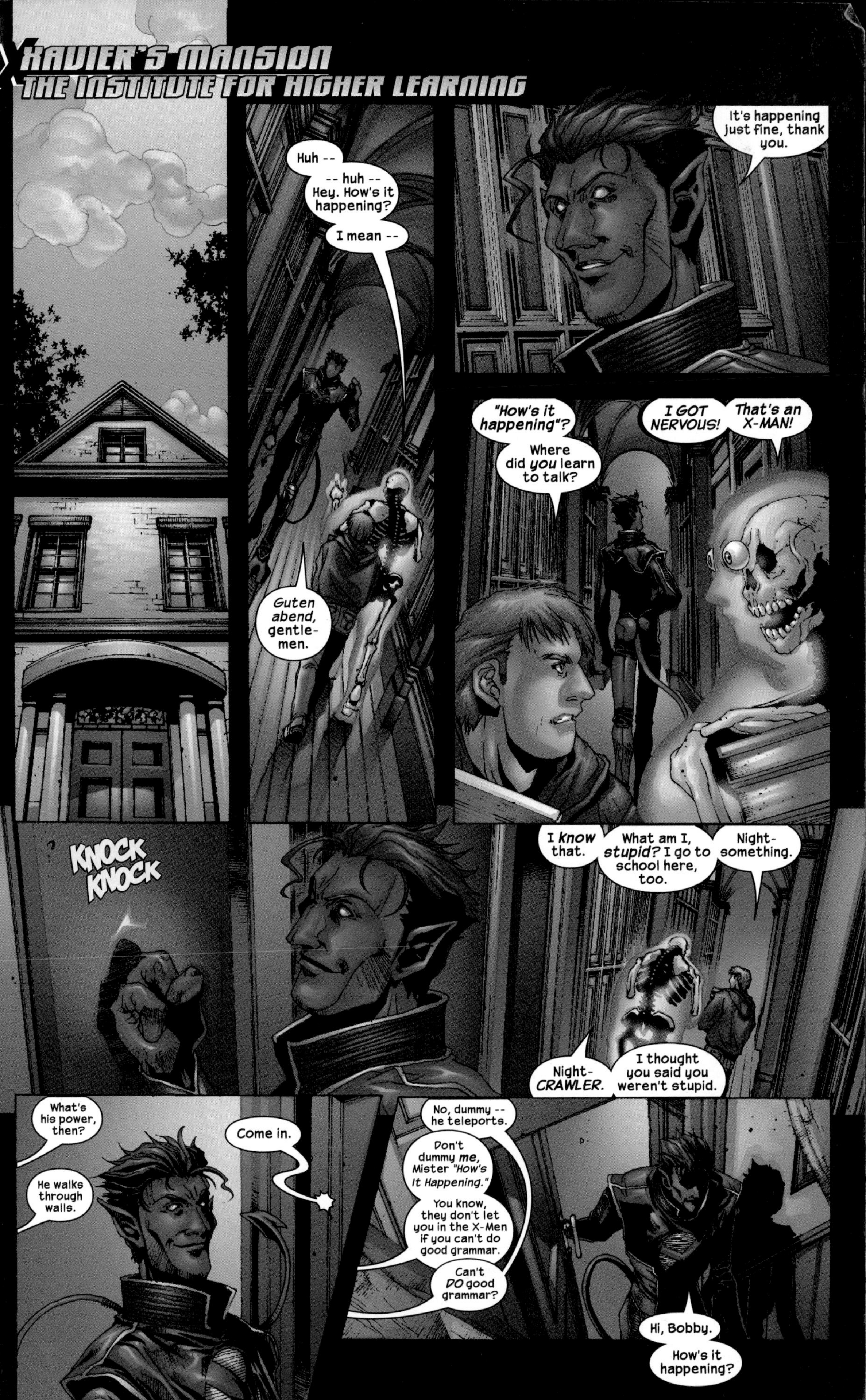
XAVIER'S MANSION
THE INSTITUTE FOR HIGHER LEARNING
Huh --
-- huh -- Hey. How's it happening?
I mean --
Guten abend, gentle-men.
It's happening just fine, thank you.
"How's it happening"?
Where did you learn to talk?
I GOT NERVOUS!
That's an X-MAN!
KNOCK KNOCK
I know that.
What am I, stupid? I go to school here, too.
Night-something.
Night-CRAWLER.
I thought you said you weren't stupid.
What's his power, then?
He walks through walls.
Come in.
No, dummy -- he teleports.
Don't dummy me, Mister "How's It Happening."
You know, they don't let you in the X-Men if you can't do good grammar.
Can't DO good grammar?
Hi, Bobby.
How's it happening?

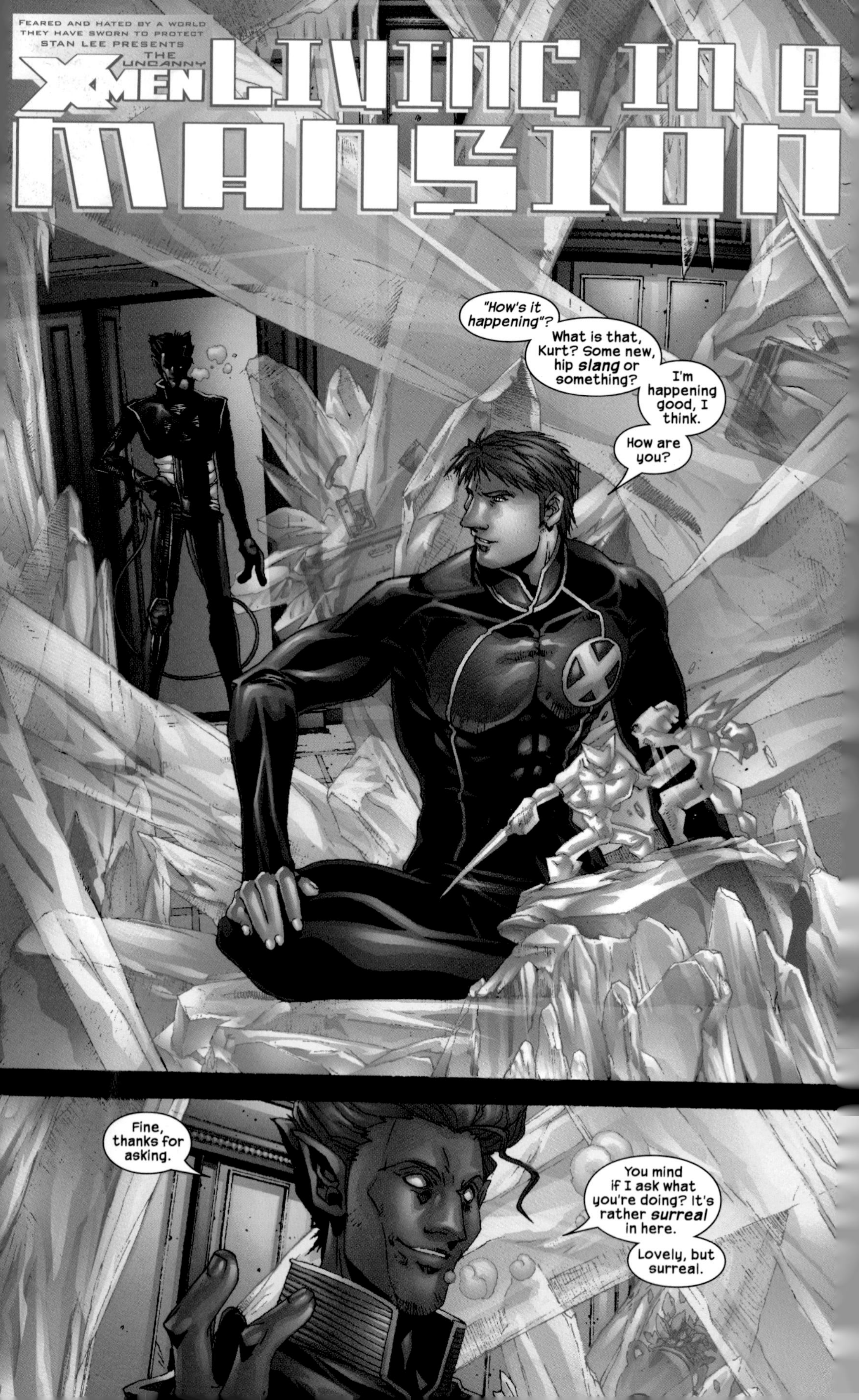
FEARED AND HATED BY A WORLD THEY HAVE SWORN TO PROTECT
STAN LEE PRESENTS
THE UNCANNY X-MEN
LIVING IN A MANSION
"How's it happening"?
What is that, Kurt? Some new, hip *slang* or something?
I'm happening good, I think.
How are you?
Fine, thanks for asking.
You mind if I ask what you're doing? It's rather *surreal* in here.
Lovely, but surreal.

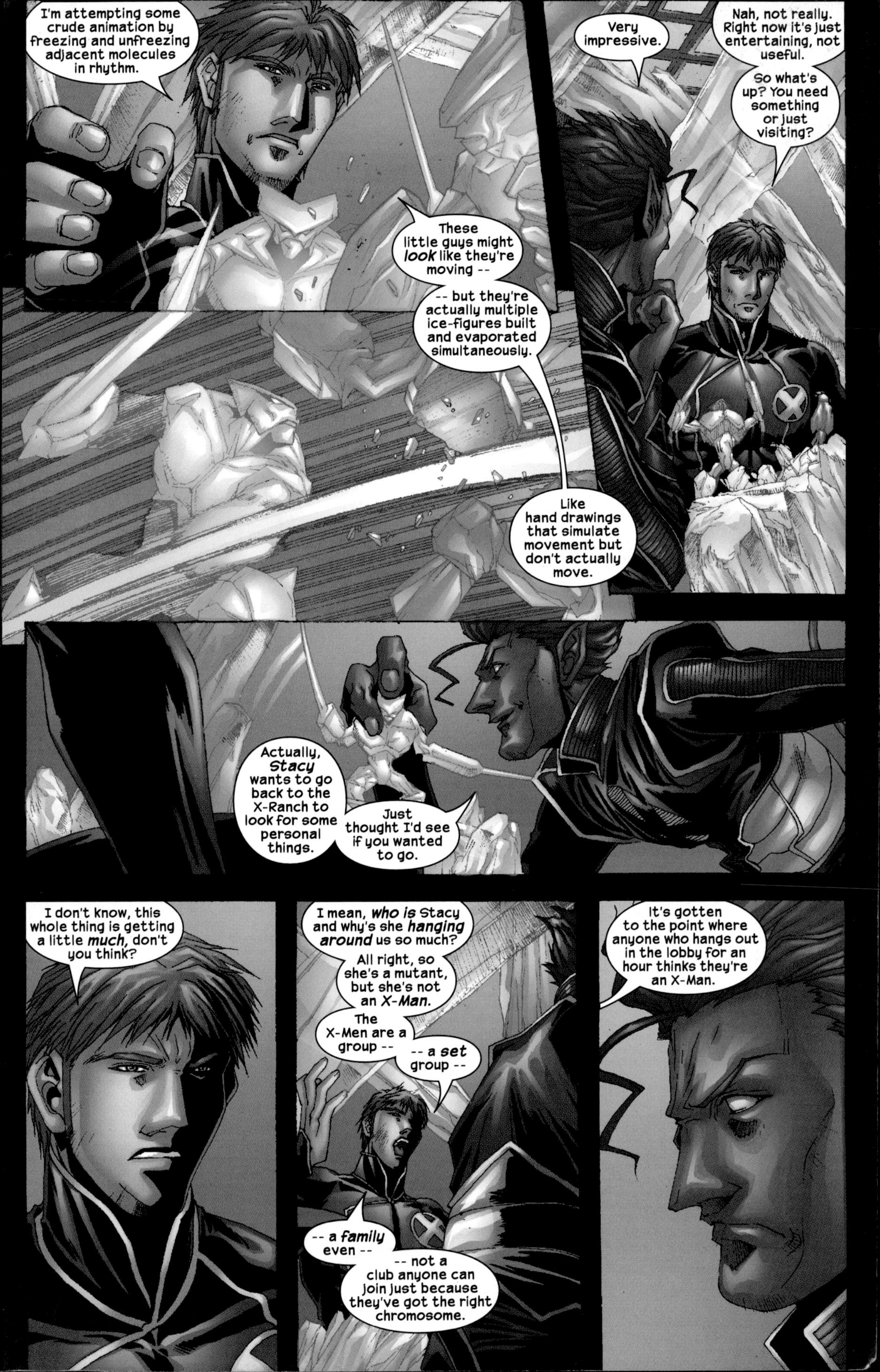
I'm attempting some crude animation by freezing and unfreezing adjacent molecules in rhythm.
These little guys might *look* like they're moving --
-- but they're actually multiple ice-figures built and evaporated simultaneously.
Like hand drawings that simulate movement but don't actually move.
Very impressive.
Nah, not really. Right now it's just entertaining, not useful.
So what's up? You need something or just visiting?
Actually, *Stacy* wants to go back to the X-Ranch to look for some personal things.
Just thought I'd see if you wanted to go.
I don't know, this whole thing is getting a little *much*, don't you think?
I mean, *who is* Stacy and why's she *hanging around* us so much?
All right, so she's a mutant, but she's not an *X-Man.*
The X-Men are a group --
-- a *set* group --
-- a *family* even --
-- not a club anyone can join just because they've got the right chromosome.
It's gotten to the point where anyone who hangs out in the lobby for an hour thinks they're an X-Man.

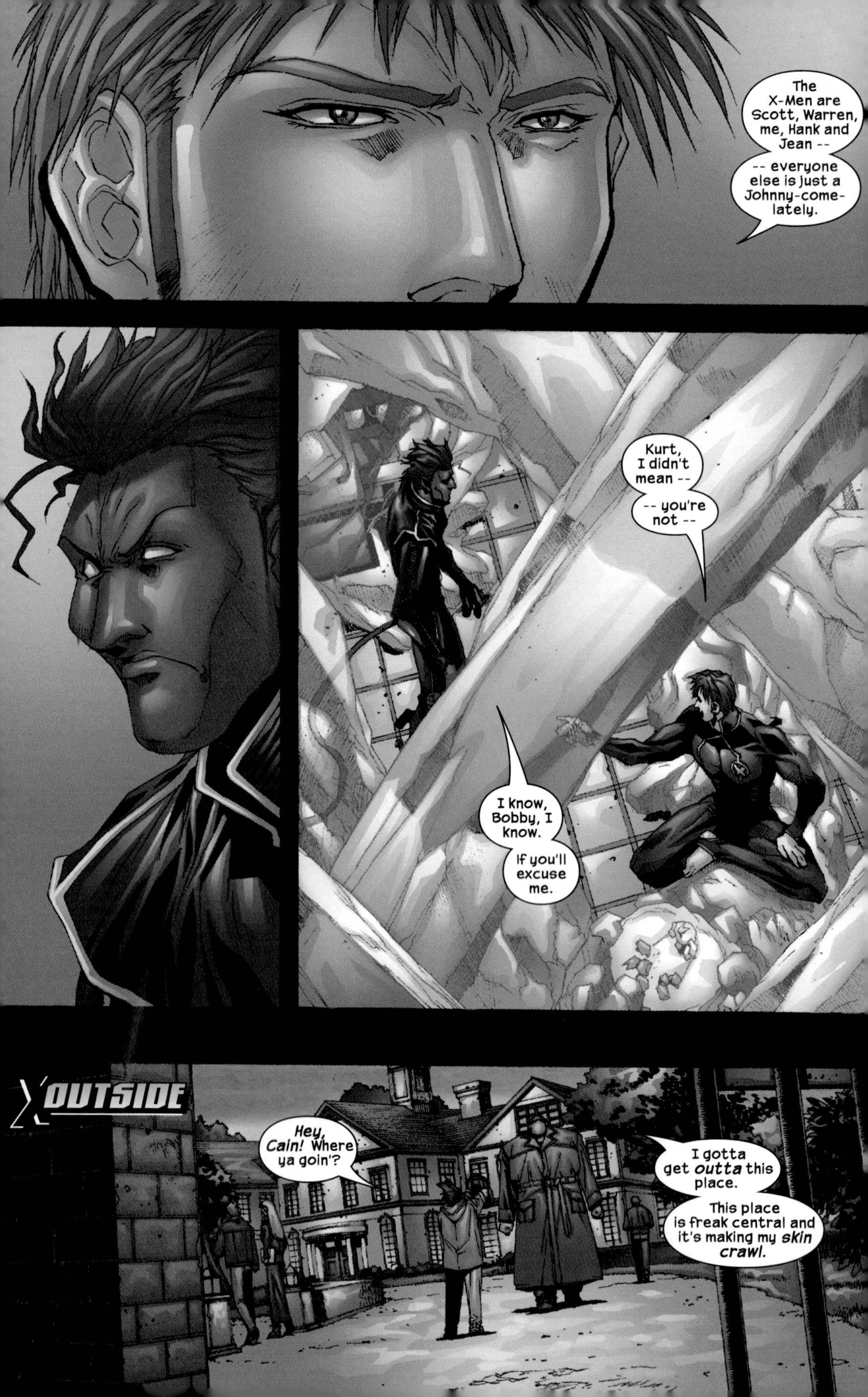
The X-Men are Scott, Warren, me, Hank and Jean --
-- everyone else is just a Johnny-come-lately.
Kurt, I didn't mean --
-- you're not --
I know, Bobby, I know.
If you'll excuse me.
OUTSIDE
Hey, Cain! Where ya goin'?
I gotta get outta this place.
This place is freak central and it's making my skin crawl.

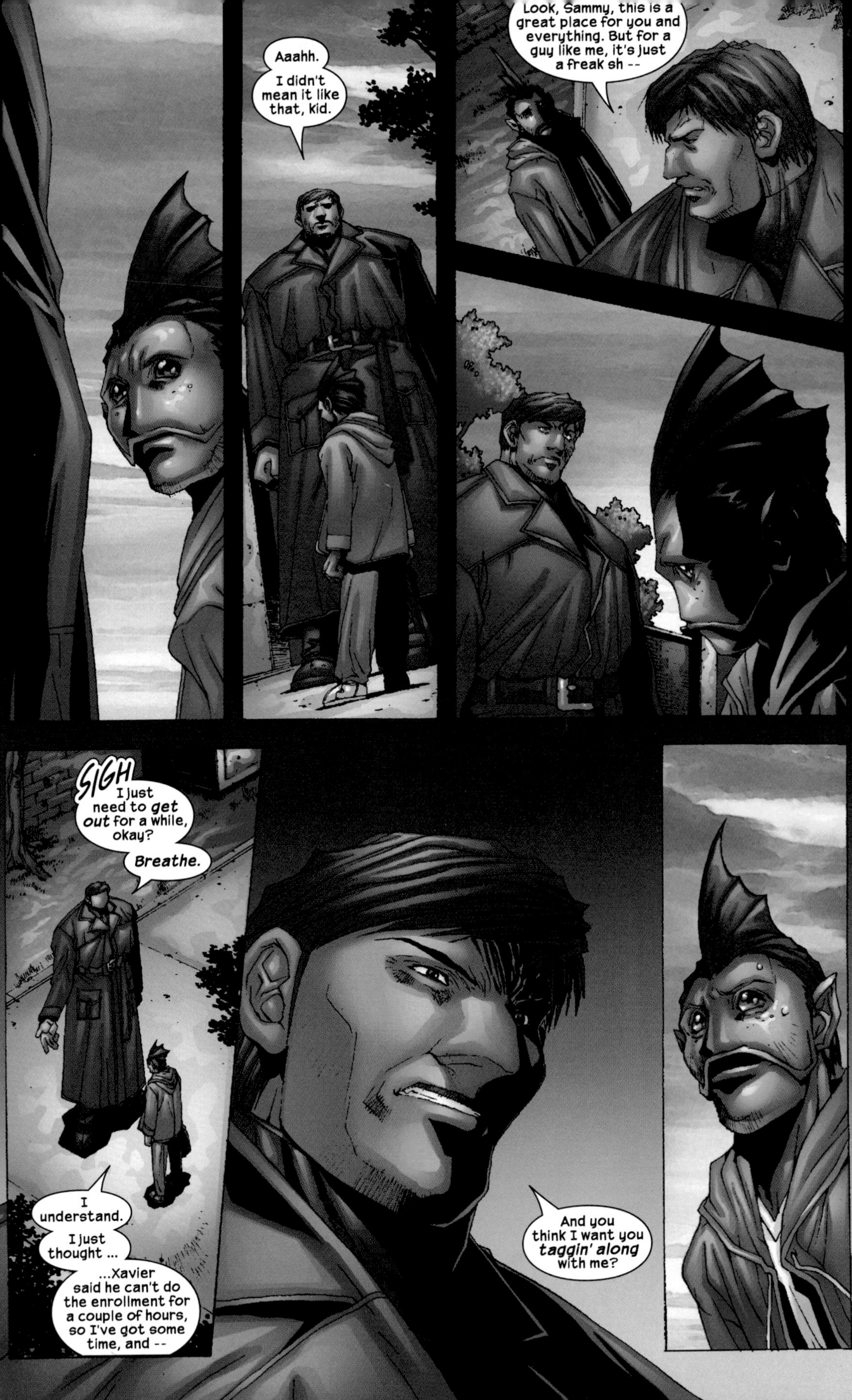
Aaahh.
I didn't mean it like that, kid.
Look, Sammy, this is a great place for you and everything. But for a guy like me, it's just a freak sh --
SIGH
I just need to *get out* for a while, okay?
Breathe.
I understand.
I just thought ...
...Xavier said he can't do the enrollment for a couple of hours, so I've got some time, and --
And you think I want you *taggin' along* with me?

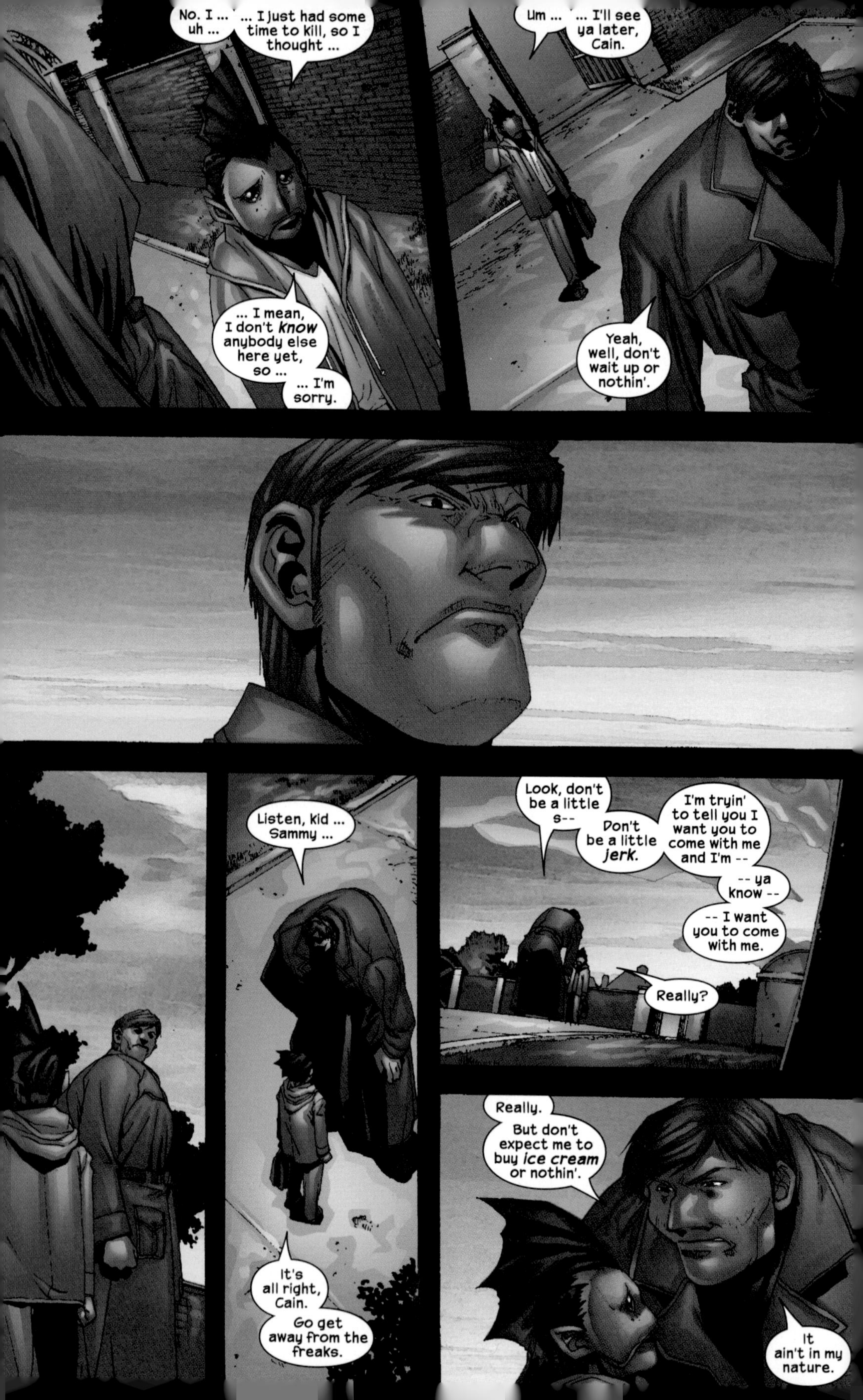
No. I ... uh ...
... I just had some time to kill, so I thought ...
... I mean, I don't *know* anybody else here yet, so ...
... I'm sorry.
Um ...
... I'll see ya later, Cain.
Yeah, well, don't wait up or nothin'.
Listen, kid ... Sammy ...
It's all right, Cain.
Go get away from the freaks.
Look, don't be a little s--
Don't be a little *jerk*.
I'm tryin' to tell you I want you to come with me and I'm --
-- ya know --
-- I want you to come with me.
Really?
Really.
But don't expect me to buy *ice cream* or nothin'.
It ain't in my nature.

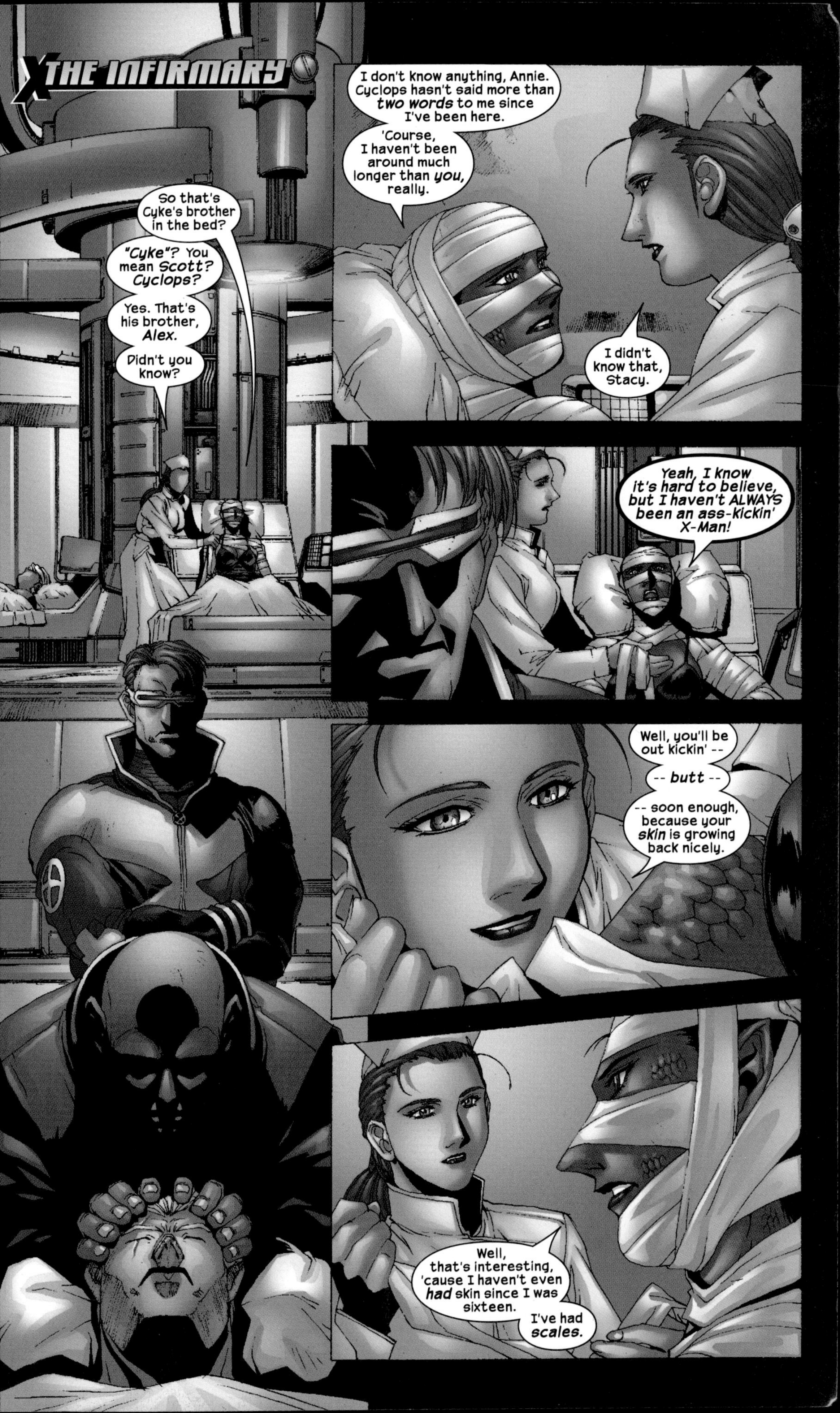
THE INFIRMARY
So that's Cyke's brother in the bed?
"Cyke"? You mean Scott? Cyclops?
Yes. That's his brother, Alex.
Didn't you know?
I don't know anything, Annie. Cyclops hasn't said more than two words to me since I've been here.
'Course, I haven't been around much longer than you, really.
I didn't know that, Stacy.
Yeah, I know it's hard to believe, but I haven't ALWAYS been an ass-kickin' X-Man!
Well, you'll be out kickin' --
-- butt --
-- soon enough, because your skin is growing back nicely.
Well, that's interesting, 'cause I haven't even had skin since I was sixteen.
I've had scales.

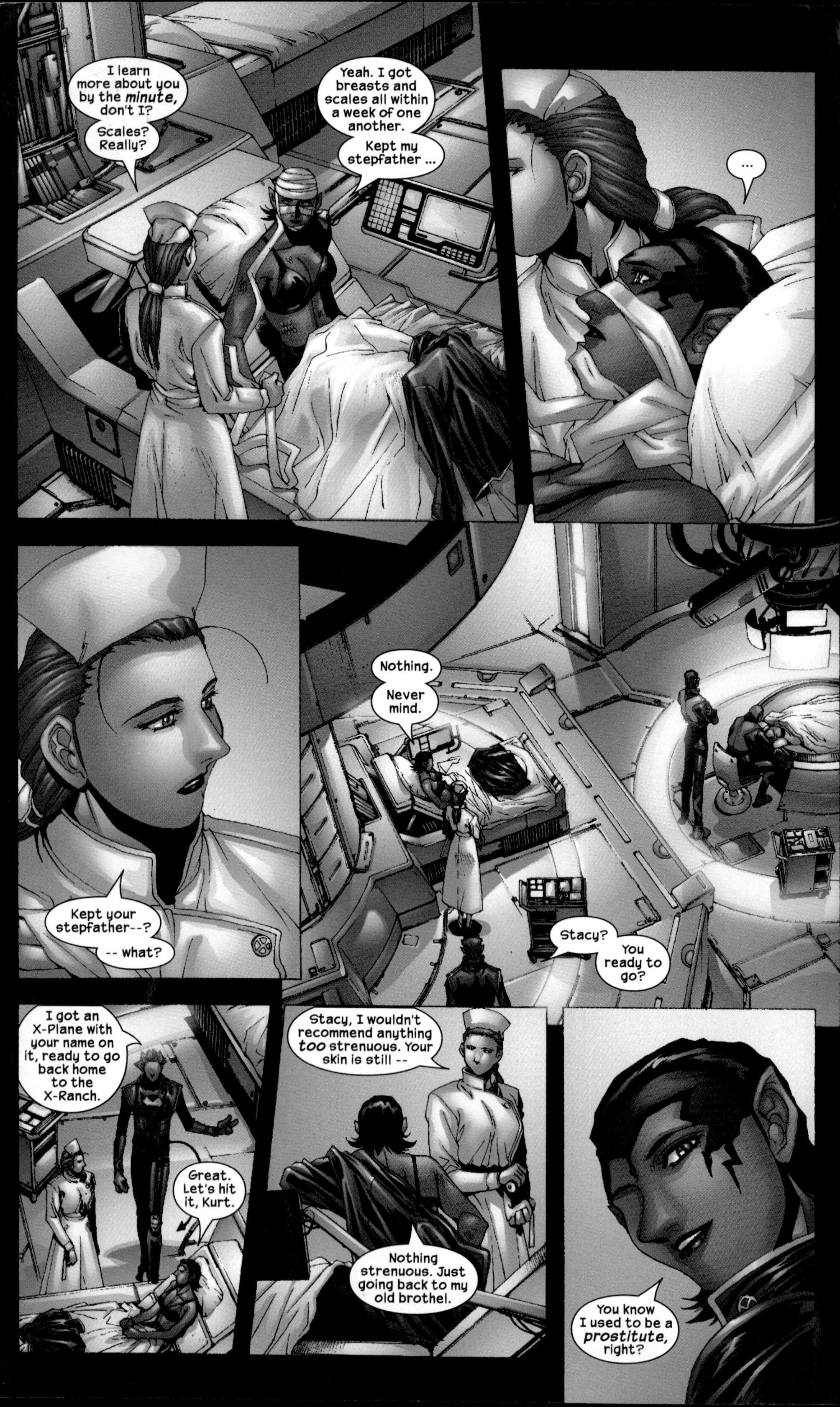

I learn more about you by the *minute,* don't I?
Scales? Really?
Yeah. I got breasts and scales all within a week of one another.
Kept my stepfather ...
...
Kept your stepfather--?
-- what?
Nothing.
Never mind.
Stacy?
You ready to go?
I got an X-Plane with your name on it, ready to go back home to the X-Ranch.
Great. Let's hit it, Kurt.
Stacy, I wouldn't recommend anything *too* strenuous. Your skin is still --
Nothing strenuous. Just going back to my old brothel.
You know I used to be a *prostitute,* right?

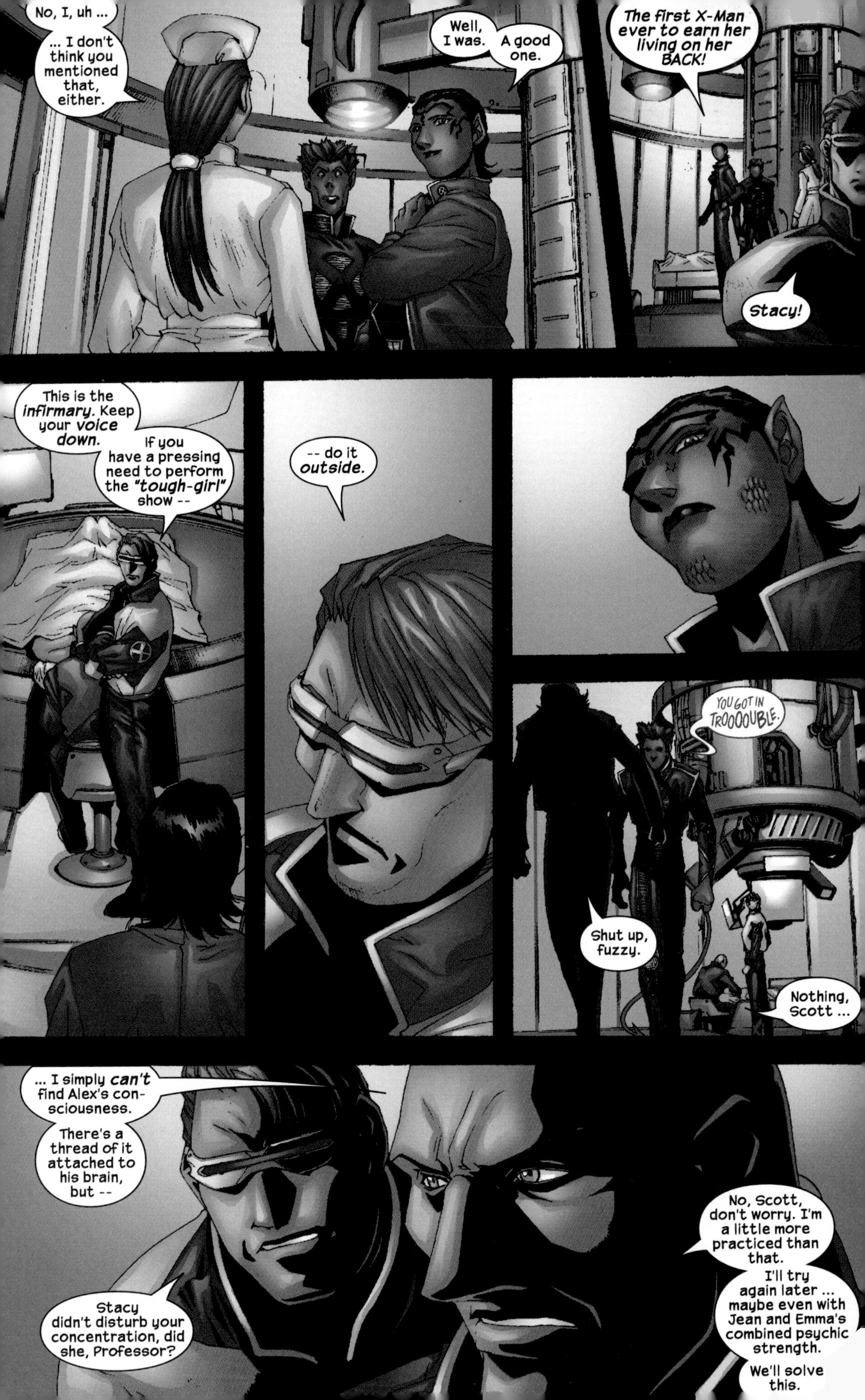
No, I, uh ...
... I don't think you mentioned that, either.
Well, I was.
A good one.
The first X-Man ever to earn her living on her BACK!
Stacy!
This is the infirmary. Keep your voice down.
If you have a pressing need to perform the "tough-girl" show --
-- do it outside.
YOU GOT IN TROOOOUBLE.
Shut up, fuzzy.
Nothing, Scott ...
... I simply can't find Alex's consciousness.
There's a thread of it attached to his brain, but --
Stacy didn't disturb your concentration, did she, Professor?
No, Scott, don't worry. I'm a little more practiced than that.
I'll try again later ... maybe even with Jean and Emma's combined psychic strength.
We'll solve this.

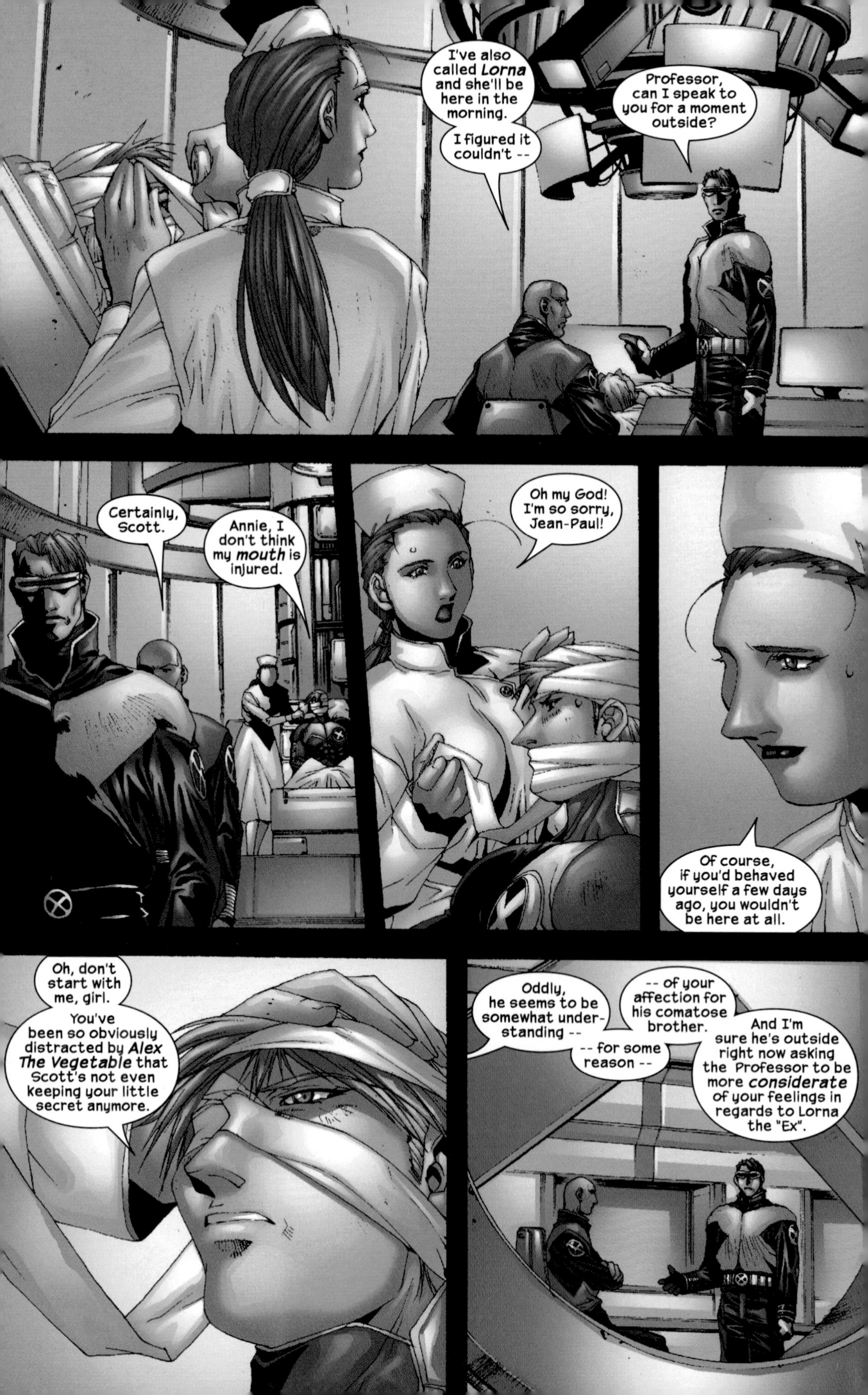
I've also called *Lorna* and she'll be here in the morning.
I figured it couldn't --
Professor, can I speak to you for a moment outside?
Certainly, Scott.
Annie, I don't think my *mouth* is injured.
Oh my God! I'm so sorry, Jean-Paul!
Of course, if you'd behaved yourself a few days ago, you wouldn't be here at all.
Oh, don't start with me, girl.
You've been so obviously distracted by *Alex The Vegetable* that Scott's not even keeping your little secret anymore.
Oddly, he seems to be somewhat under-standing --
-- for some reason --
-- of your affection for his comatose brother.
And I'm sure he's outside right now asking the Professor to be more *considerate* of your feelings in regards to Lorna the "Ex".

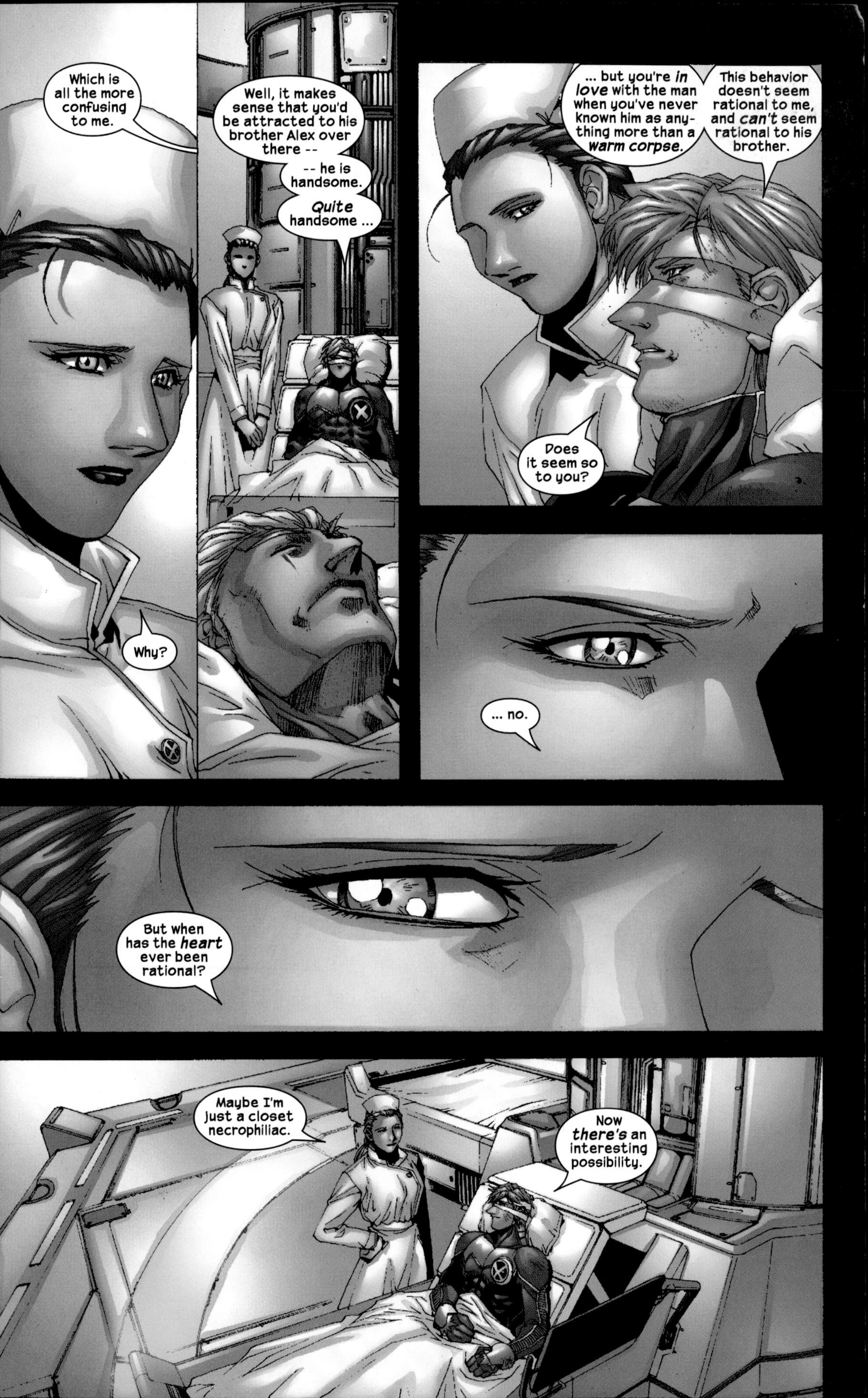
Which is all the more confusing to me.
Well, it makes sense that you'd be attracted to his brother Alex over there --
-- he is handsome.
Quite handsome ...
Why?
... but you're in love with the man when you've never known him as any-thing more than a warm corpse.
This behavior doesn't seem rational to me, and can't seem rational to his brother.
Does it seem so to you?
... no.
But when has the heart ever been rational?
Maybe I'm just a closet necrophiliac.
Now there's an interesting possibility.

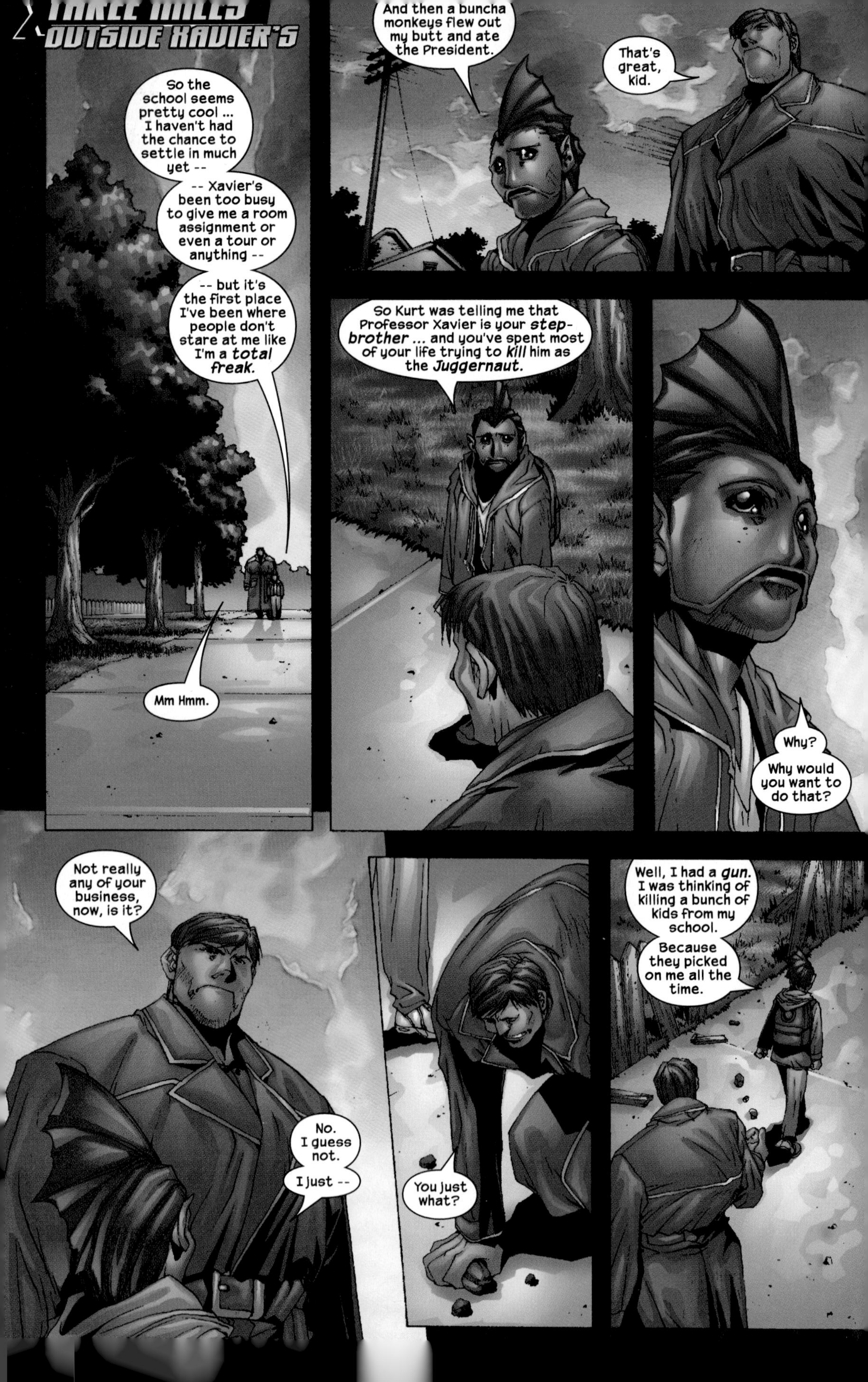
THREE MILES OUTSIDE XAVIER'S
So the school seems pretty cool ... I haven't had the chance to settle in much yet --
-- Xavier's been too busy to give me a room assignment or even a tour or anything --
-- but it's the first place I've been where people don't stare at me like I'm a *total freak.*
Mm Hmm.
And then a buncha monkeys flew out my butt and ate the President.
That's great, kid.
So Kurt was telling me that Professor Xavier is your *step-brother ...* and you've spent most of your life trying to *kill* him as the *Juggernaut.*
Why?
Why would you want to do that?
Not really any of your business, now, is it?
No. I guess not.
I just --
You just what?
Well, I had a *gun.* I was thinking of killing a bunch of kids from my school.
Because they picked on me all the time.

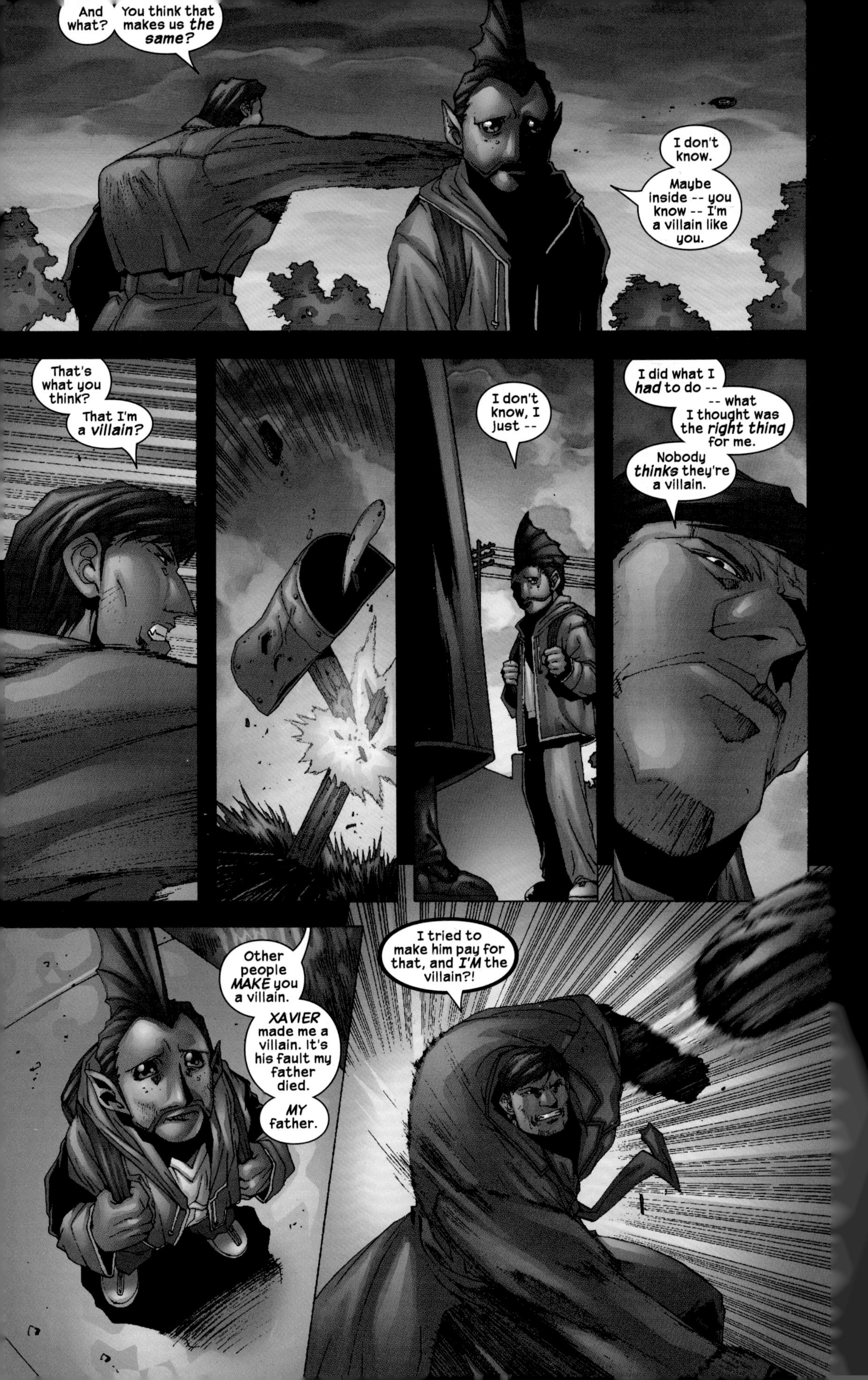

And what?
You think that makes us *the same?*
I don't know.
Maybe inside -- you know -- I'm a villain like you.
That's what you think?
That I'm a *villain?*
I don't know, I just --
I did what I *had* to do --
-- what I thought was the *right thing* for me.
Nobody *thinks* they're a villain.
Other people *MAKE* you a villain.
XAVIER made me a villain. It's his fault my father died.
MY father.
I tried to make him pay for that, and *I'M* the villain?!

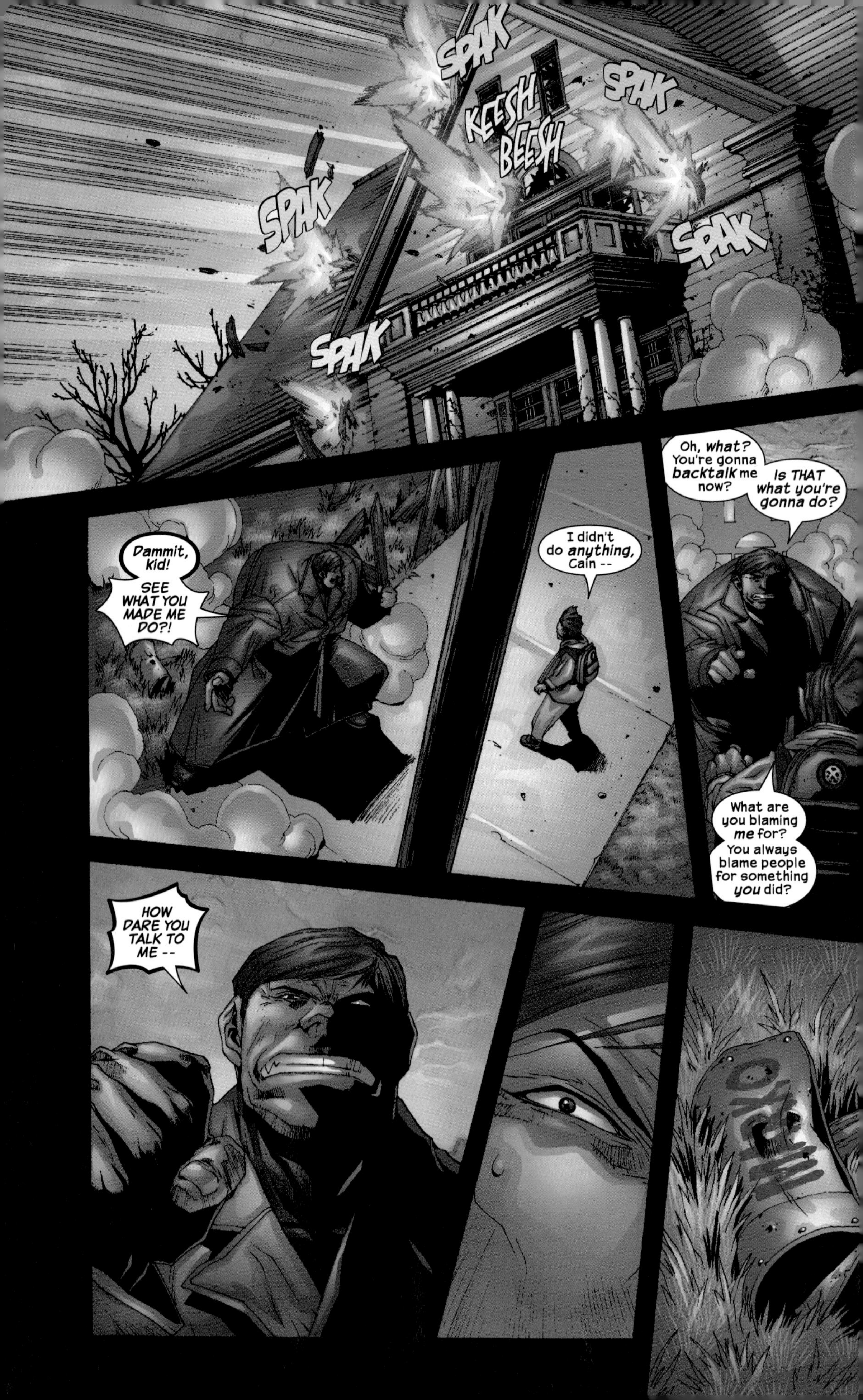
SPAK
KEESH
BEESH
SPAK
SPAK
SPAK
SPAK
Dammit, kid!
SEE WHAT YOU MADE ME DO?!
I didn't do anything, Cain --
Oh, what? You're gonna backtalk me now?
Is THAT what you're gonna do?
What are you blaming me for? You always blame people for something you did?
HOW DARE YOU TALK TO ME --

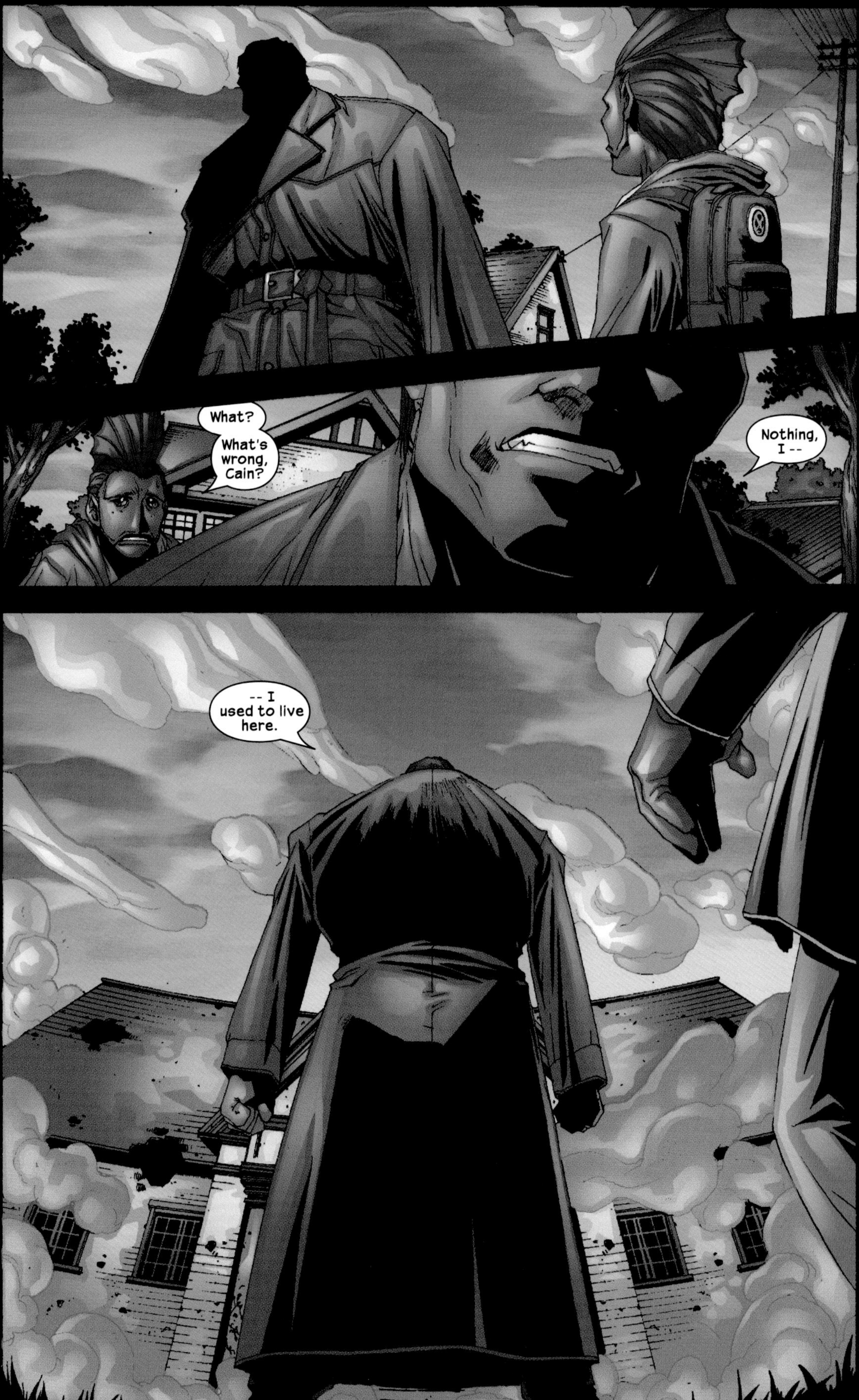
What?
What's wrong, Cain?
Nothing, I --
-- I used to live here.

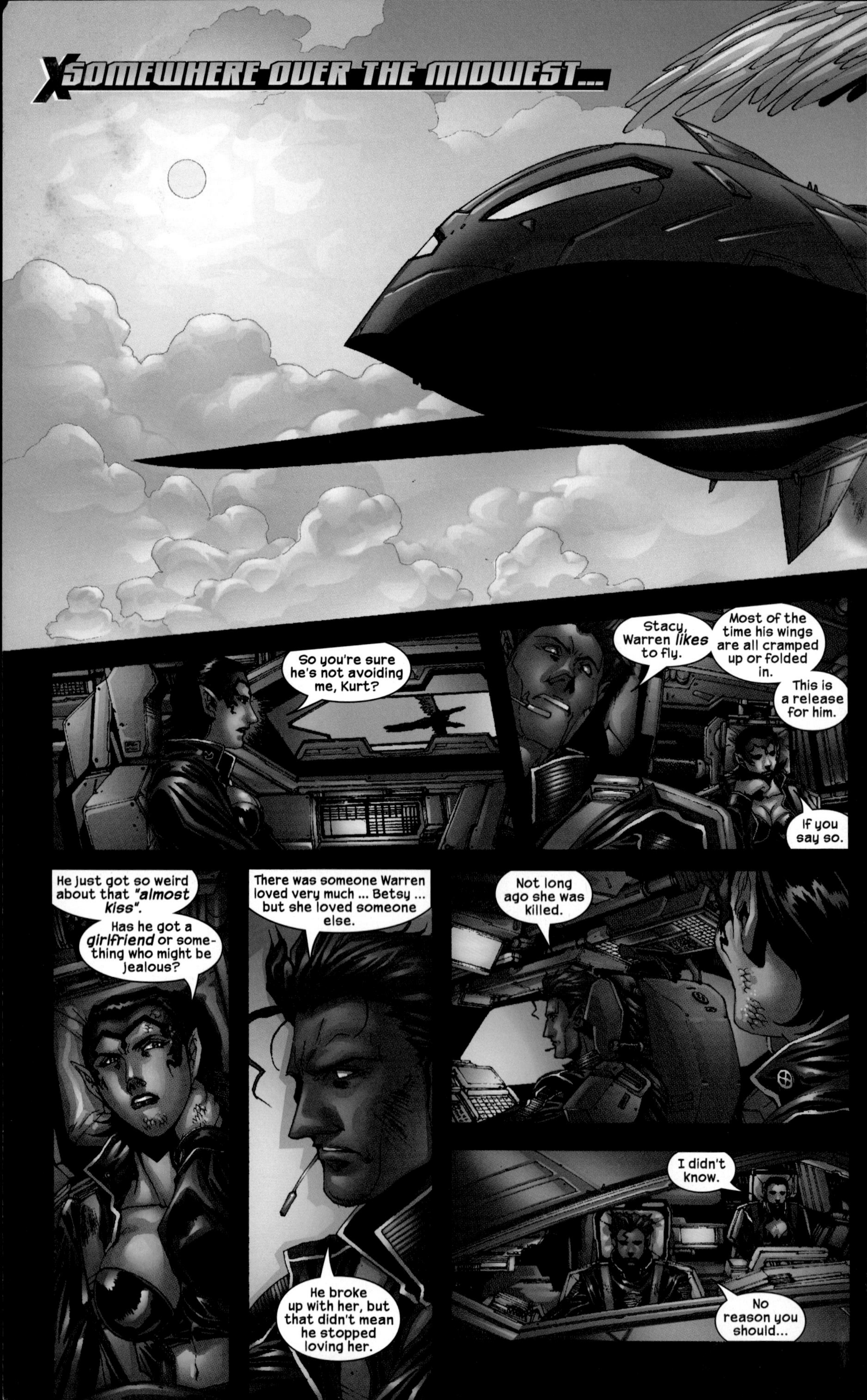
SOMEWHERE OVER THE MIDWEST...
So you're sure he's not avoiding me, Kurt?
Stacy, Warren likes to fly.
Most of the time his wings are all cramped up or folded in.
This is a release for him.
If you say so.
He just got so weird about that "almost kiss".
Has he got a girlfriend or something who might be jealous?
There was someone Warren loved very much ... Betsy ... but she loved someone else.
He broke up with her, but that didn't mean he stopped loving her.
Not long ago she was killed.
I didn't know.
No reason you should...

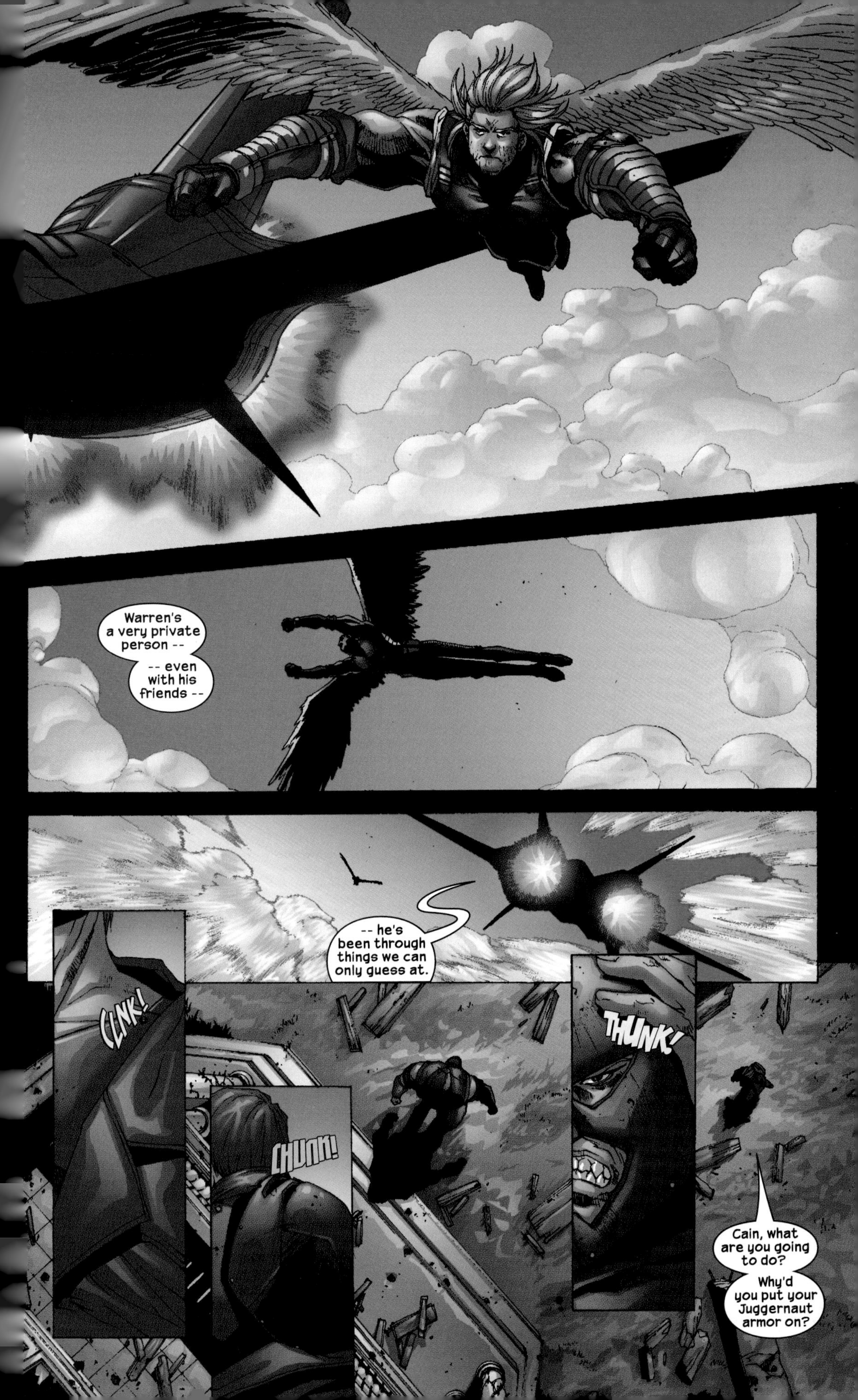
Warren's a very private person --
-- even with his friends --
-- he's been through things we can only guess at.
CLNK!
CHUNK!
THUNK!
Cain, what are you going to do?
Why'd you put your Juggernaut armor on?

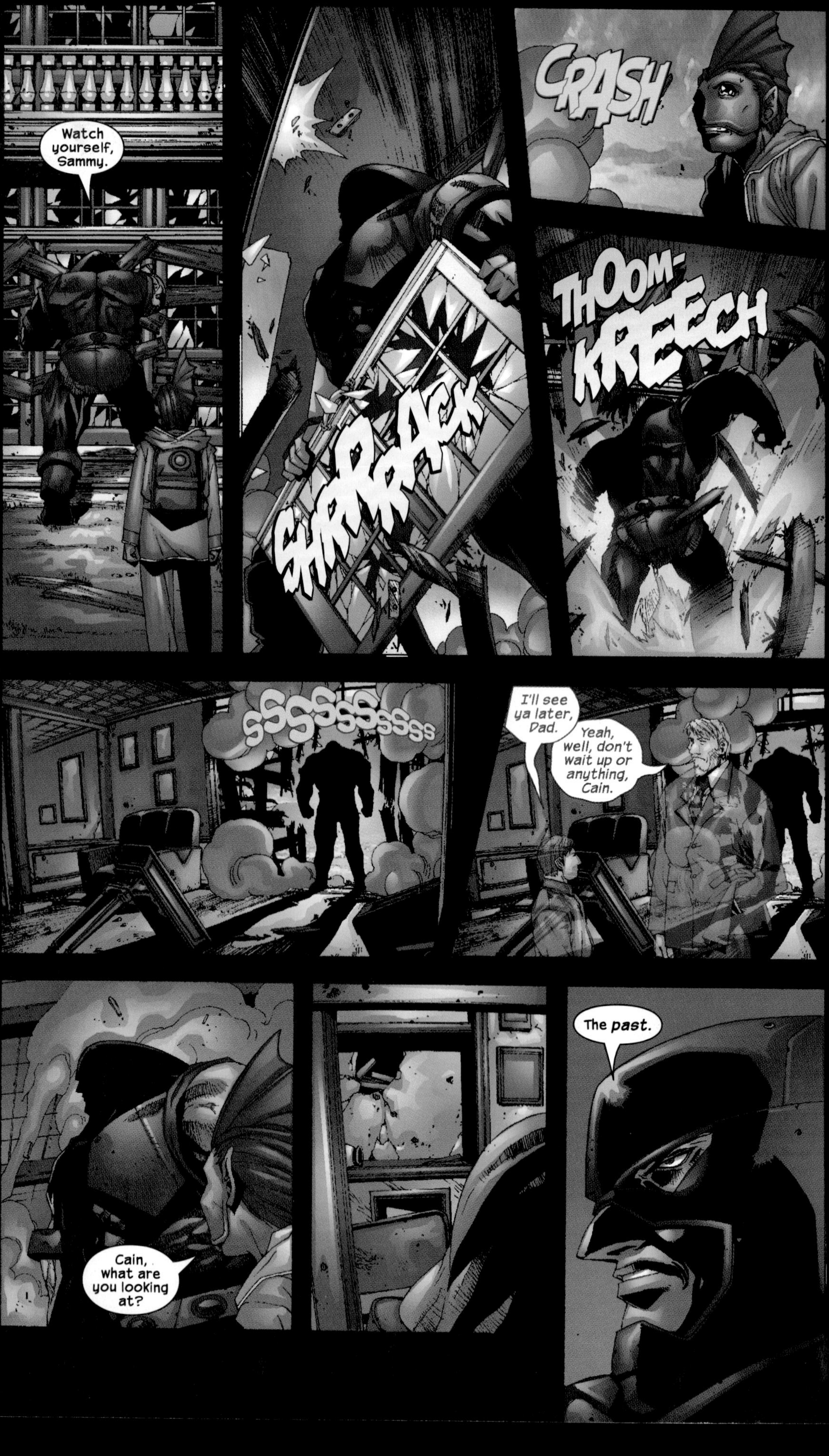
Watch yourself, Sammy.
SHRRACK
CRASH
THOOM-KREECH
SSSSSSssss
I'll see ya later, Dad.
Yeah, well, don't wait up or anything, Cain.
Cain, what are you looking at?
The *past*.

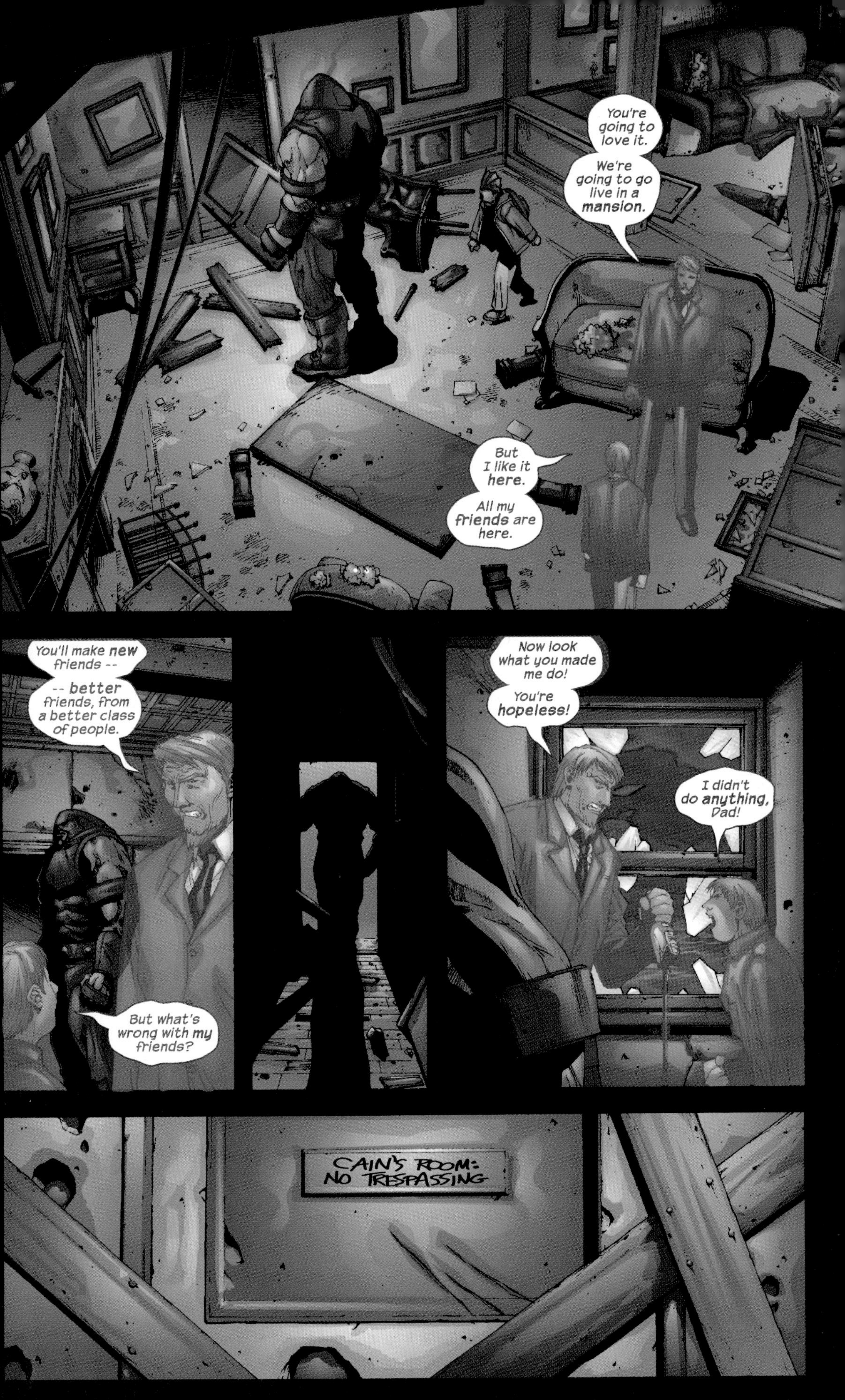
You're going to love it.
We're going to go live in a mansion.
But I like it here.
All my friends are here.
You'll make new friends --
-- better friends, from a better class of people.
But what's wrong with my friends?
Now look what you made me do!
You're hopeless!
I didn't do anything, Dad!
CAIN'S ROOM: NO TRESPASSING

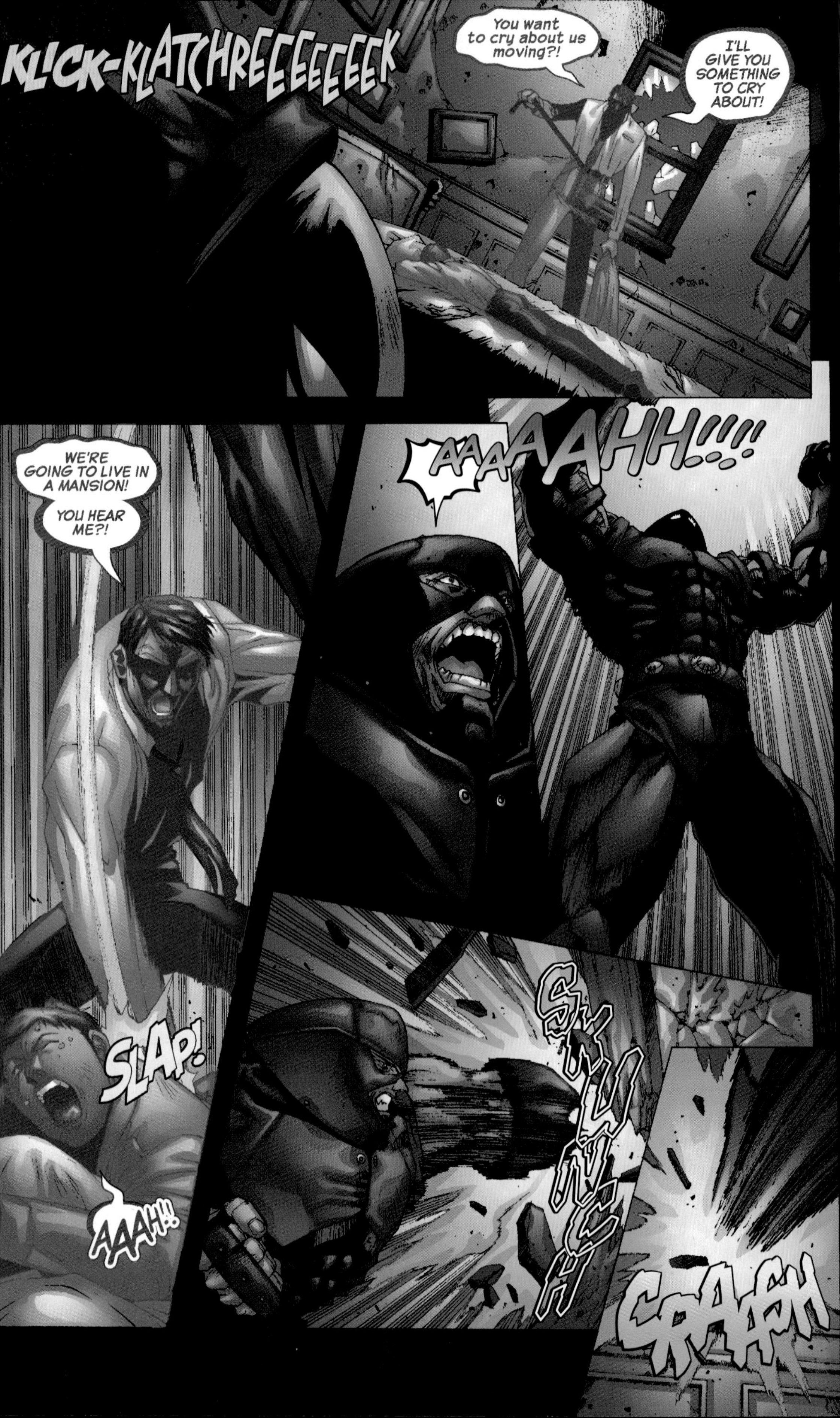
KLICK-KLATCHREEEEEEEEK
You want to cry about us moving?!
I'LL GIVE YOU SOMETHING TO CRY ABOUT!
WE'RE GOING TO LIVE IN A MANSION!
YOU HEAR ME?!
SLAP!
AAAH!!
AAAAAHH!!!!
SWUNCH
CRASH

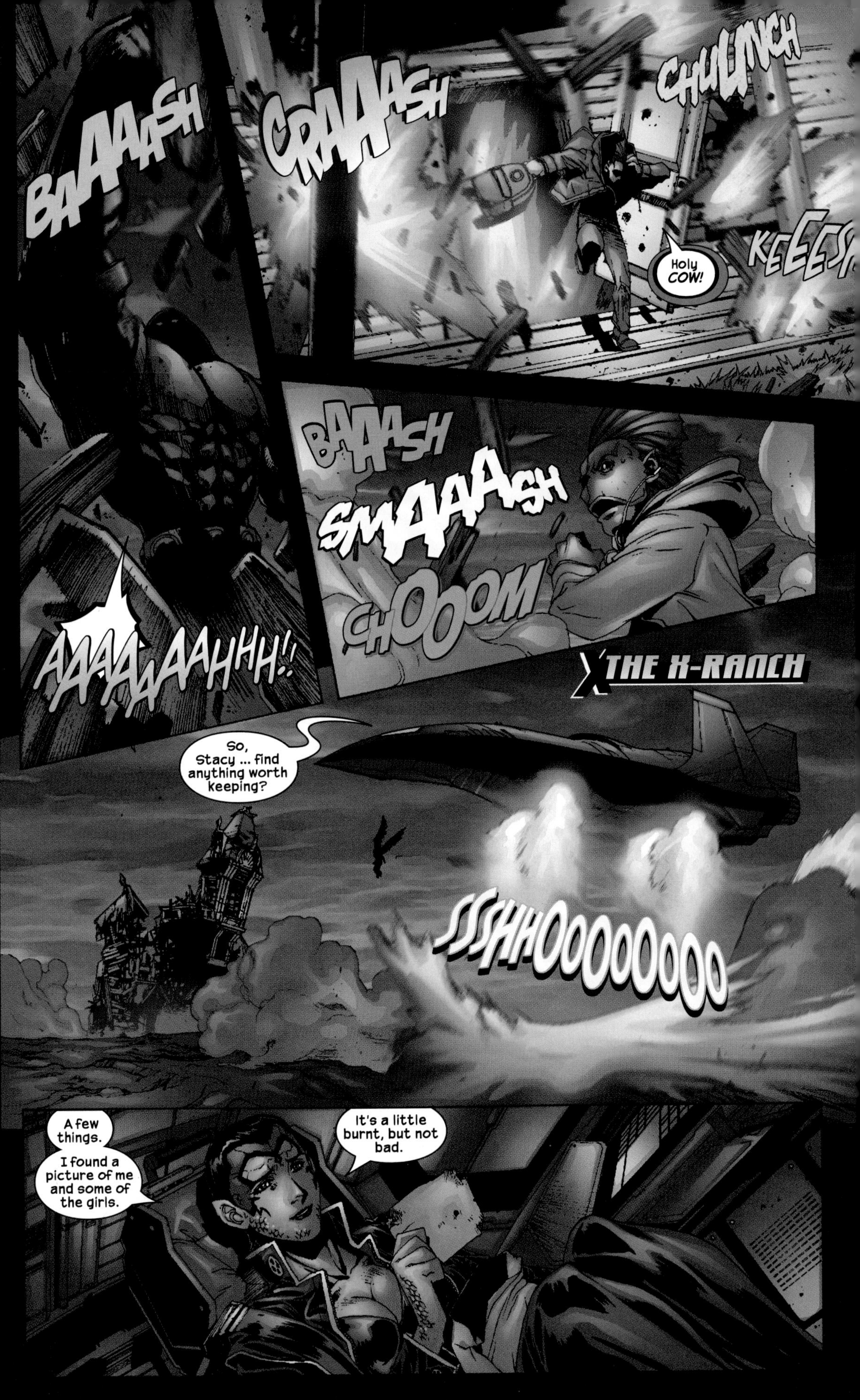

BAAAASH
CRAAASH
CHUUNCH
Holy COW!
KEEEESH
BAAASH
SMAAASH
CHOOOM
AAAAAAAHHH!!
THE X-RANCH
So, Stacy ... find anything worth keeping?
SSSHHOOOOOOOO
A few things.
I found a picture of me and some of the girls.
It's a little burnt, but not bad.

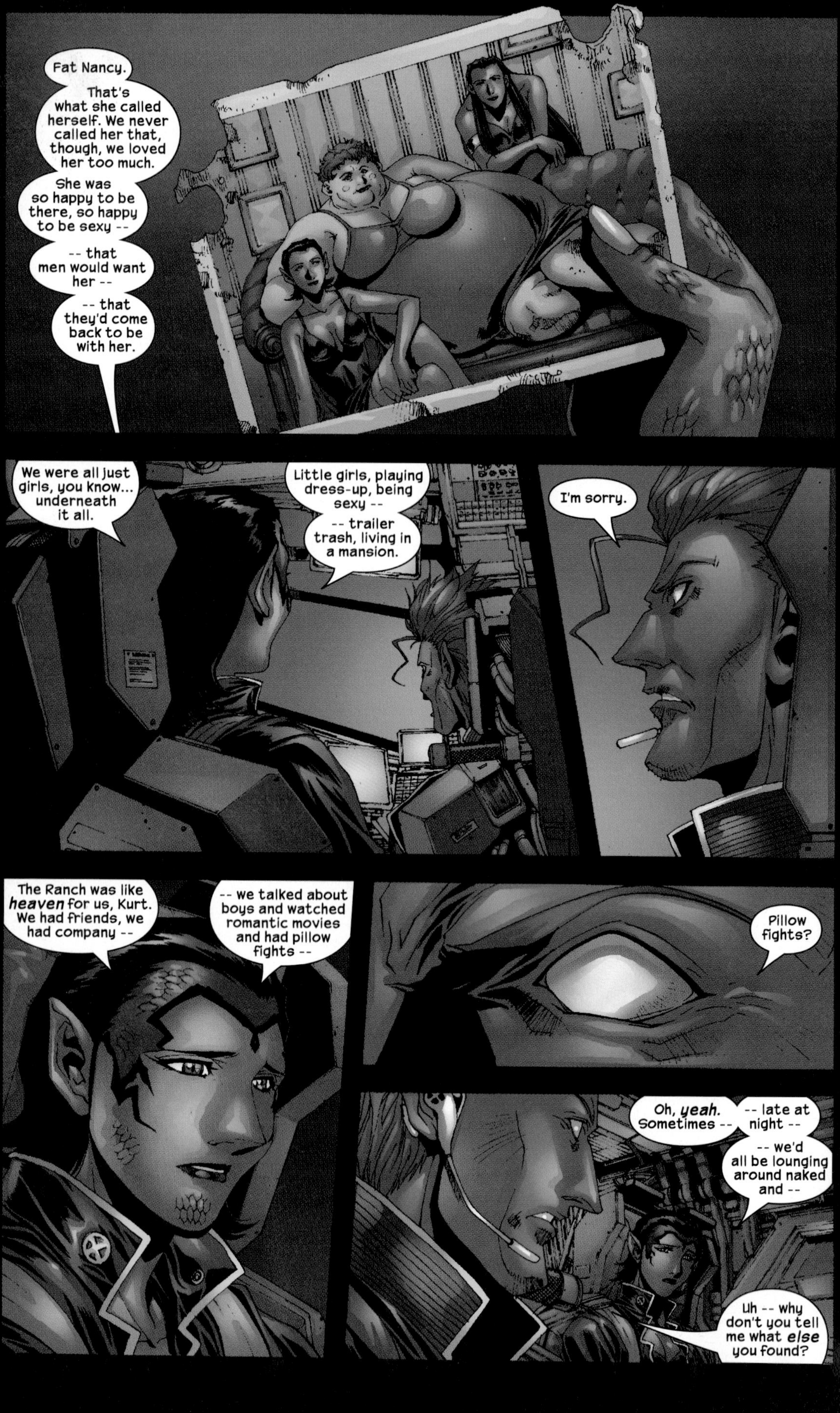
Fat Nancy.
That's what she called herself. We never called her that, though, we loved her too much.
She was so happy to be there, so happy to be sexy --
-- that men would want her --
-- that they'd come back to be with her.
We were all just girls, you know... underneath it all.
Little girls, playing dress-up, being sexy --
-- trailer trash, living in a mansion.
I'm sorry.
The Ranch was like *heaven* for us, Kurt. We had friends, we had company --
-- we talked about boys and watched romantic movies and had pillow fights --
Pillow fights?
Oh, *yeah*. Sometimes --
-- late at night --
-- we'd all be lounging around naked and --
Uh -- why don't you tell me what *else* you found?

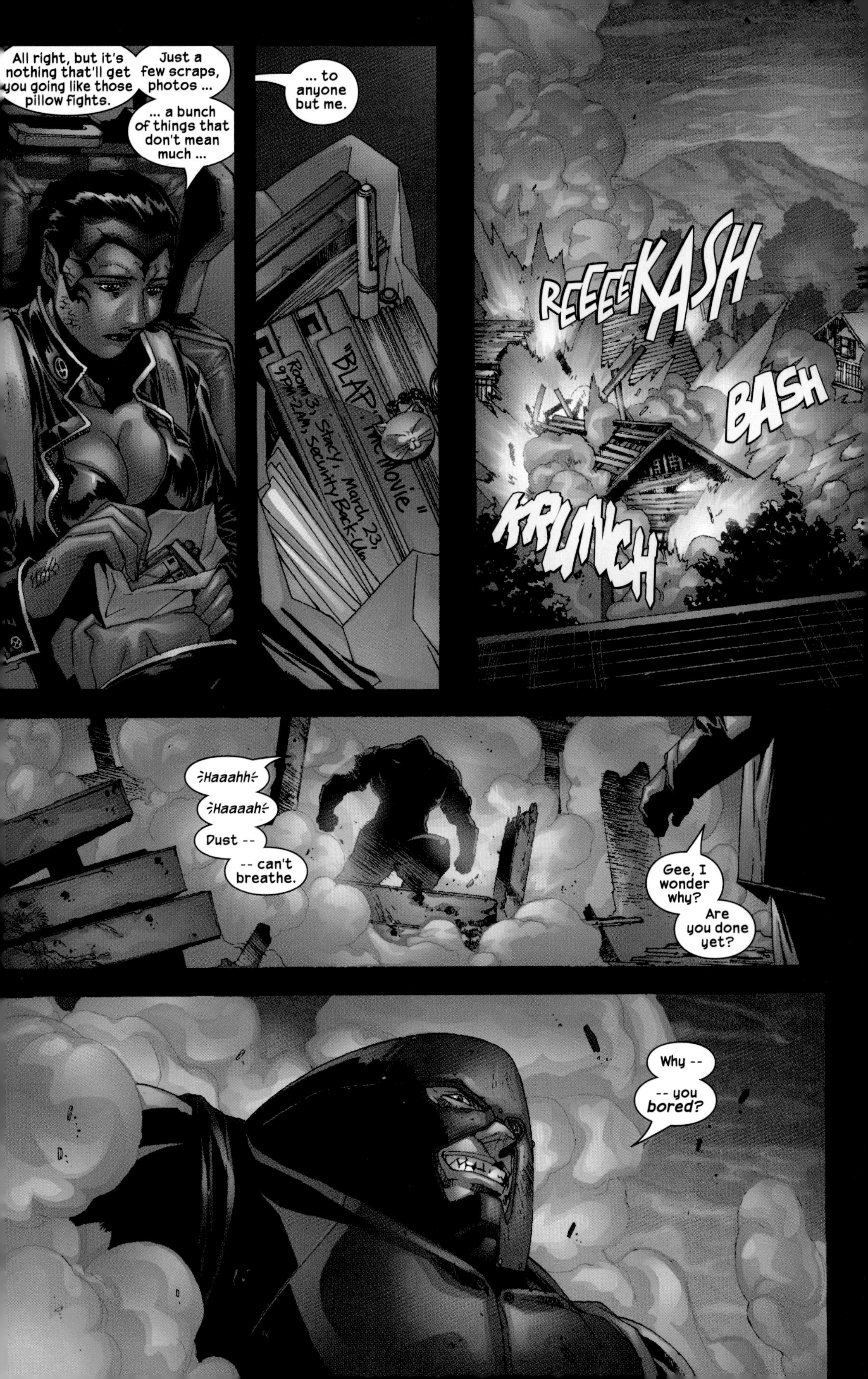
All right, but it's nothing that'll get you going like those pillow fights.
Just a few scraps, photos ...
... a bunch of things that don't mean much ...
... to anyone but me.
"BLAP: The Movie"
Room 3, Stacy, March 23, 9PM-2AM, Security Back-Up
REEEEEKASH
BASH
KRUNCH
Haaahh
Haaaah
Dust --
-- can't breathe.
Gee, I wonder why?
Are you done yet?
Why --
-- you *bored?*

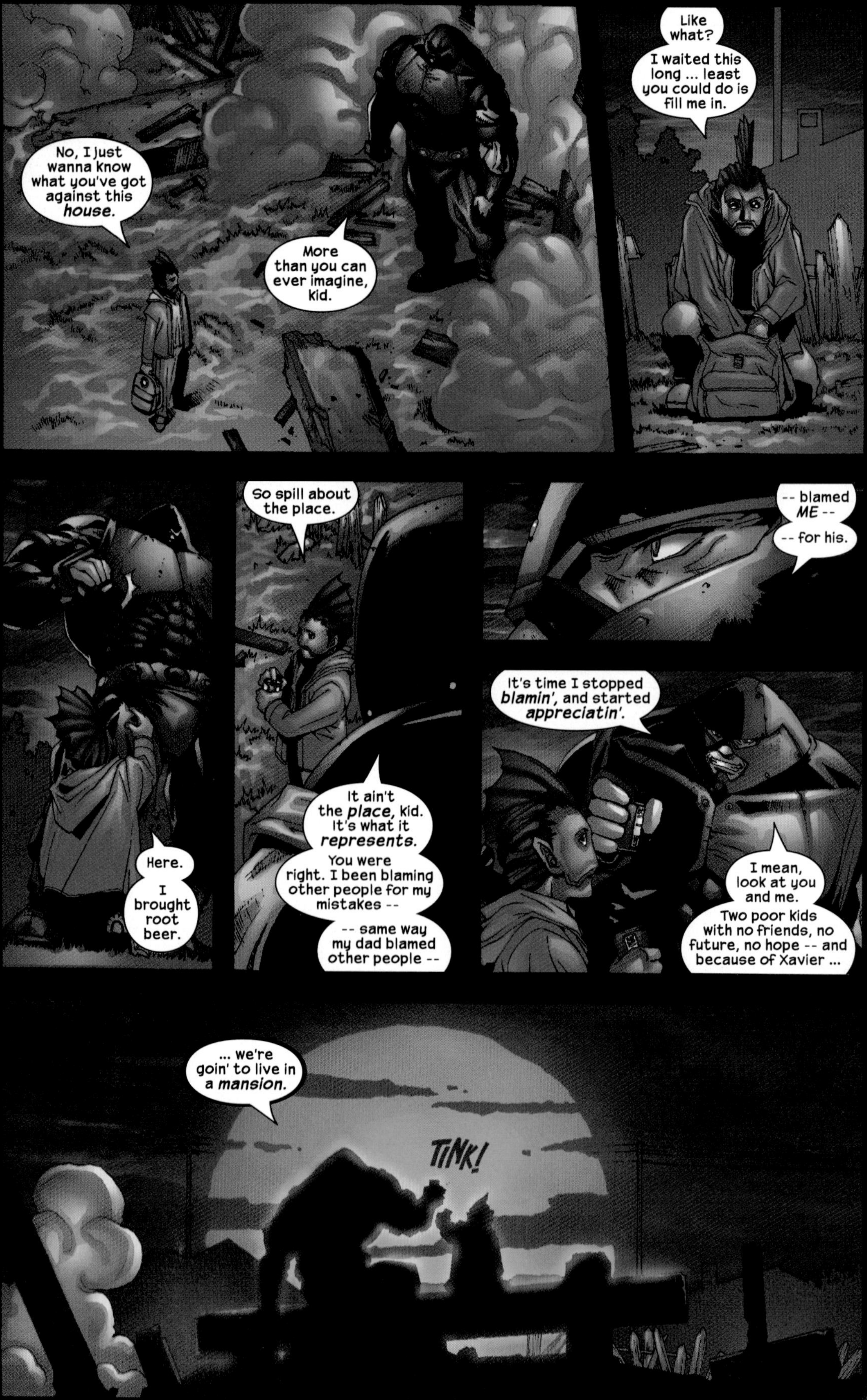
No, I just wanna know what you've got against this *house.*
More than you can ever imagine, kid.
Like what?
I waited this long ... least you could do is fill me in.
Here.
I brought root beer.
So spill about the place.
It ain't the *place,* kid. It's what it *represents.*
You were right. I been blaming other people for my mistakes --
-- same way my dad blamed other people --
-- blamed *ME* --
-- for his.
It's time I stopped *blamin',* and started *appreciatin'.*
I mean, look at you and me.
Two poor kids with no friends, no future, no hope -- and because of Xavier ...
... we're goin' to live in a *mansion.*
TINK!

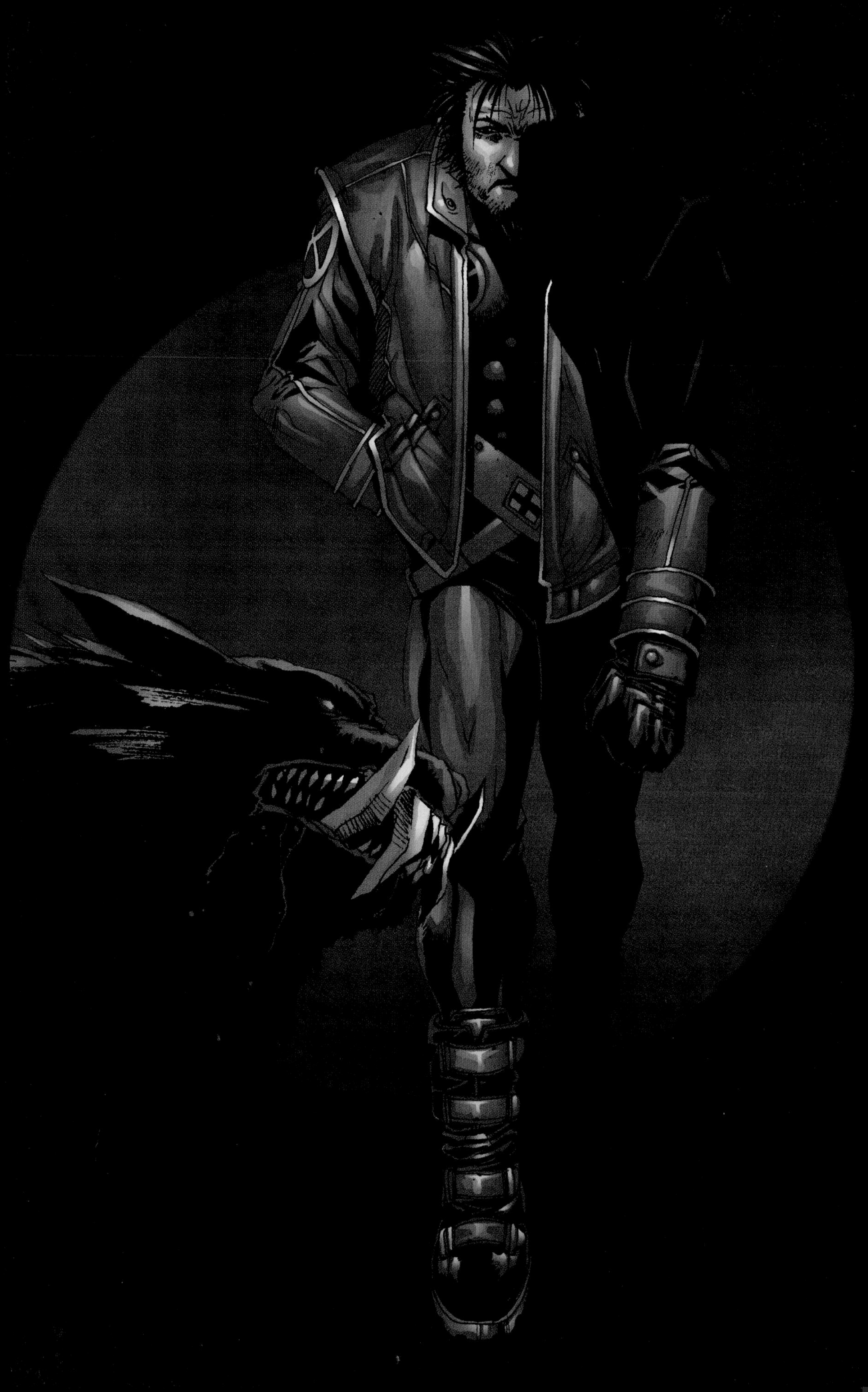

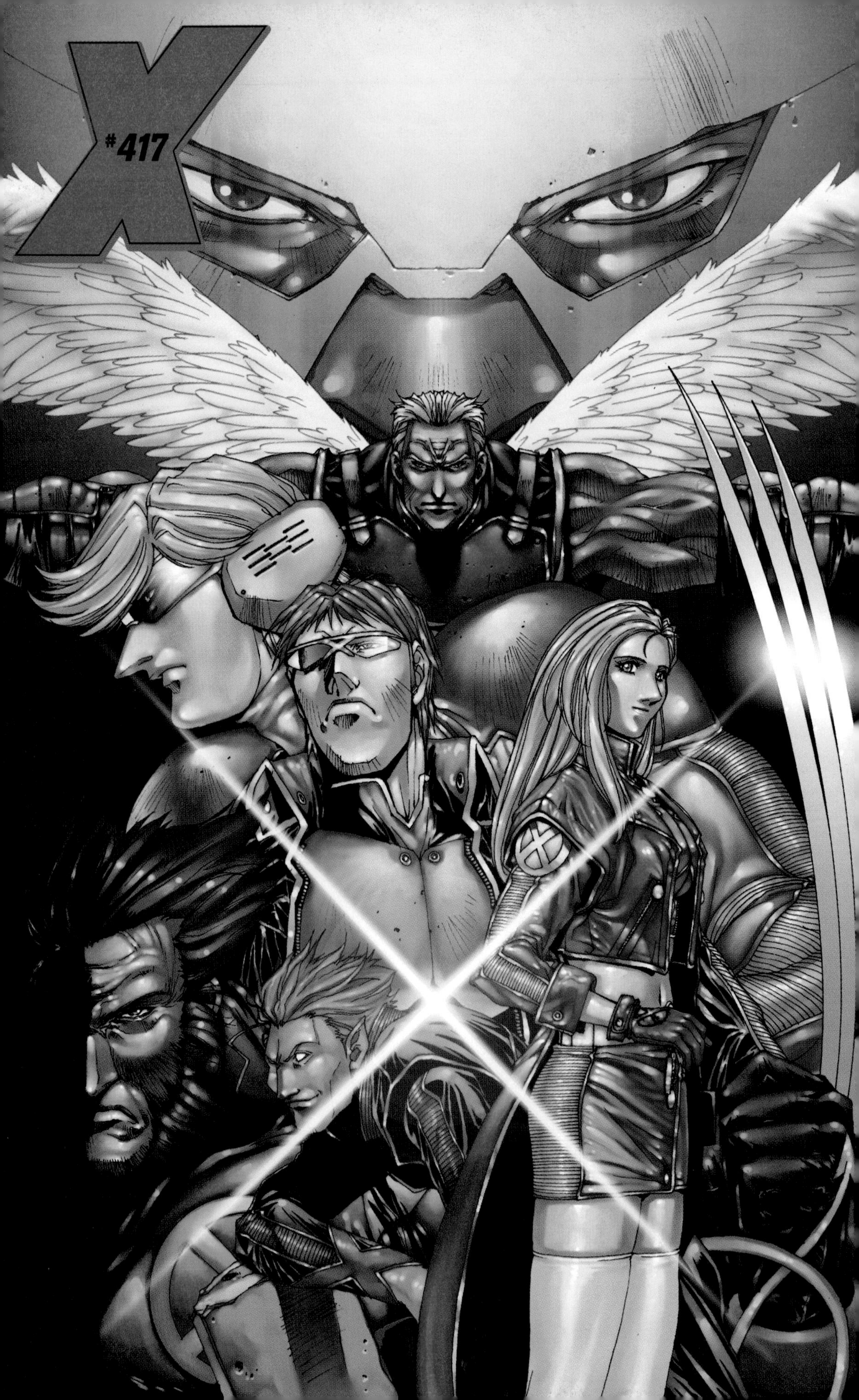
X
#417

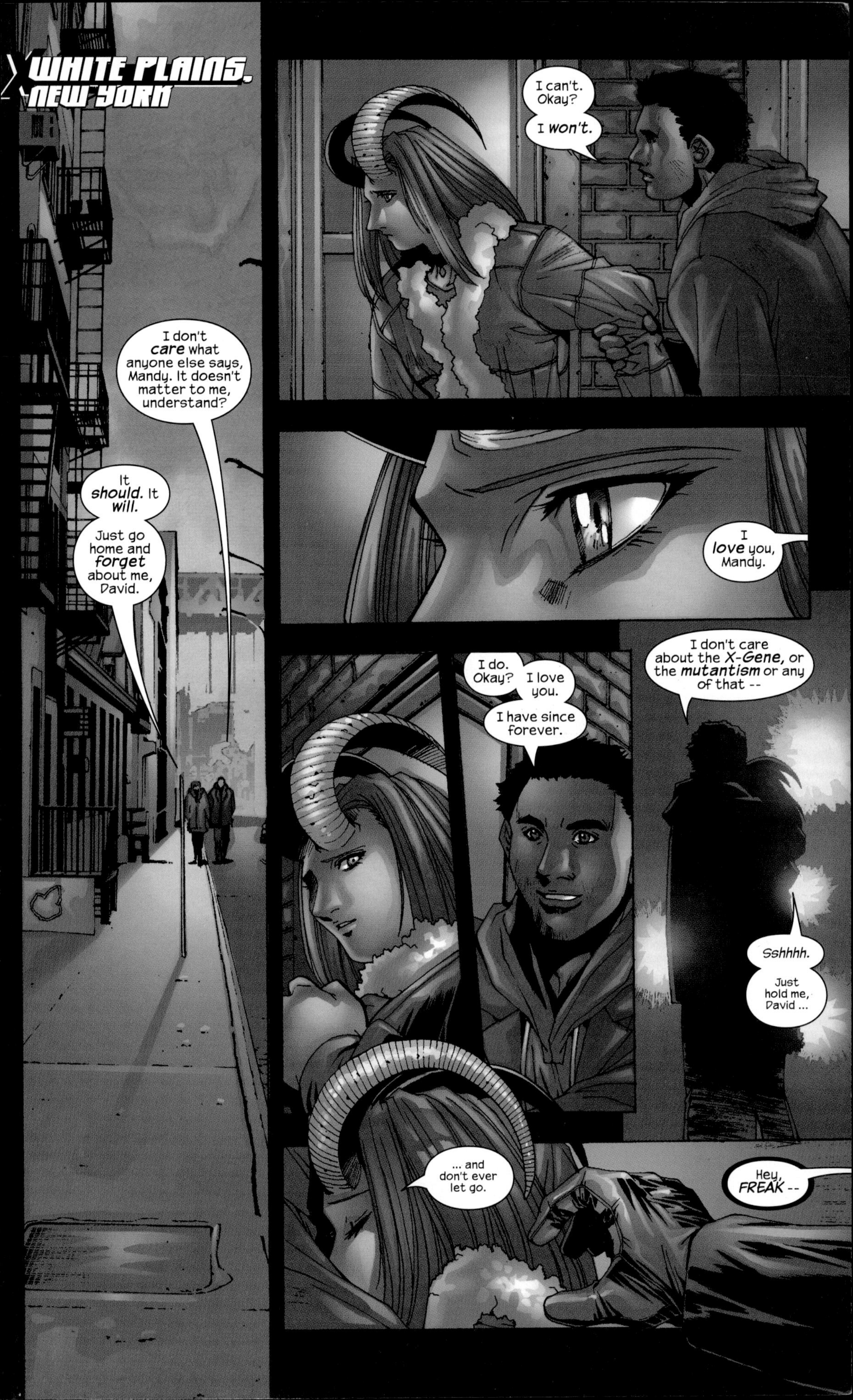
WHITE PLAINS, NEW YORK
I don't care what anyone else says, Mandy. It doesn't matter to me, understand?
It should. It will.
Just go home and forget about me, David.
I can't. Okay?
I won't.
I love you, Mandy.
I do. Okay?
I love you.
I have since forever.
I don't care about the X-Gene, or the mutantism or any of that --
Sshhhh.
Just hold me, David ...
... and don't ever let go.
Hey, FREAK --

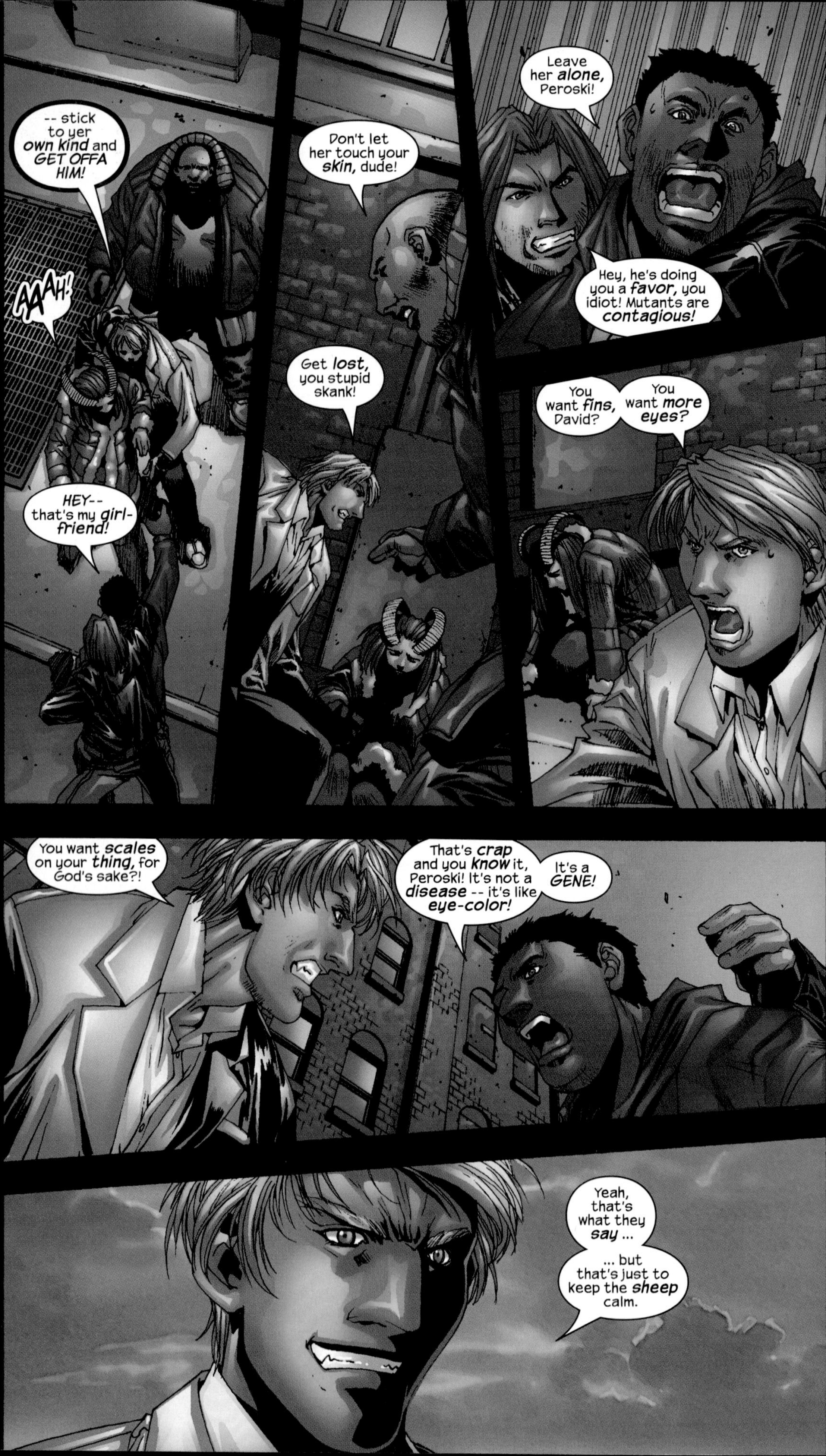
-- stick to yer own kind and GET OFFA HIM!
AAAH!
HEY-- that's my girl-friend!
Don't let her touch your skin, dude!
Get lost, you stupid skank!
Leave her alone, Peroski!
Hey, he's doing you a favor, you idiot! Mutants are contagious!
You want fins, David?
You want more eyes?
You want scales on your thing, for God's sake?!
That's crap and you know it, Peroski! It's not a disease -- it's like eye-color!
It's a GENE!
Yeah, that's what they say ...
... but that's just to keep the sheep calm.

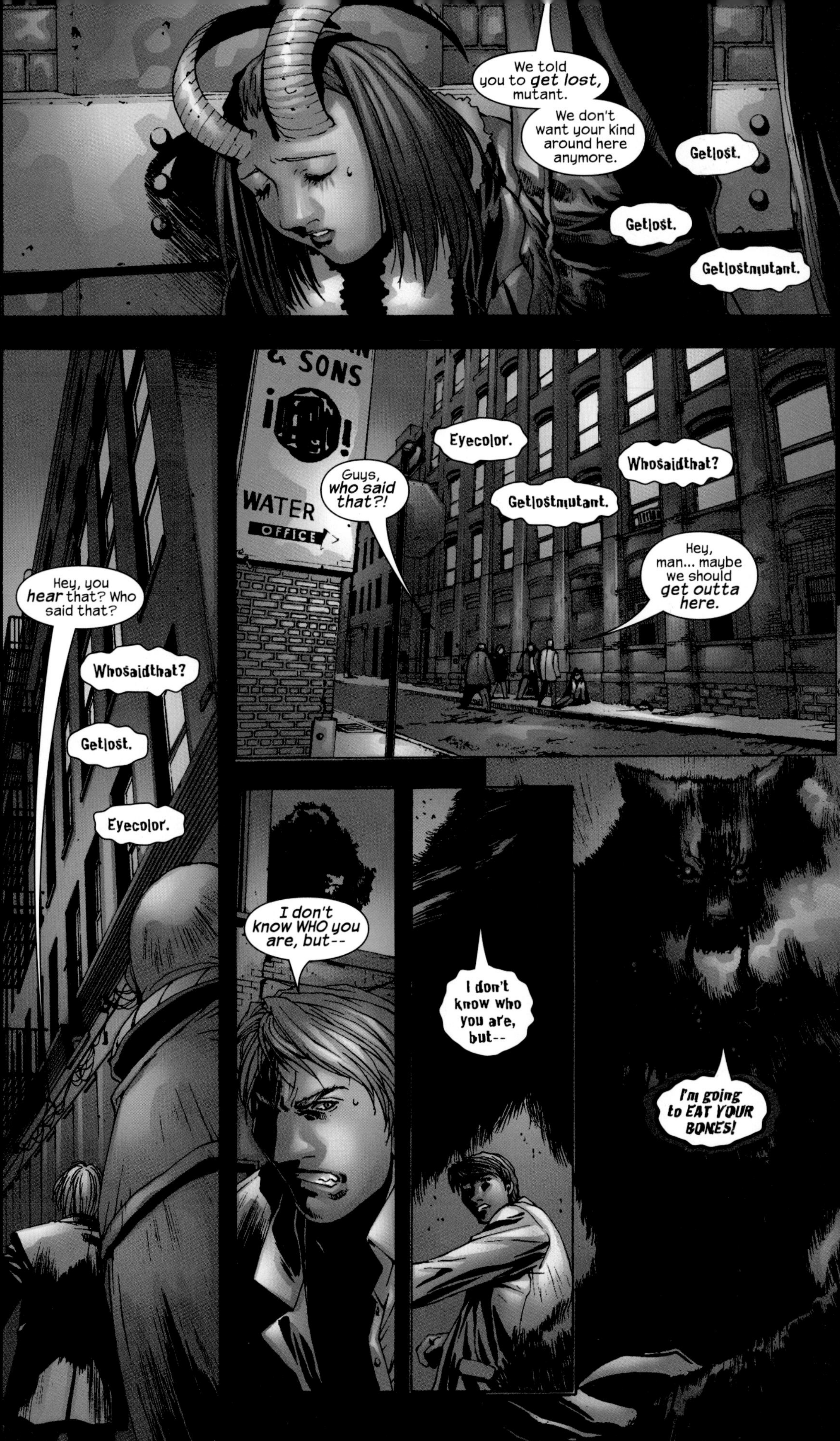
We told you to get lost, mutant.
We don't want your kind around here anymore.
Getlost.
Getlost.
Getlostmutant.
& SONS
WATER
OFFICE
Hey, you hear that? Who said that?
Whosaidthat?
Getlost.
Eyecolor.
Eyecolor.
Guys, who said that?!
Getlostmutant.
Whosaidthat?
Hey, man... maybe we should get outta here.
I don't know WHO you are, but--
I don't know who you are, but--
I'm going to EAT YOUR BONES!

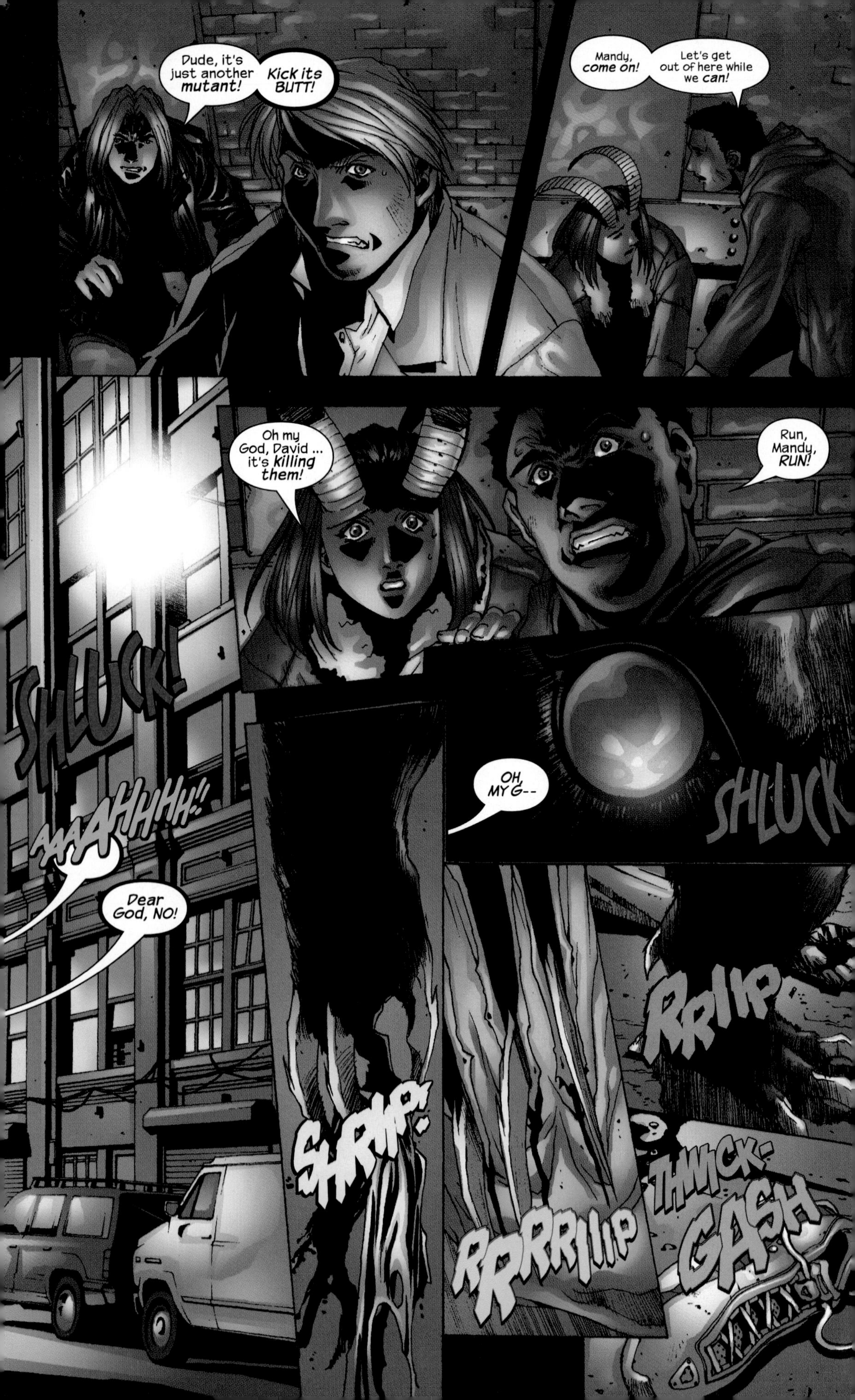
Dude, it's just another mutant!
Kick its BUTT!
Mandy, come on!
Let's get out of here while we can!
Oh my God, David ... it's killing them!
Run, Mandy, RUN!
SHLUCK!
AAAAHHHH!!
Dear God, NO!
OH, MY G--
SHLUCK
SHRIP!
RRRRIIIP
THWICK-GASH

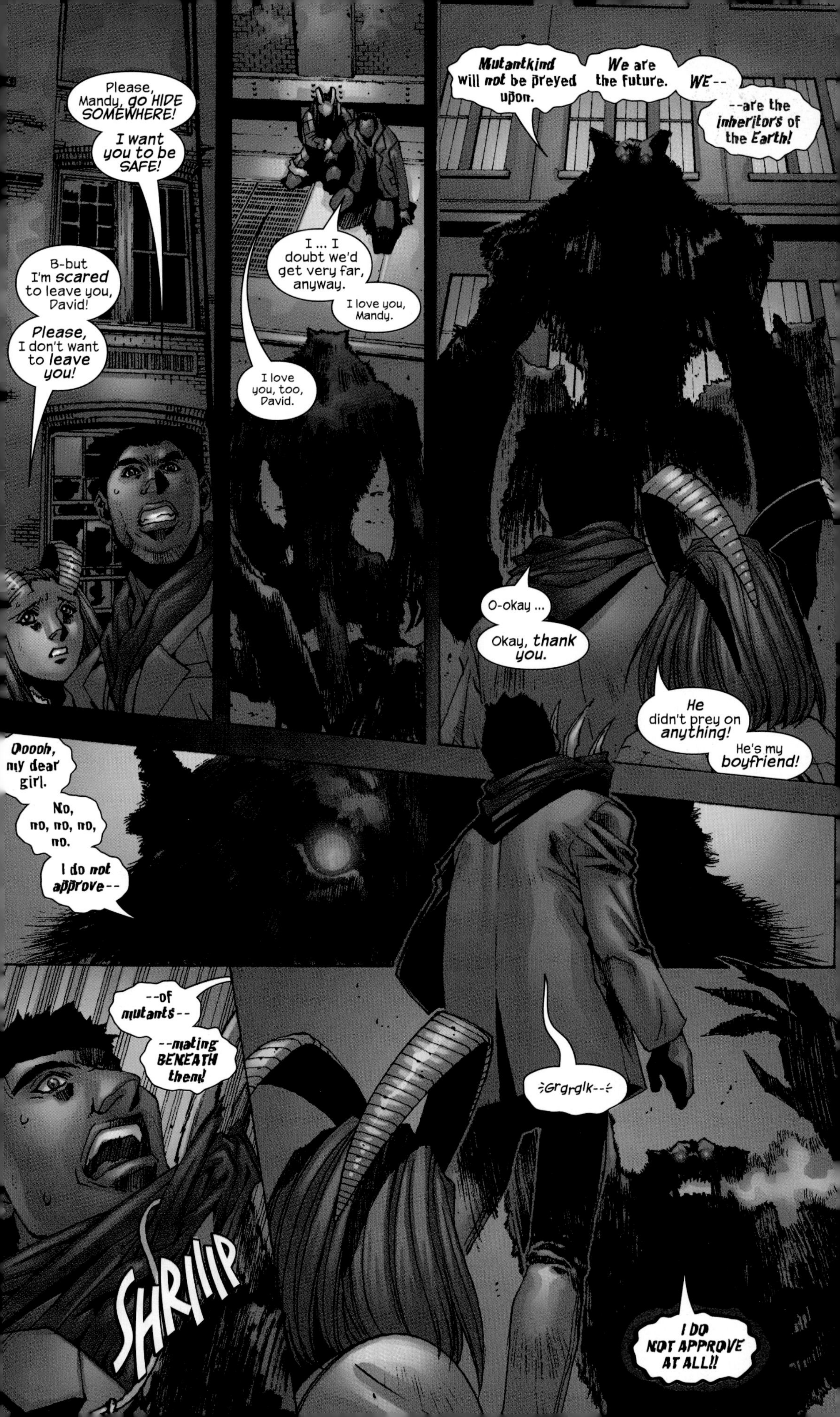
Please, Mandy, go HIDE SOMEWHERE!
I want you to be SAFE!
B-but I'm scared to leave you, David!
Please, I don't want to leave you!
I ... I doubt we'd get very far, anyway.
I love you, Mandy.
I love you, too, David.
Mutantkind will not be preyed upon.
We are the future.
WE--
--are the inheritors of the Earth!
O-okay ...
Okay, thank you.
He didn't prey on anything!
He's my boyfriend!
Ooooh, my dear girl.
No, no, no, no, no.
I do not approve--
--of mutants--
--mating BENEATH them!
Grgrglk--
SHRIIIP
I DO NOT APPROVE AT ALL!!

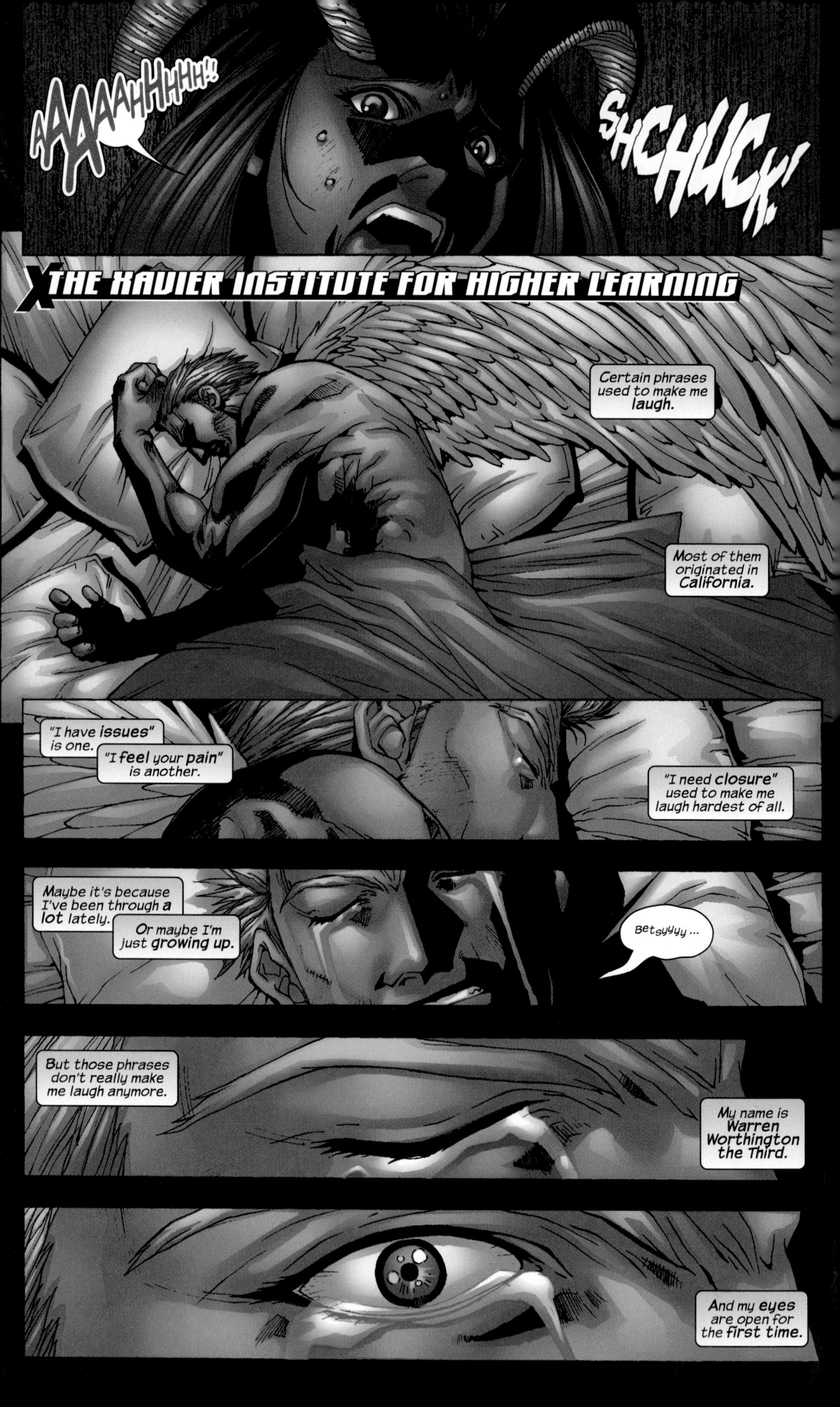

AAAAAHHHHH!!
SHCHUCK!
THE XAVIER INSTITUTE FOR HIGHER LEARNING
Certain phrases used to make me laugh.
Most of them originated in California.
"I have issues" is one.
"I feel your pain" is another.
"I need closure" used to make me laugh hardest of all.
Maybe it's because I've been through a lot lately.
Or maybe I'm just growing up.
Betsyyyy ...
But those phrases don't really make me laugh anymore.
My name is Warren Worthington the Third.
And my eyes are open for the first time.

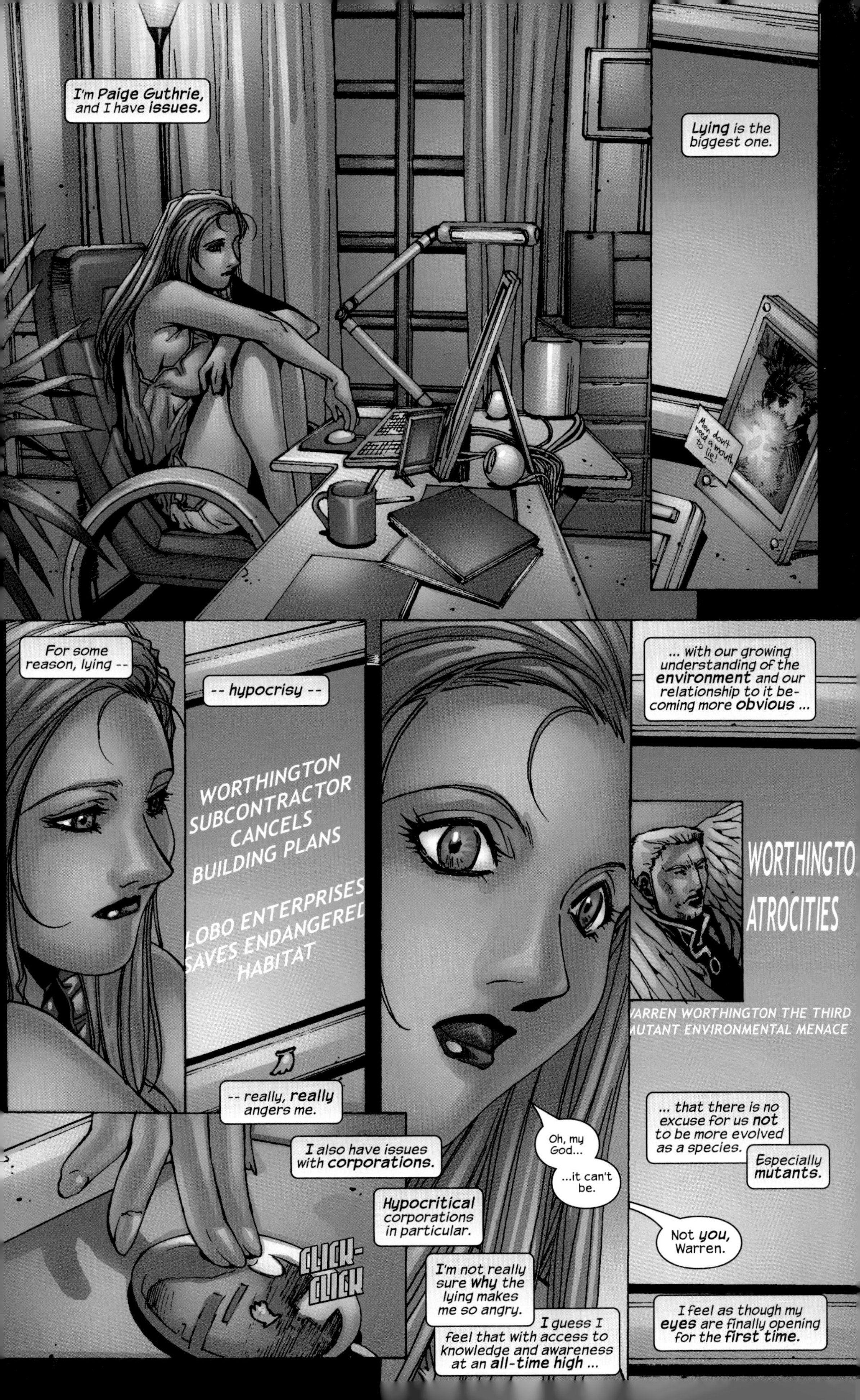

I'm Paige Guthrie, and I have issues.
Lying is the biggest one.
Men don't need a mouth to lie!
For some reason, lying --
-- hypocrisy --
WORTHINGTON SUBCONTRACTOR CANCELS BUILDING PLANS
LOBO ENTERPRISES SAVES ENDANGERED HABITAT
-- really, really angers me.
... with our growing understanding of the environment and our relationship to it becoming more obvious ...
WORTHINGTO
ATROCITIES
ARREN WORTHINGTON THE THIRD
UTANT ENVIRONMENTAL MENACE
... that there is no excuse for us not to be more evolved as a species.
Especially mutants.
I also have issues with corporations.
Hypocritical corporations in particular.
CLICK-CLICK
I'm not really sure why the lying makes me so angry.
I guess I feel that with access to knowledge and awareness at an all-time high ...
Oh, my God...
...it can't be.
Not you, Warren.
I feel as though my eyes are finally opening for the first time.

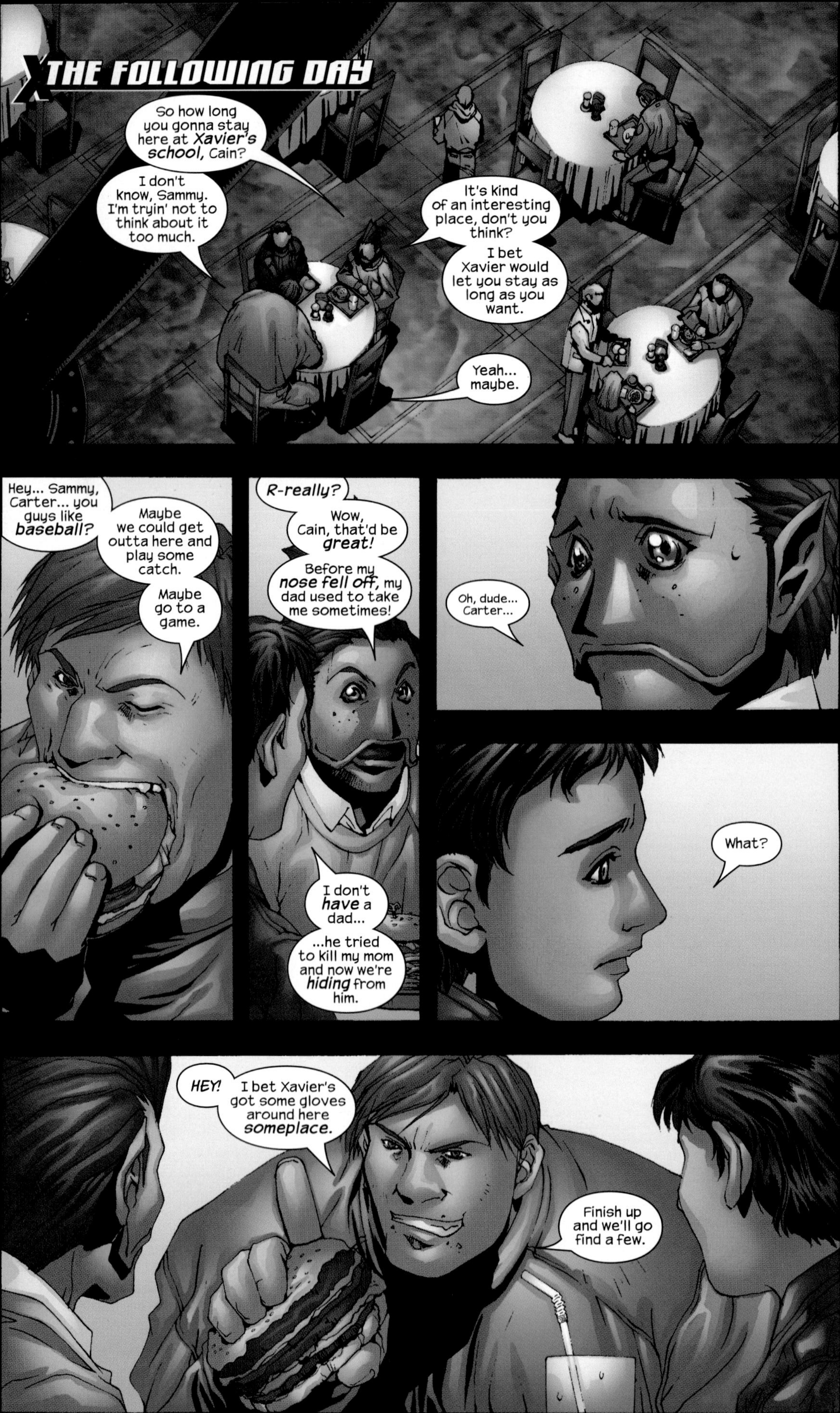
THE FOLLOWING DAY
So how long you gonna stay here at Xavier's school, Cain?
I don't know, Sammy. I'm tryin' not to think about it too much.
It's kind of an interesting place, don't you think?
I bet Xavier would let you stay as long as you want.
Yeah... maybe.
Hey... Sammy, Carter... you guys like baseball?
Maybe we could get outta here and play some catch.
Maybe go to a game.
R-really?
Wow, Cain, that'd be great!
Before my nose fell off, my dad used to take me sometimes!
I don't have a dad...
...he tried to kill my mom and now we're hiding from him.
Oh, dude... Carter...
What?
HEY!
I bet Xavier's got some gloves around here someplace.
Finish up and we'll go find a few.

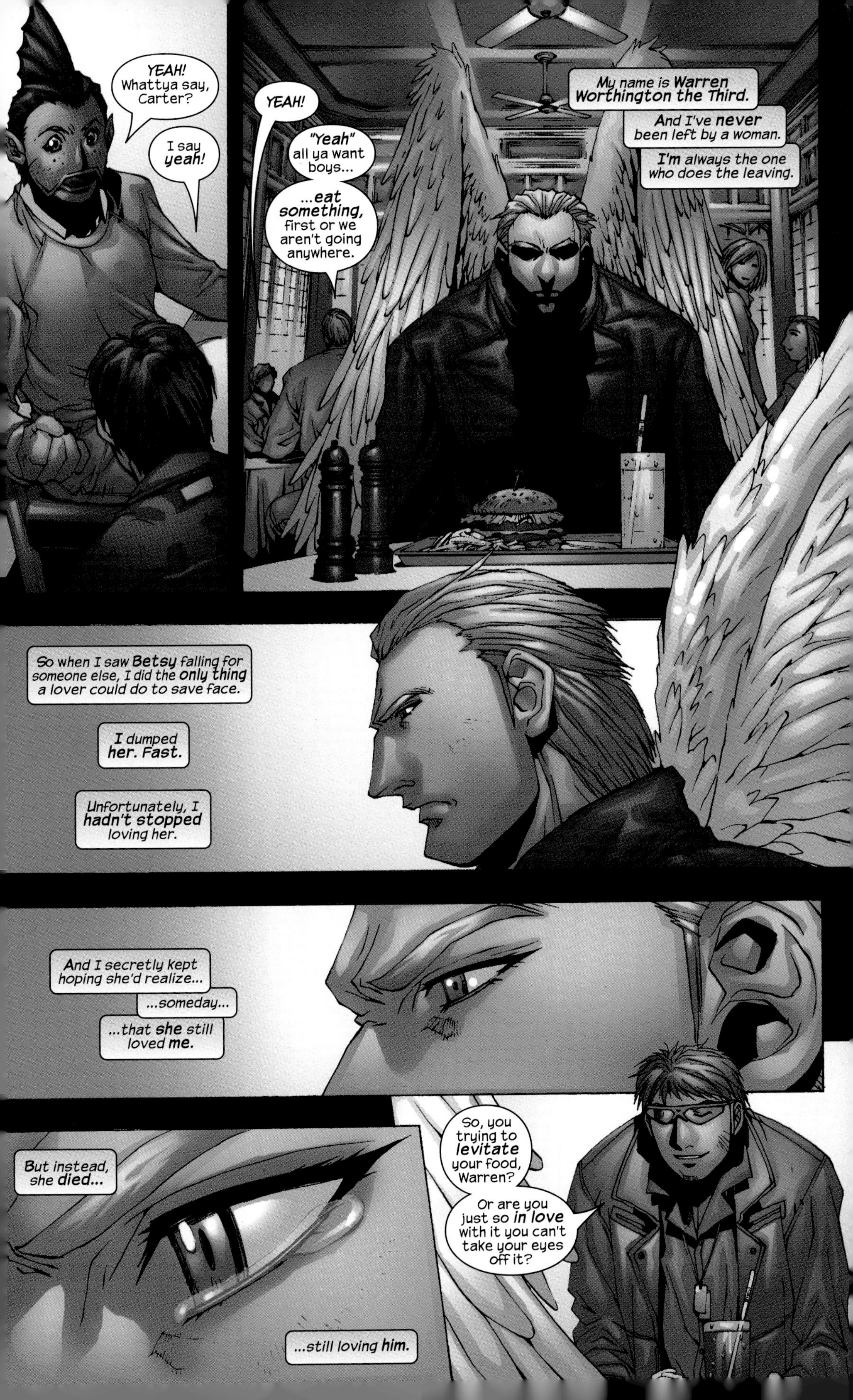
YEAH! Whattya say, Carter?
I say yeah!
YEAH!
"Yeah" all ya want boys...
...eat something, first or we aren't going anywhere.
My name is Warren Worthington the Third.
And I've never been left by a woman.
I'm always the one who does the leaving.
So when I saw Betsy falling for someone else, I did the only thing a lover could do to save face.
I dumped her. Fast.
Unfortunately, I hadn't stopped loving her.
And I secretly kept hoping she'd realize...
...someday...
...that she still loved me.
But instead, she died...
...still loving him.
So, you trying to levitate your food, Warren?
Or are you just so in love with it you can't take your eyes off it?

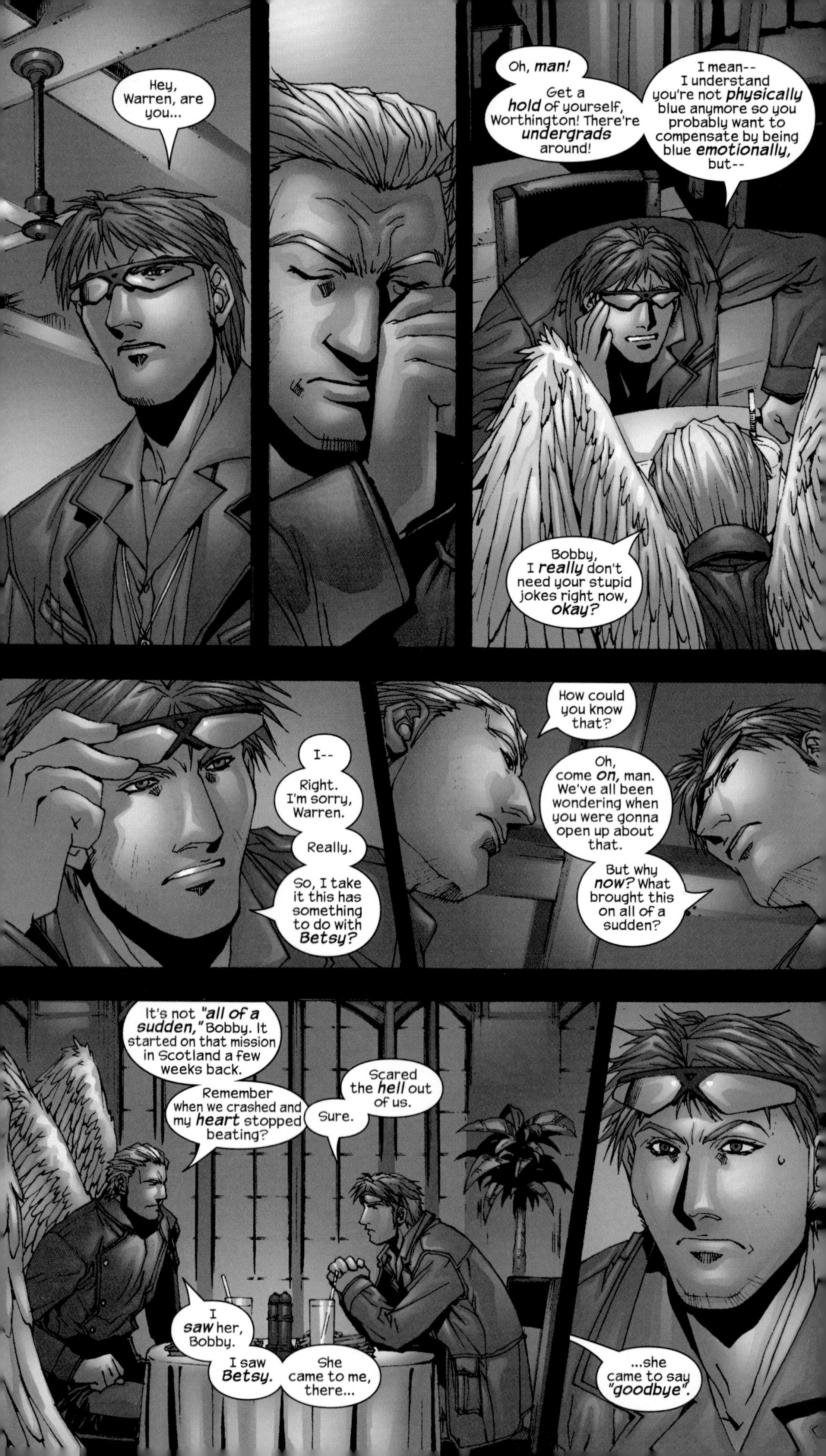

Hey, Warren, are you...
Oh, *man!*
Get a **hold** of yourself, Worthington! There're *undergrads* around!
I mean-- I understand you're not **physically** blue anymore so you probably want to compensate by being blue **emotionally,** but--
Bobby, I **really** don't need your stupid jokes right now, **okay?**
I--
Right. I'm sorry, Warren.
Really.
So, I take it this has something to do with **Betsy?**
How could you know that?
Oh, come **on,** man. We've all been wondering when you were gonna open up about that.
But why **now?** What brought this on all of a sudden?
It's not **"all of a sudden,"** Bobby. It started on that mission in Scotland a few weeks back.
Remember when we crashed and my **heart** stopped beating?
Sure.
Scared the **hell** out of us.
I **saw** her, Bobby.
I saw **Betsy.**
She came to me, there...
...she came to say **"goodbye".**

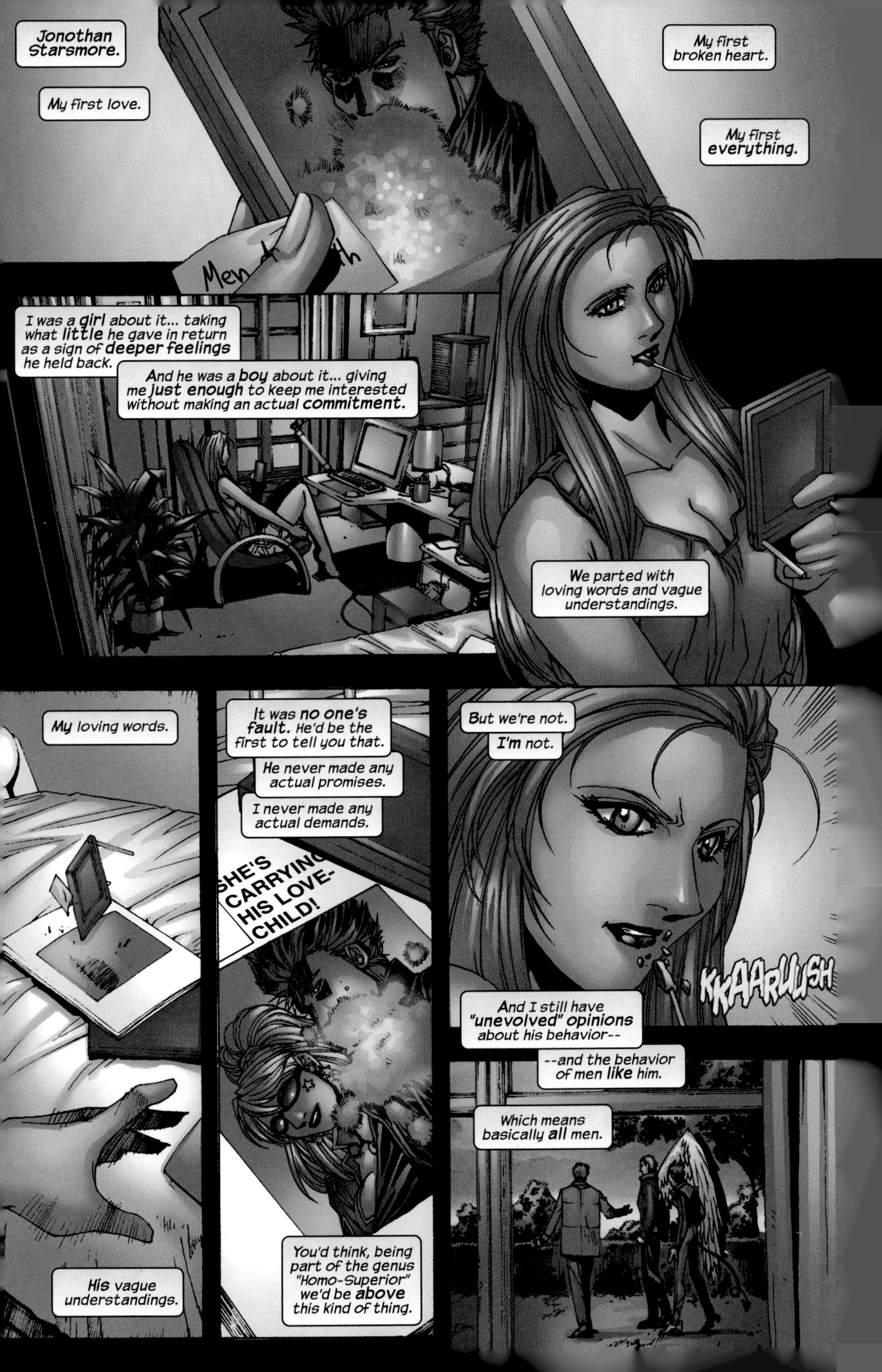

Jonothan Starsmore.
My first love.
My first broken heart.
My first everything.
Men
I was a girl about it... taking what little he gave in return as a sign of deeper feelings he held back.
And he was a boy about it... giving me just enough to keep me interested without making an actual commitment.
We parted with loving words and vague understandings.
My loving words.
His vague understandings.
It was no one's fault. He'd be the first to tell you that.
He never made any actual promises.
I never made any actual demands.
SHE'S CARRYIN HIS LOVE-CHILD!
You'd think, being part of the genus "Homo-Superior" we'd be above this kind of thing.
But we're not.
I'm not.
KKAARUUSH
And I still have "unevolved" opinions about his behavior--
--and the behavior of men like him.
Which means basically all men.

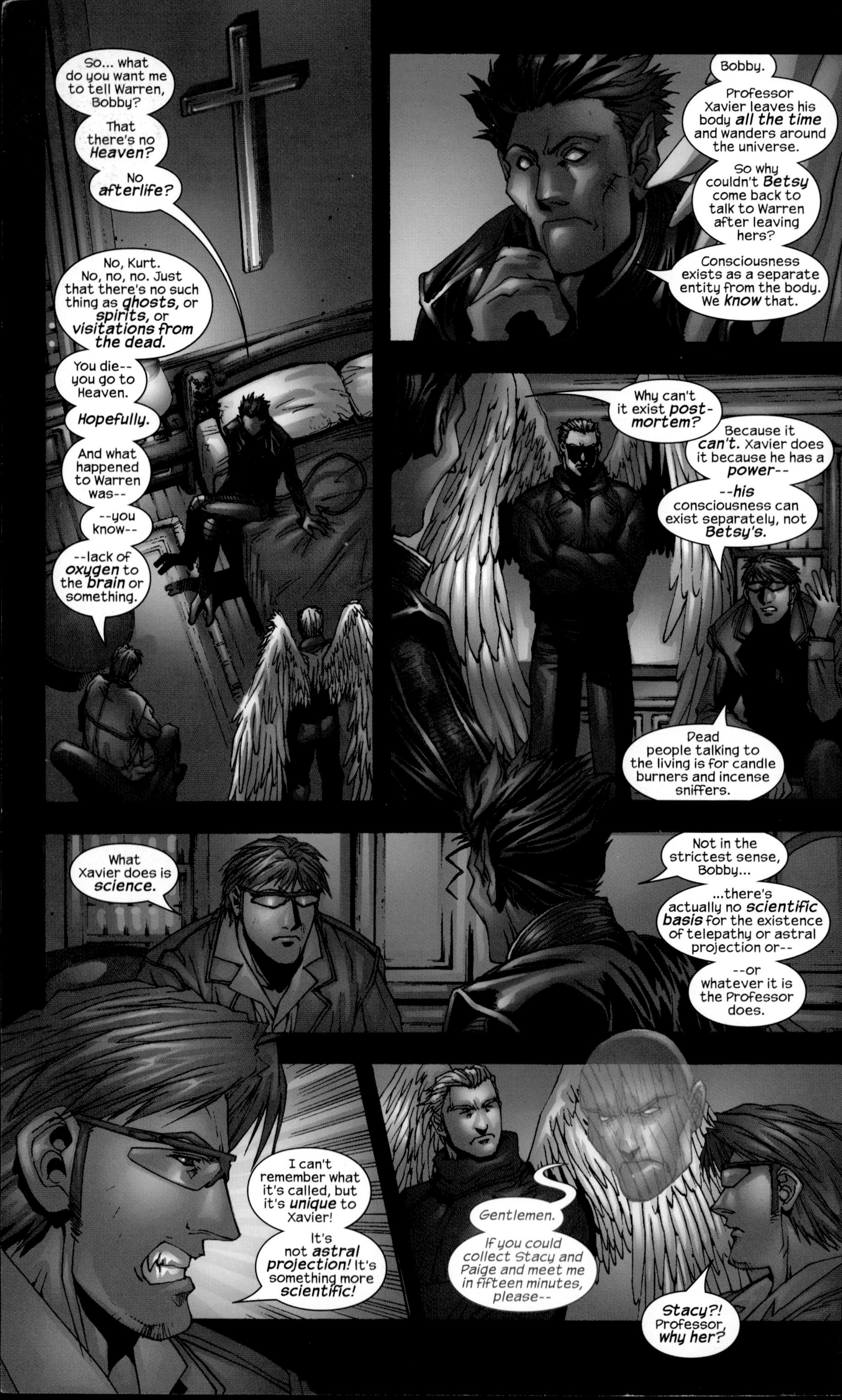
So... what do you want me to tell Warren, Bobby?
That there's no Heaven?
No afterlife?
No, Kurt. No, no, no. Just that there's no such thing as ghosts, or spirits, or visitations from the dead.
You die-- you go to Heaven.
Hopefully.
And what happened to Warren was--
--you know--
--lack of oxygen to the brain or something.
Bobby.
Professor Xavier leaves his body all the time and wanders around the universe.
So why couldn't Betsy come back to talk to Warren after leaving hers?
Consciousness exists as a separate entity from the body. We know that.
Why can't it exist post-mortem?
Because it can't. Xavier does it because he has a power--
--his consciousness can exist separately, not Betsy's.
Dead people talking to the living is for candle burners and incense sniffers.
What Xavier does is science.
Not in the strictest sense, Bobby...
...there's actually no scientific basis for the existence of telepathy or astral projection or--
--or whatever it is the Professor does.
I can't remember what it's called, but it's unique to Xavier!
It's not astral projection! It's something more scientific!
Gentlemen.
If you could collect Stacy and Paige and meet me in fifteen minutes, please--
Stacy?! Professor, why her?

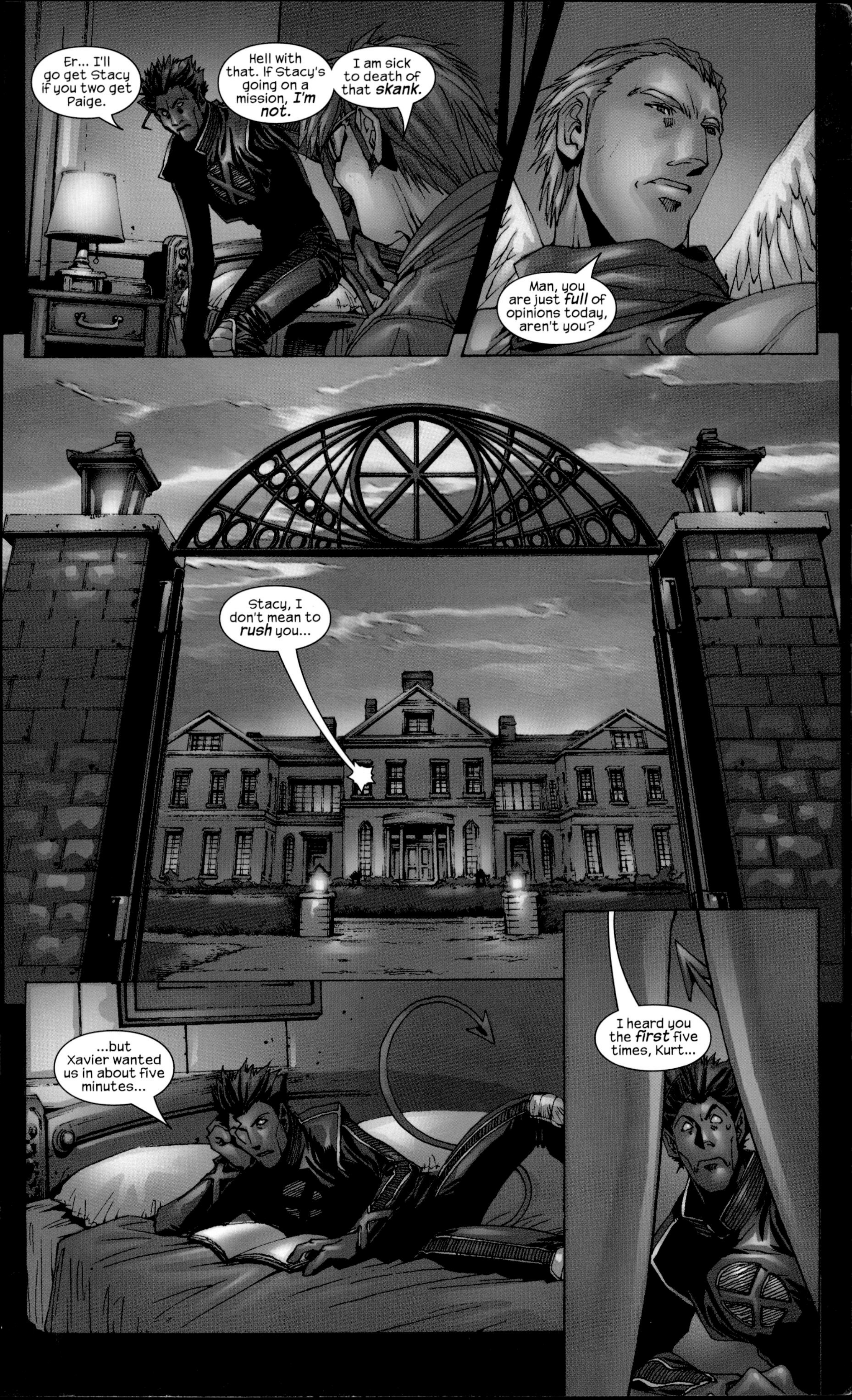
Er... I'll go get Stacy if you two get Paige.
Hell with that. If Stacy's going on a mission, I'm not.
I am sick to death of that skank.
Man, you are just full of opinions today, aren't you?
Stacy, I don't mean to rush you...
...but Xavier wanted us in about five minutes...
I heard you the first five times, Kurt...

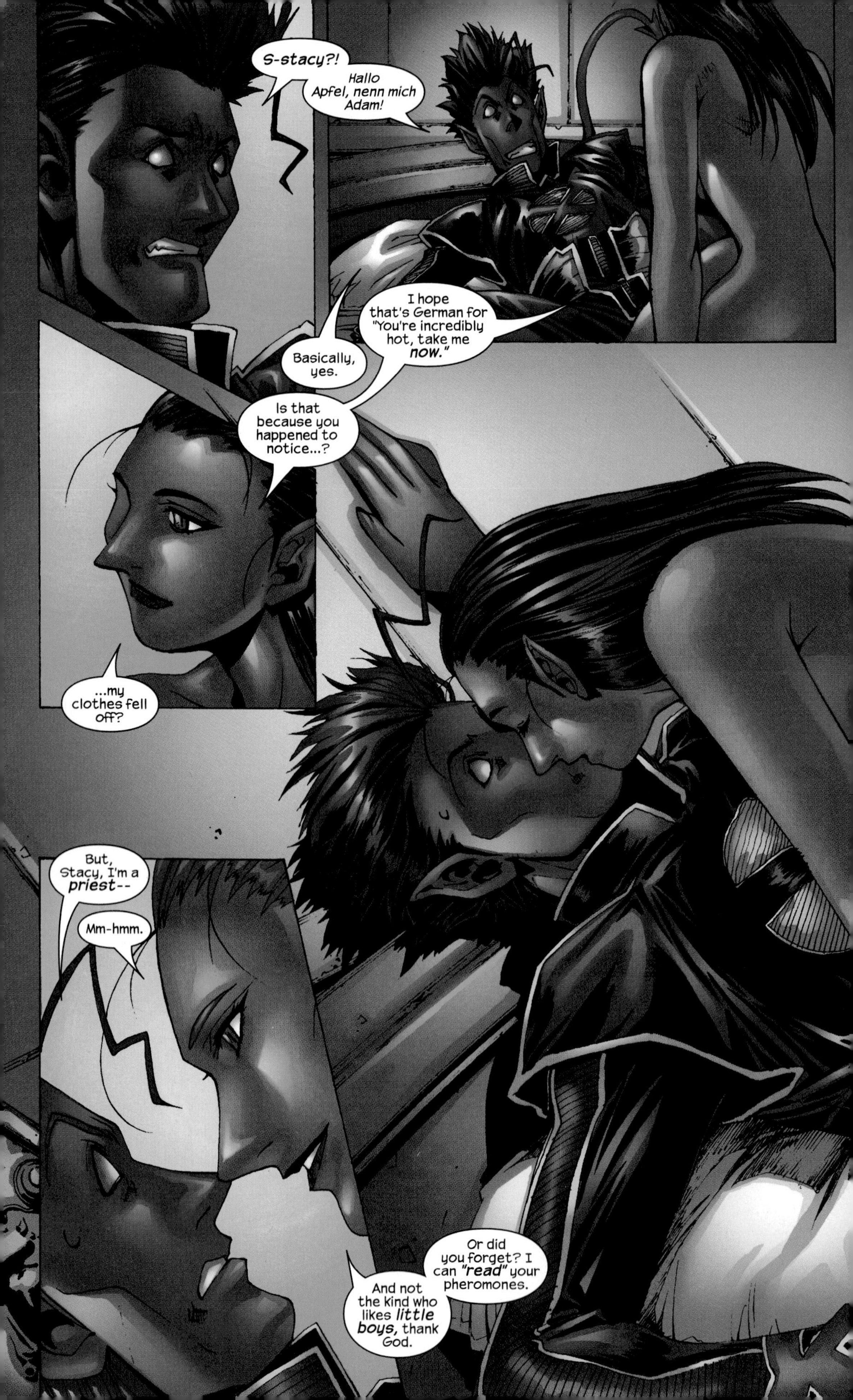

S-stacy?!
Hallo Apfel, nenn mich Adam!
I hope that's German for "You're incredibly hot, take me now."
Basically, yes.
Is that because you happened to notice...?
...my clothes fell off?
But, Stacy, I'm a priest--
Mm-hmm.
Or did you forget? I can "read" your pheromones.
And not the kind who likes little boys, thank God.

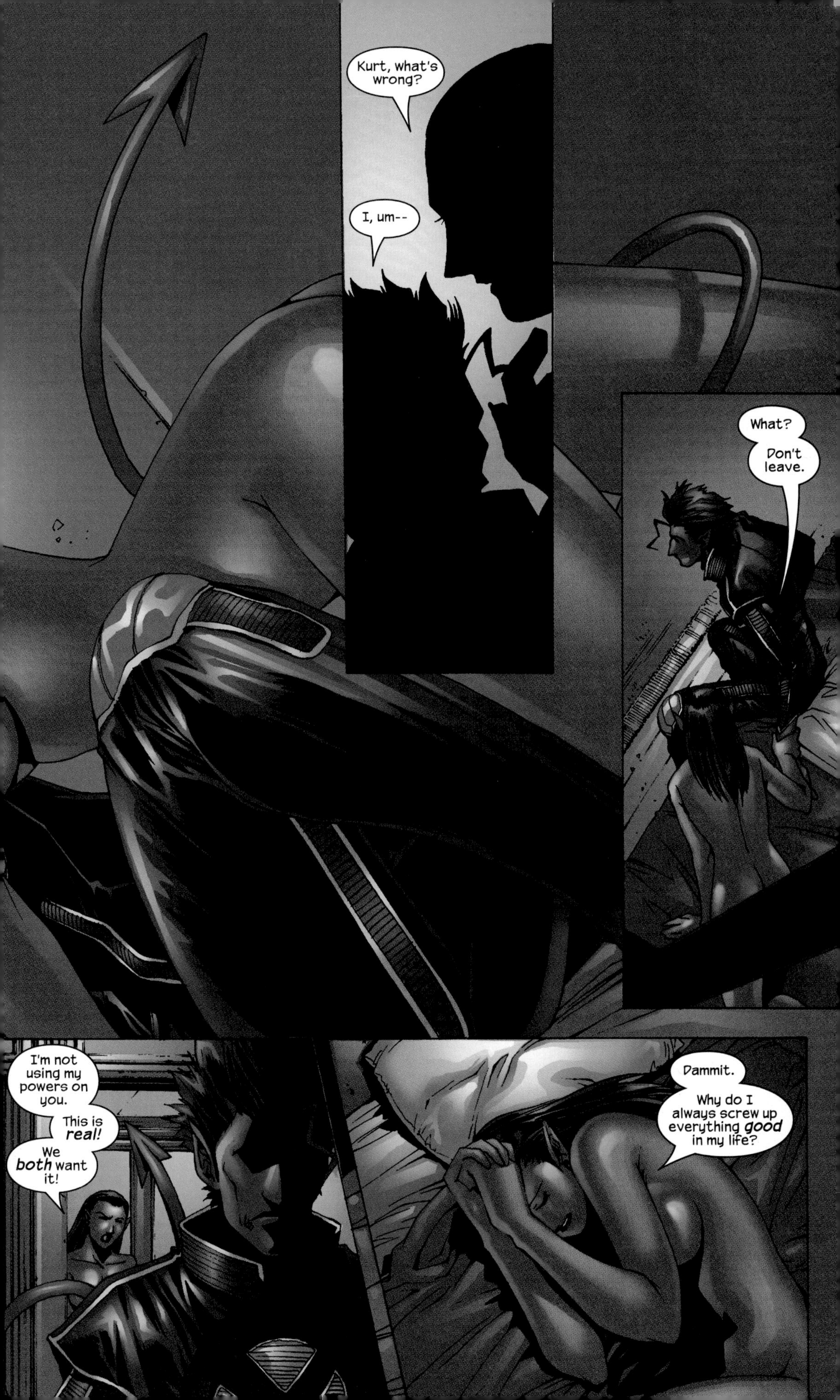
Kurt, what's wrong?
I, um--
What?
Don't leave.
I'm not using my powers on you.
This is *real!*
We *both* want it!
Dammit.
Why do I always screw up everything *good* in my life?

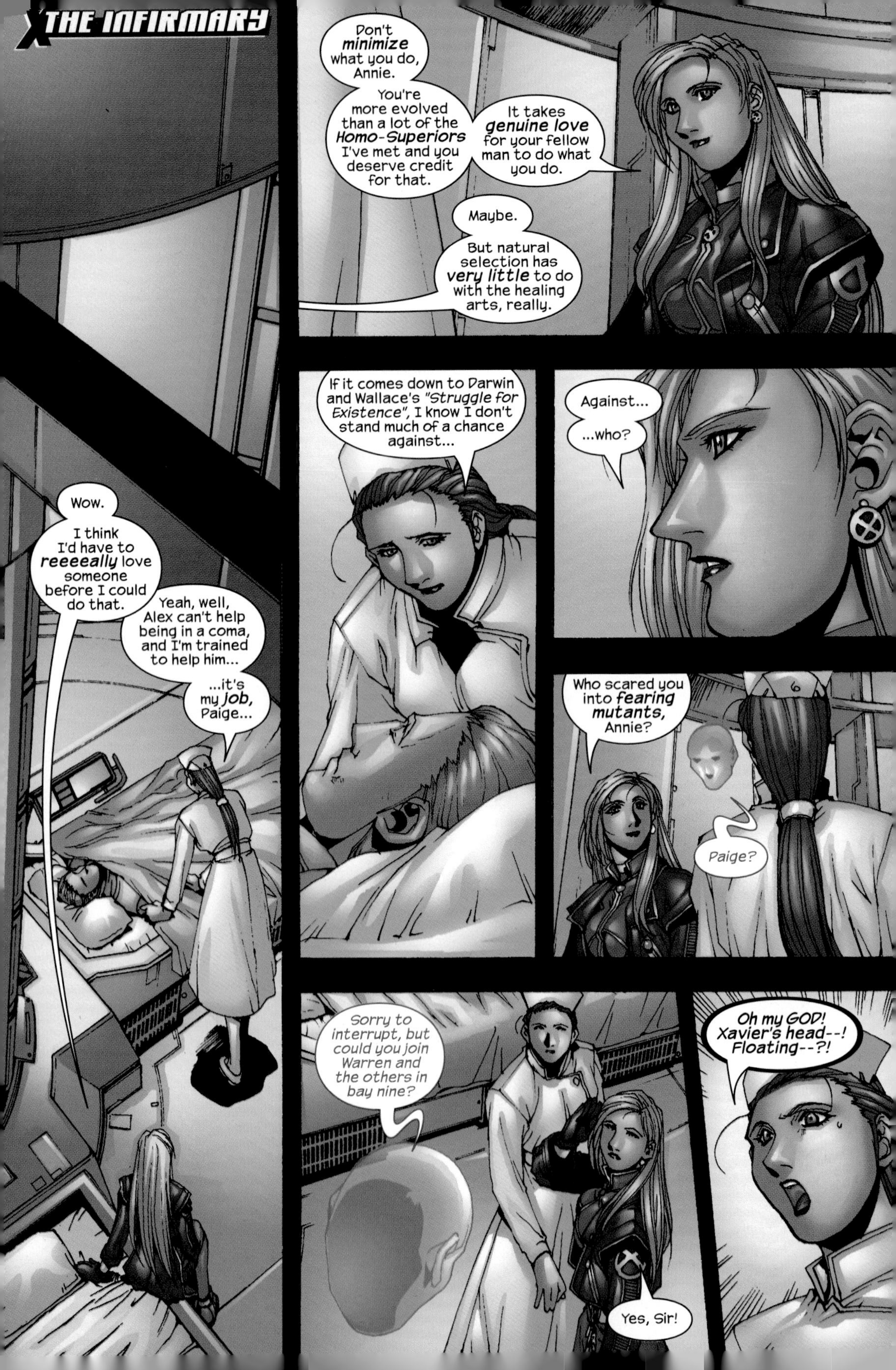
THE INFIRMARY
Don't minimize what you do, Annie.
You're more evolved than a lot of the Homo-Superiors I've met and you deserve credit for that.
It takes genuine love for your fellow man to do what you do.
Maybe.
But natural selection has very little to do with the healing arts, really.
Wow.
I think I'd have to reeeeally love someone before I could do that.
Yeah, well, Alex can't help being in a coma, and I'm trained to help him...
...it's my job, Paige...
If it comes down to Darwin and Wallace's "Struggle for Existence", I know I don't stand much of a chance against...
Against...
...who?
Who scared you into fearing mutants, Annie?
Paige?
Sorry to interrupt, but could you join Warren and the others in bay nine?
Yes, Sir!
Oh my GOD! Xavier's head--! Floating--?!

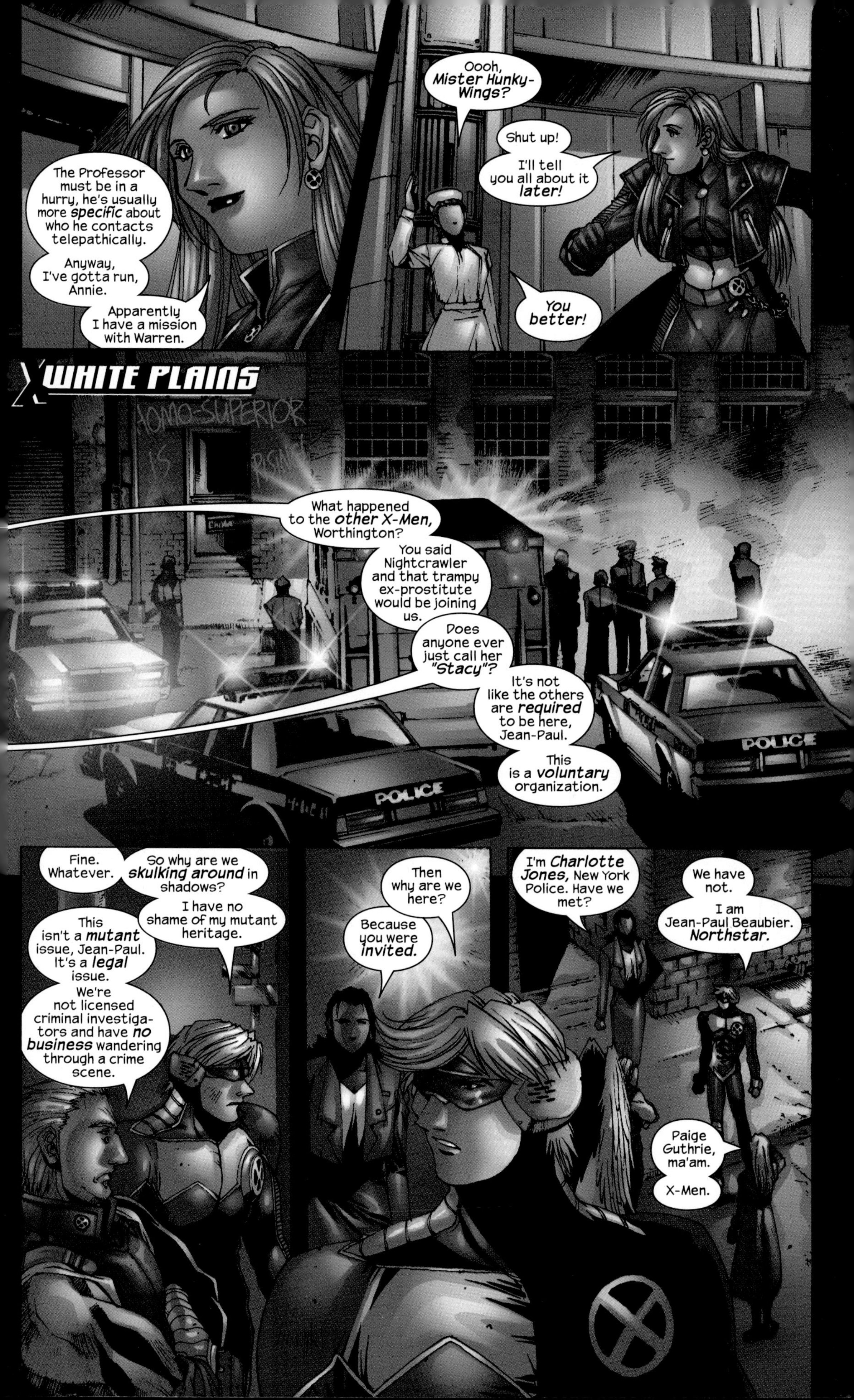
The Professor must be in a hurry, he's usually more *specific* about who he contacts telepathically.
Anyway, I've gotta run, Annie.
Apparently I have a mission with Warren.
Oooh, *Mister Hunky-Wings?*
Shut up!
I'll tell you all about it *later!*
You better!
WHITE PLAINS
HOMO-SUPERIOR IS RISING
What happened to the *other X-Men,* Worthington?
You said Nightcrawler and that trampy ex-prostitute would be joining us.
Does anyone ever just call her *"Stacy"?*
It's not like the others are *required* to be here, Jean-Paul.
This is a *voluntary* organization.
POLICE
POLICE
Fine. Whatever.
So why are we *skulking around* in shadows?
I have no shame of my mutant heritage.
This isn't a *mutant* issue, Jean-Paul. It's a *legal* issue.
We're not licensed criminal investigators and have *no business* wandering through a crime scene.
Then why are we here?
Because you were *invited.*
I'm *Charlotte Jones,* New York Police. Have we met?
We have not.
I am Jean-Paul Beaubier. *Northstar.*
Paige Guthrie, ma'am.
X-Men.

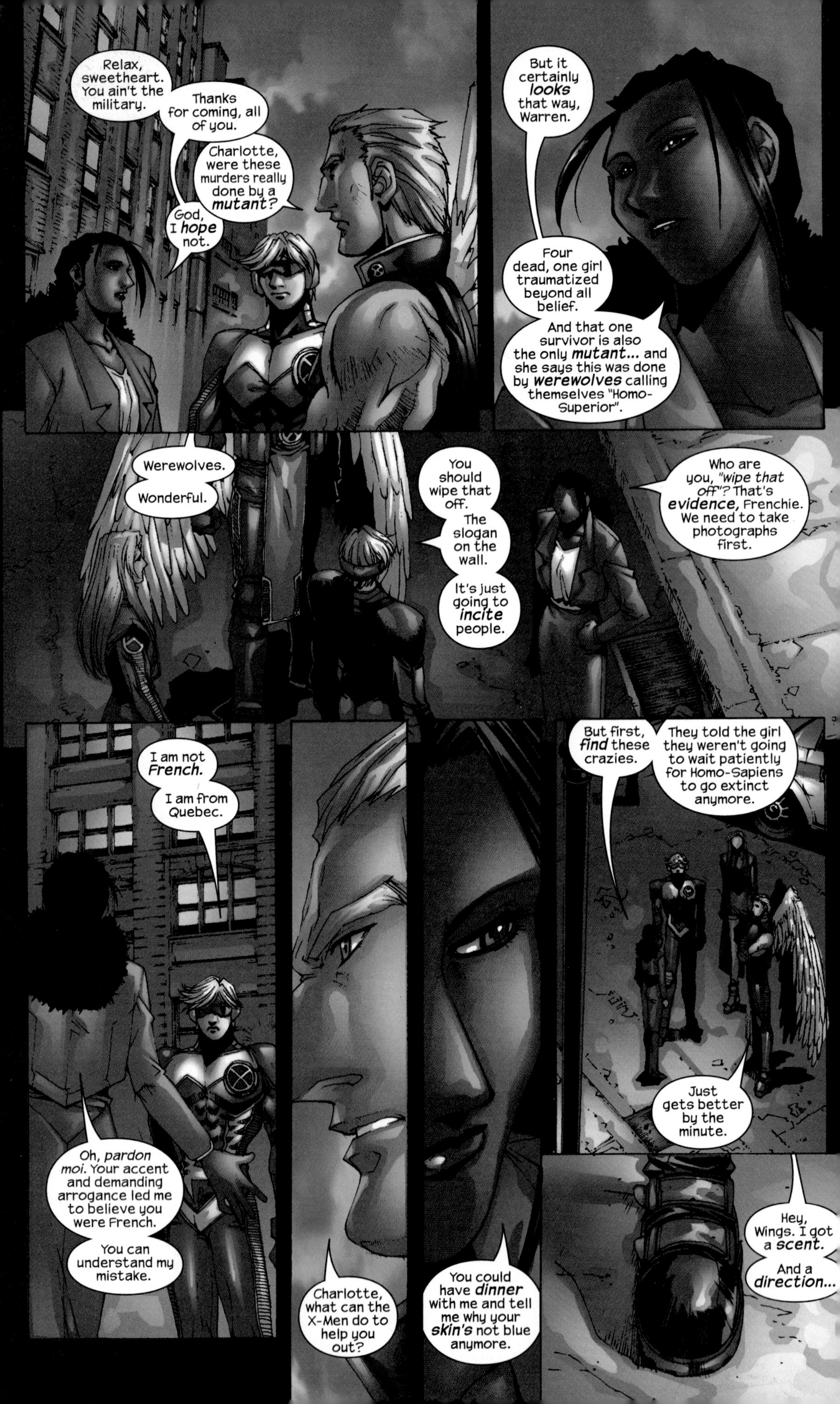
Relax, sweetheart. You ain't the military.
Thanks for coming, all of you.
Charlotte, were these murders really done by a *mutant*?
God, I *hope* not.
But it certainly *looks* that way, Warren.
Four dead, one girl traumatized beyond all belief.
And that one survivor is also the only *mutant...* and she says this was done by *werewolves* calling themselves "Homo-Superior".
Werewolves.
Wonderful.
You should wipe that off.
The slogan on the wall.
It's just going to *incite* people.
Who are you, *"wipe that off"*? That's *evidence,* Frenchie. We need to take photographs first.
I am not *French.*
I am from Quebec.
Oh, *pardon moi*. Your accent and demanding arrogance led me to believe you were French.
You can understand my mistake.
Charlotte, what can the X-Men do to help you out?
You could have *dinner* with me and tell me why your *skin's* not blue anymore.
They told the girl they weren't going to wait patiently for Homo-Sapiens to go extinct anymore.
But first, *find* these crazies.
Just gets better by the minute.
Hey, Wings. I got a *scent.*
And a *direction...*

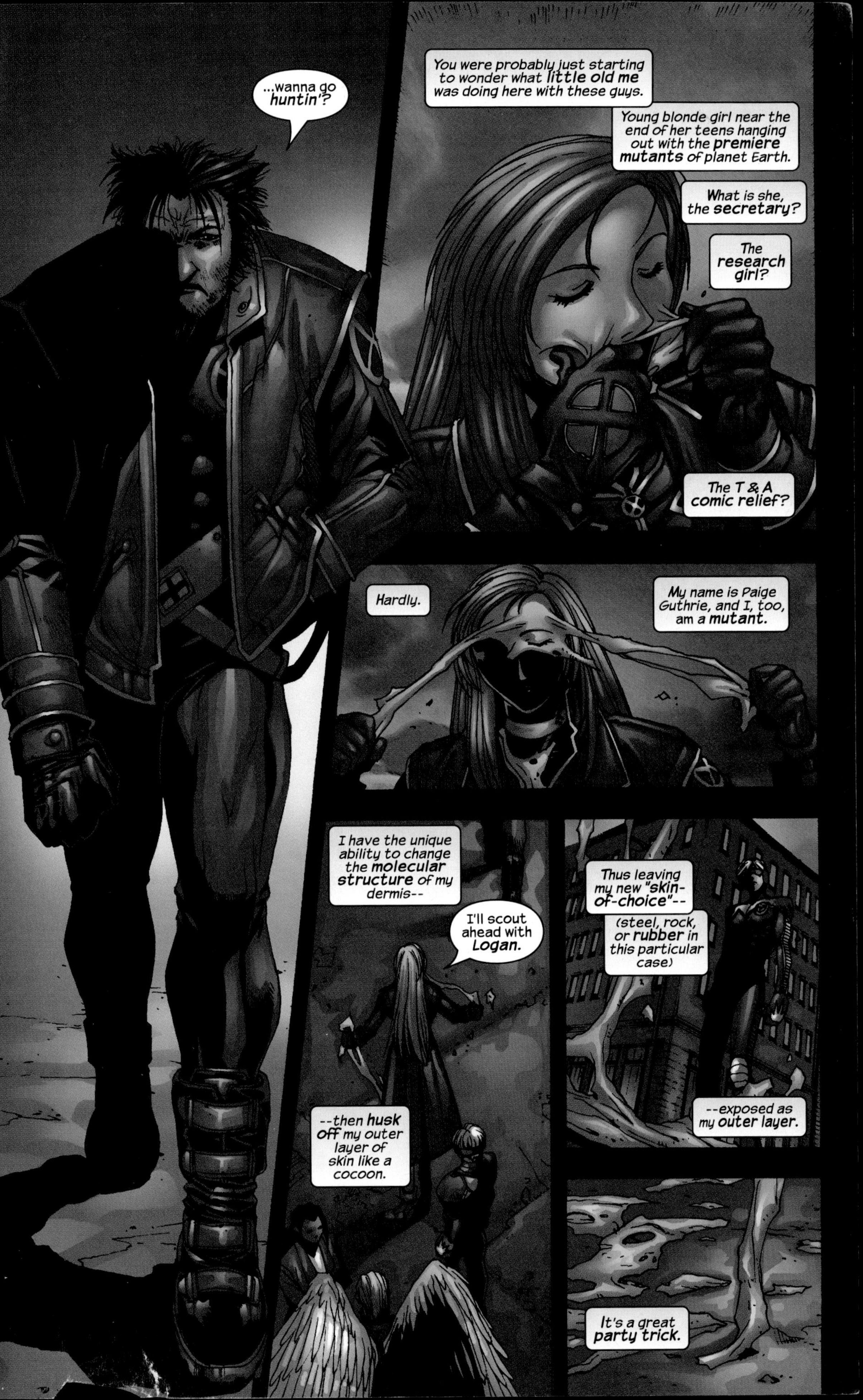
...wanna go huntin'?
You were probably just starting to wonder what little old me was doing here with these guys.
Young blonde girl near the end of her teens hanging out with the premiere mutants of planet Earth.
What is she, the secretary?
The research girl?
The T & A comic relief?
Hardly.
My name is Paige Guthrie, and I, too, am a mutant.
I have the unique ability to change the molecular structure of my dermis--
I'll scout ahead with Logan.
--then husk off my outer layer of skin like a cocoon.
Thus leaving my new "skin-of-choice"--
(steel, rock, or rubber in this particular case)
--exposed as my outer layer.
It's a great party trick.

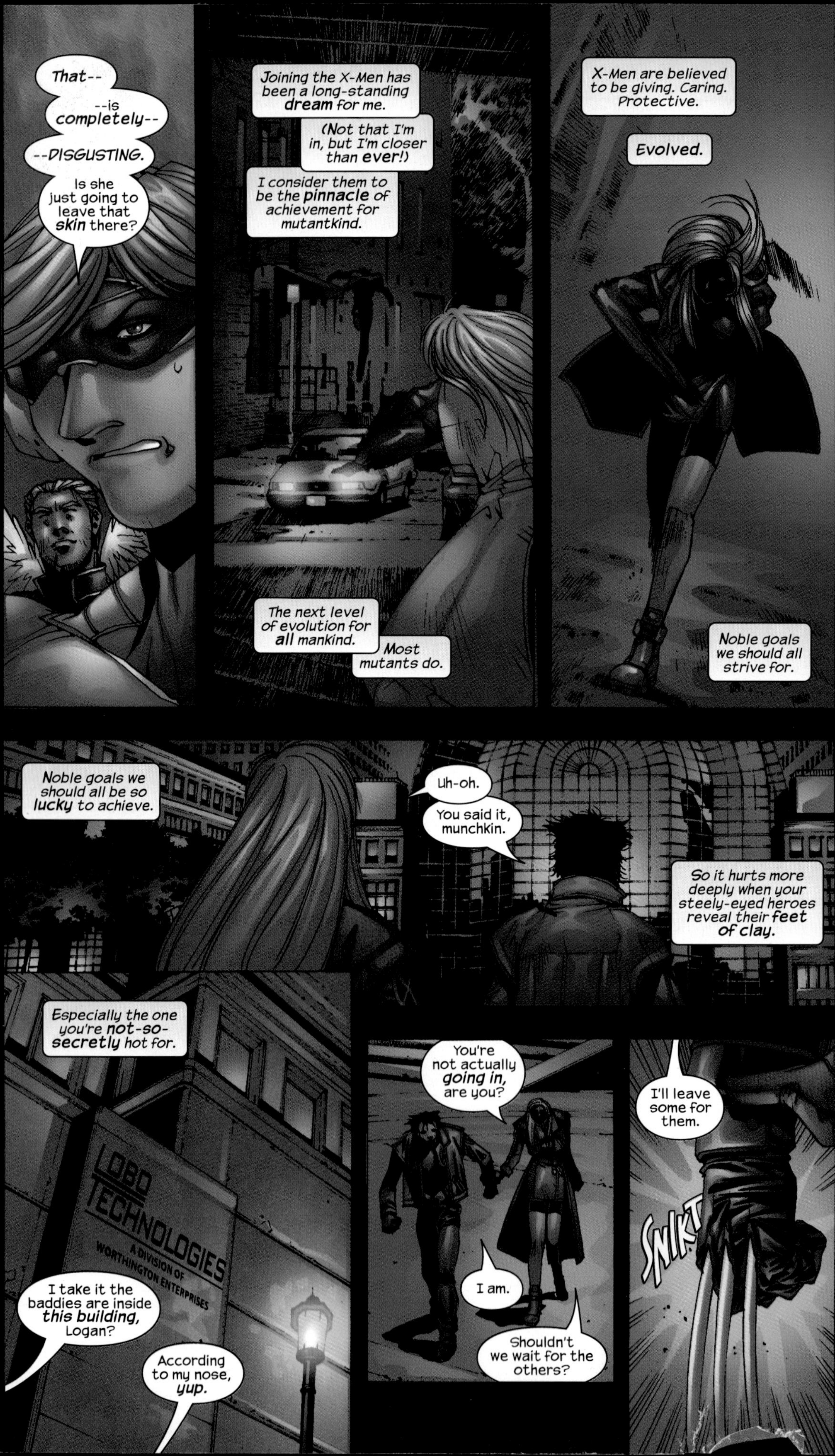

That--
--is completely--
--DISGUSTING.
Is she just going to leave that skin there?
Joining the X-Men has been a long-standing dream for me.
(Not that I'm in, but I'm closer than ever!)
I consider them to be the pinnacle of achievement for mutantkind.
The next level of evolution for all mankind.
Most mutants do.
X-Men are believed to be giving. Caring. Protective.
Evolved.
Noble goals we should all strive for.
Noble goals we should all be so lucky to achieve.
Uh-oh.
You said it, munchkin.
So it hurts more deeply when your steely-eyed heroes reveal their feet of clay.
Especially the one you're not-so-secretly hot for.
LOBO TECHNOLOGIES
A DIVISION OF WORTHINGTON ENTERPRISES
I take it the baddies are inside this building, Logan?
According to my nose, yup.
You're not actually going in, are you?
I am.
Shouldn't we wait for the others?
I'll leave some for them.
SNIKT

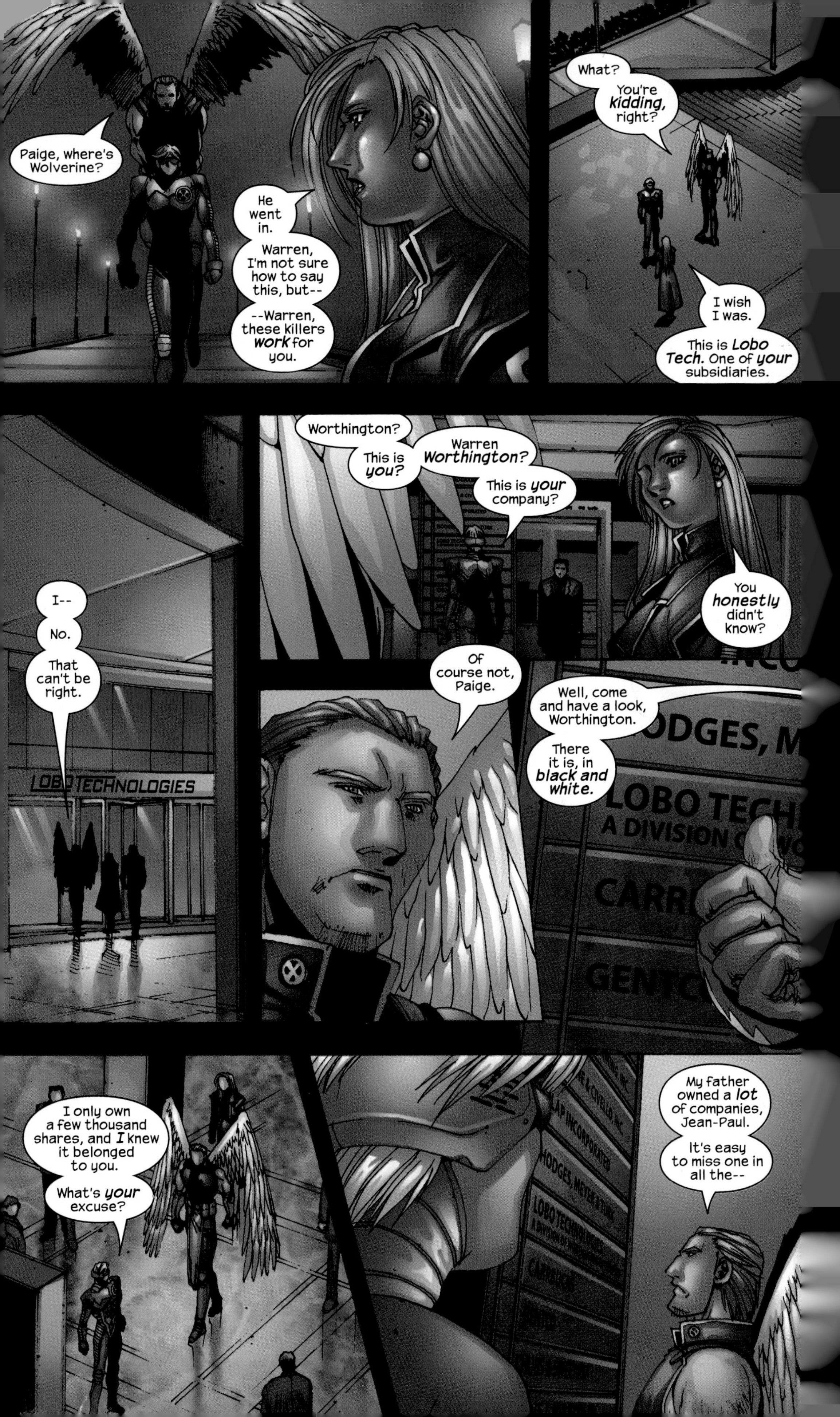
Paige, where's Wolverine?
He went in.
Warren, I'm not sure how to say this, but--
--Warren, these killers work for you.
What?
You're kidding, right?
I wish I was.
This is Lobo Tech. One of your subsidiaries.
I--
No.
That can't be right.
LOBO TECHNOLOGIES
Worthington?
This is you?
Warren Worthington?
This is your company?
You honestly didn't know?
Of course not, Paige.
Well, come and have a look, Worthington.
There it is, in black and white.
I only own a few thousand shares, and I knew it belonged to you.
What's your excuse?
My father owned a lot of companies, Jean-Paul.
It's easy to miss one in all the--

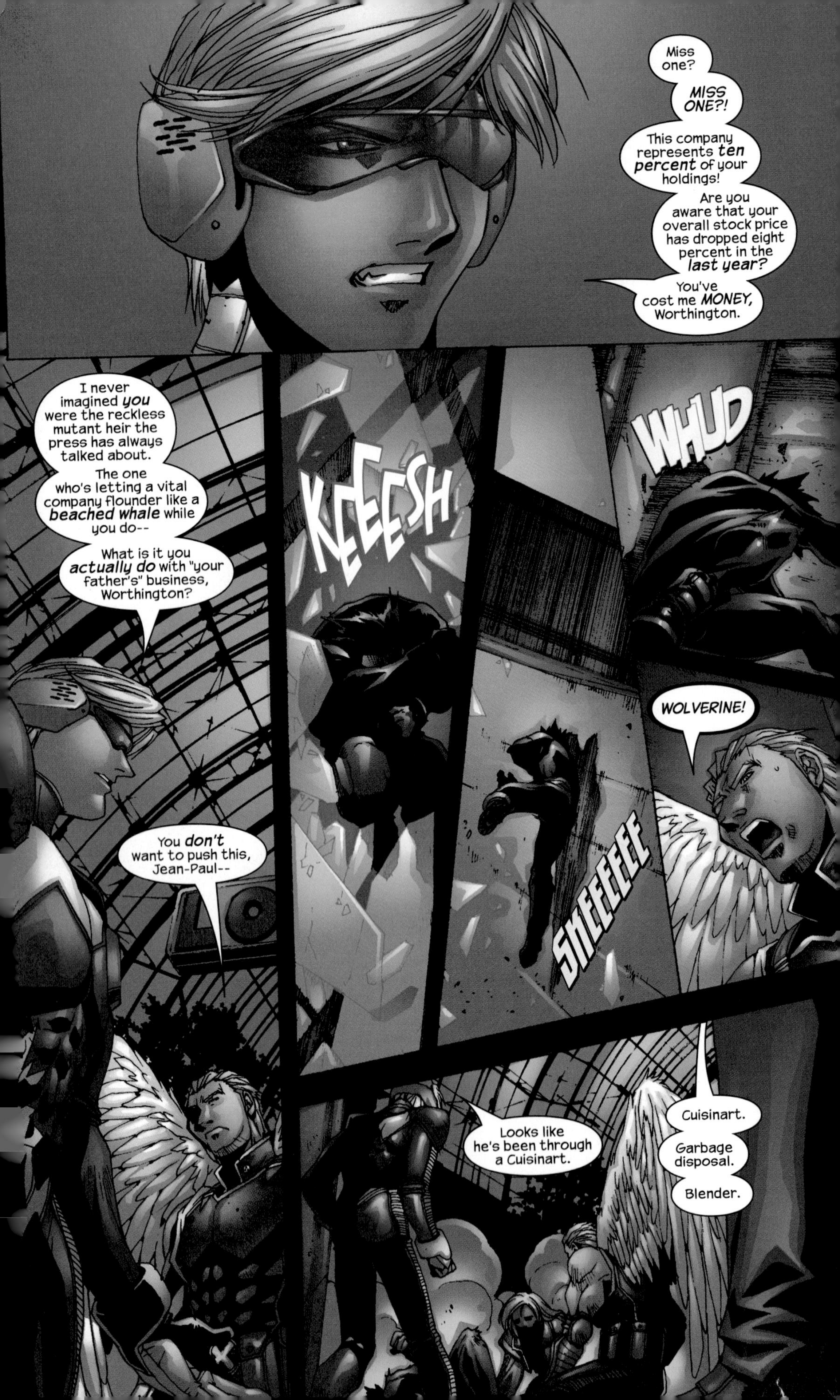
Miss one?
MISS ONE?!
This company represents ten percent of your holdings!
Are you aware that your overall stock price has dropped eight percent in the last year?
You've cost me MONEY, Worthington.
I never imagined you were the reckless mutant heir the press has always talked about.
The one who's letting a vital company flounder like a beached whale while you do--
What is it you actually do with "your father's" business, Worthington?
You don't want to push this, Jean-Paul--
KEEESH
SHEEEEEE
WHUD
WOLVERINE!
Looks like he's been through a Cuisinart.
Cuisinart.
Garbage disposal.
Blender.

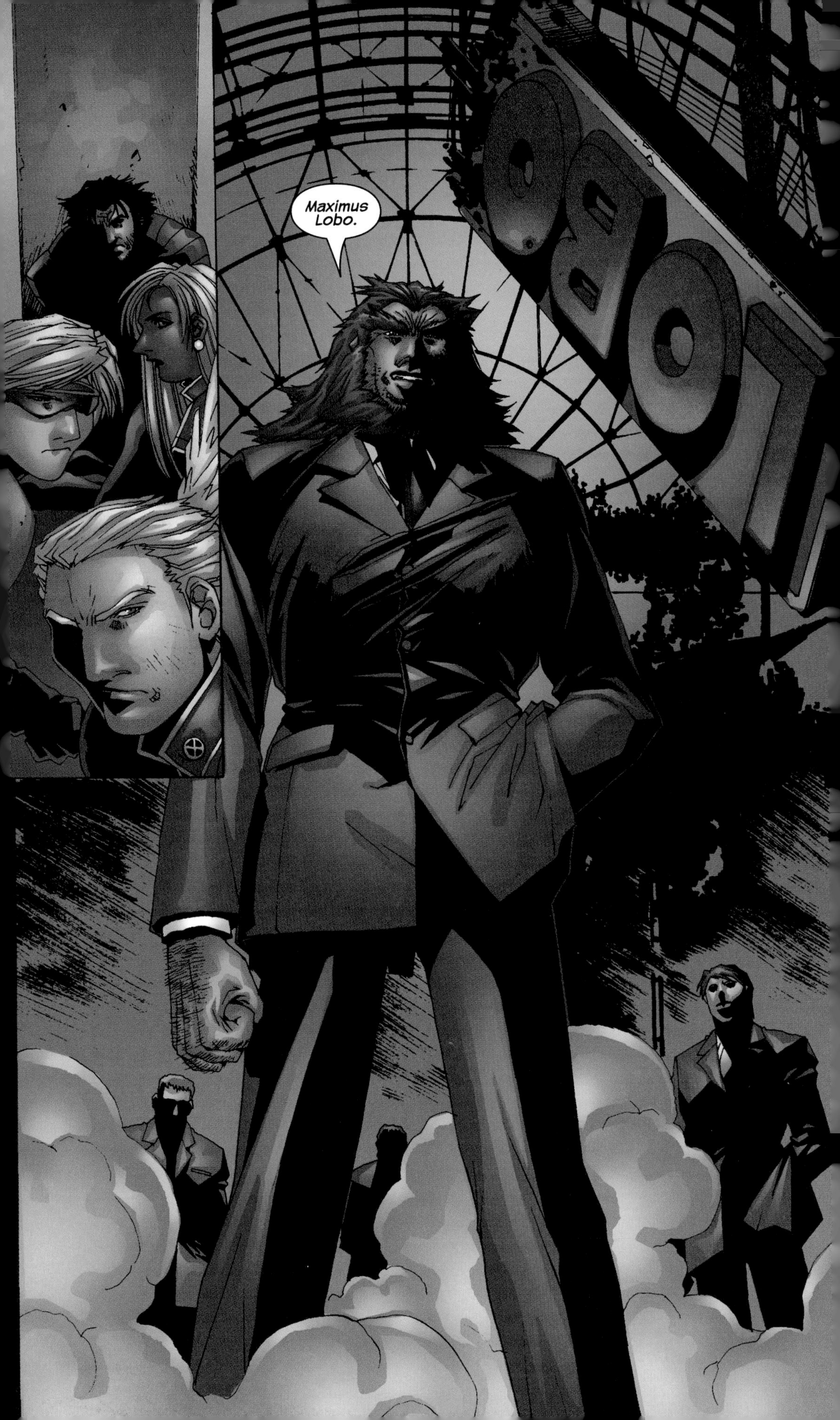
Maximus Lobo.

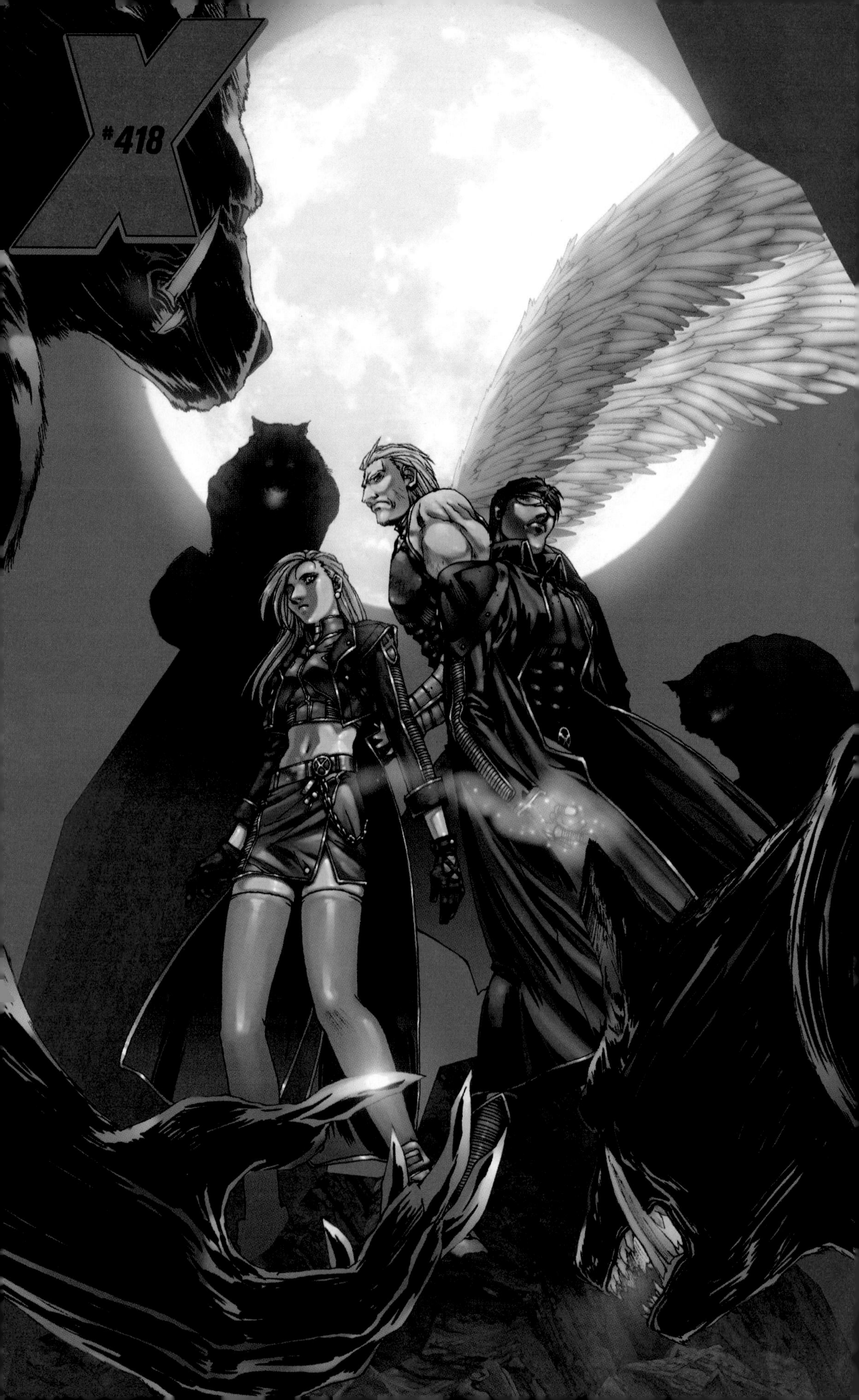
X
#418

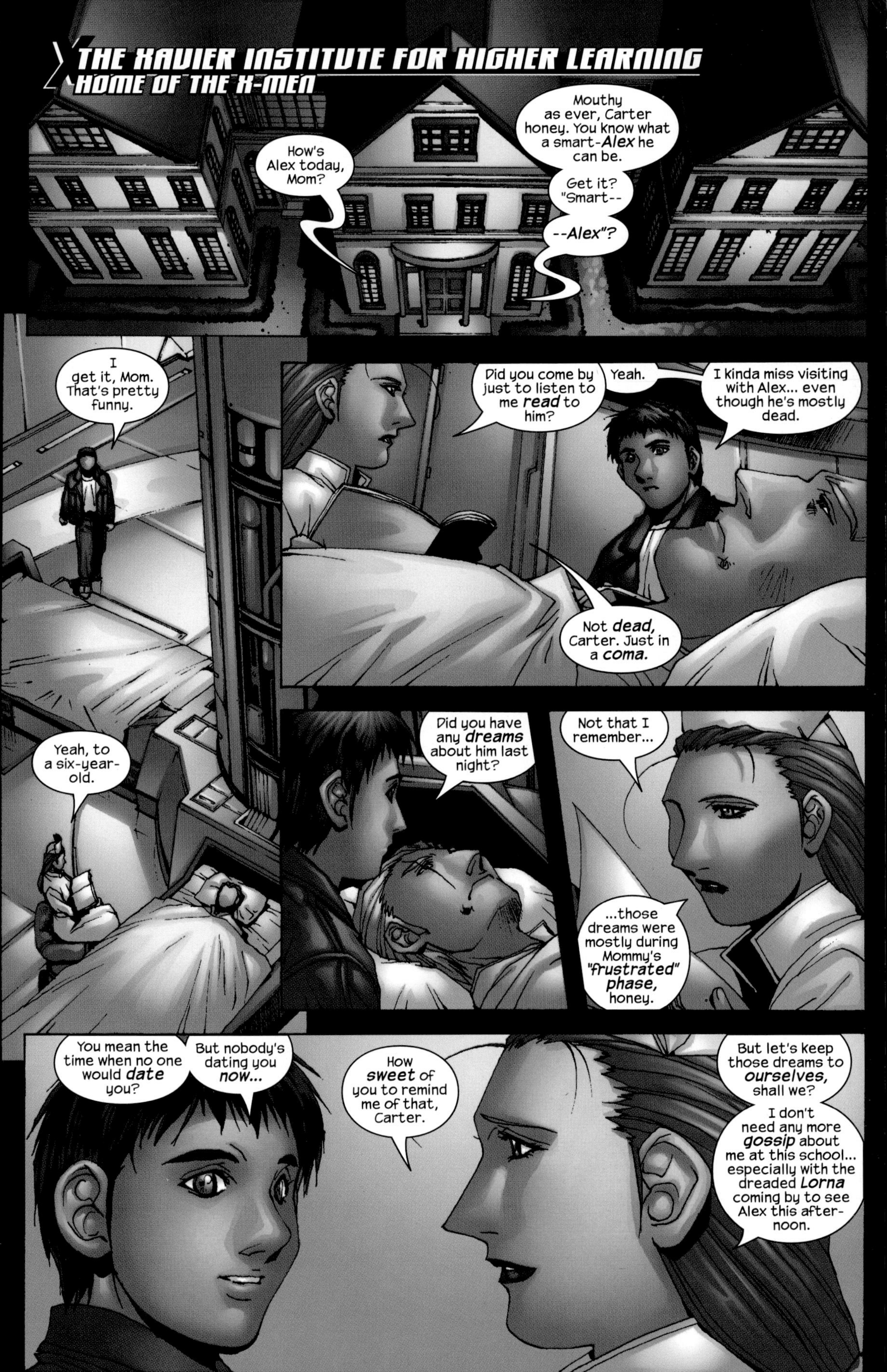
THE XAVIER INSTITUTE FOR HIGHER LEARNING
HOME OF THE X-MEN
How's Alex today, Mom?
Mouthy as ever, Carter honey. You know what a smart-*Alex* he can be.
Get it? "Smart--
--*Alex*"?
I get it, Mom. That's pretty funny.
Yeah, to a six-year-old.
Did you come by just to listen to me *read* to him?
Yeah.
I kinda miss visiting with Alex... even though he's mostly dead.
Not *dead,* Carter. Just in a *coma.*
Did you have any *dreams* about him last night?
Not that I remember...
...those dreams were mostly during Mommy's *"frustrated" phase,* honey.
You mean the time when no one would *date* you?
But nobody's dating you *now...*
How *sweet* of you to remind me of that, Carter.
But let's keep those dreams to *ourselves,* shall we?
I don't need any more *gossip* about me at this school... especially with the dreaded *Lorna* coming by to see Alex this after-noon.

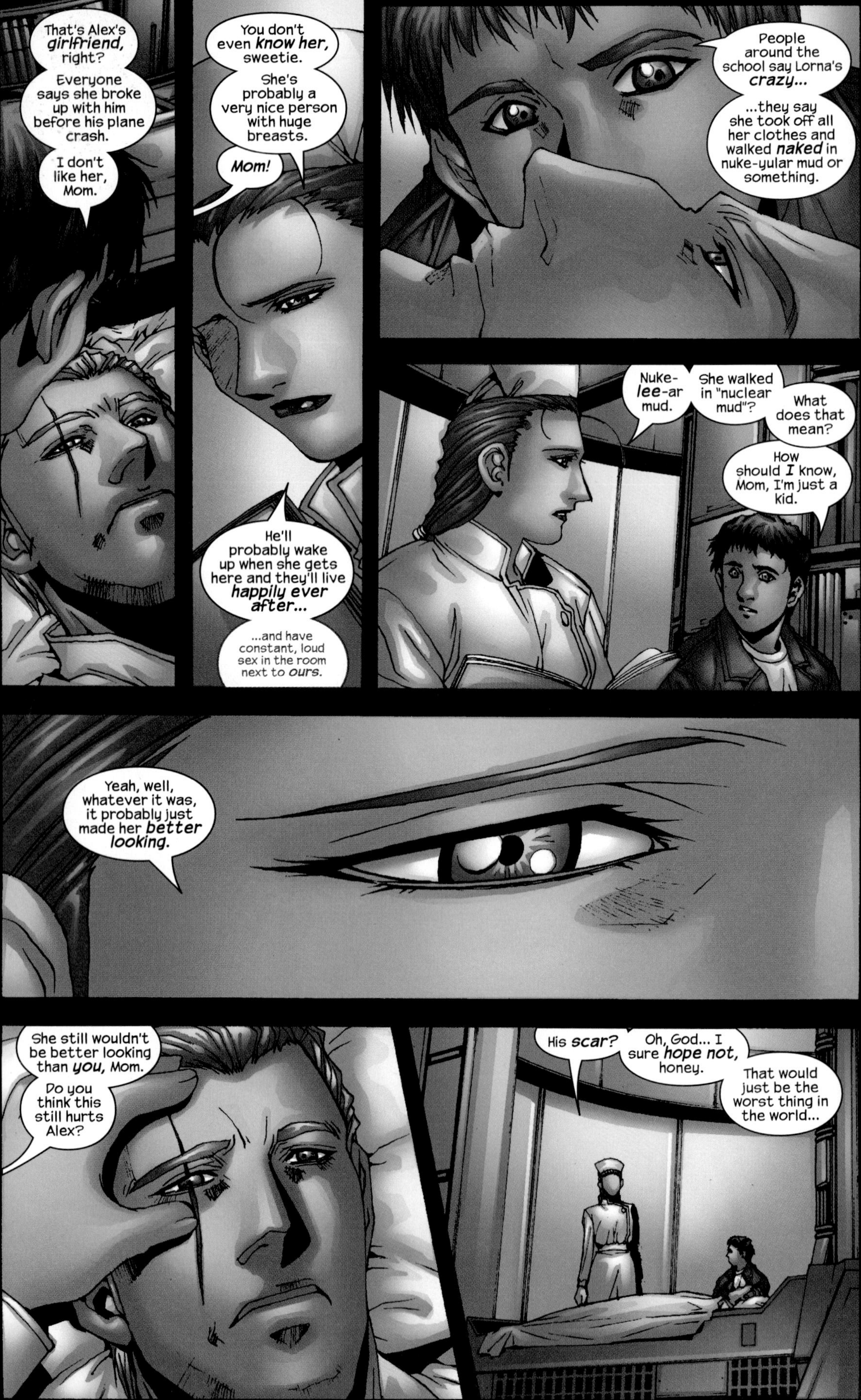
That's Alex's girlfriend, right?
Everyone says she broke up with him before his plane crash.
I don't like her, Mom.
You don't even know her, sweetie.
She's probably a very nice person with huge breasts.
Mom!
People around the school say Lorna's crazy...
...they say she took off all her clothes and walked naked in nuke-yular mud or something.
He'll probably wake up when she gets here and they'll live happily ever after...
...and have constant, loud sex in the room next to ours.
Nuke-lee-ar mud.
She walked in "nuclear mud"?
What does that mean?
How should I know, Mom, I'm just a kid.
Yeah, well, whatever it was, it probably just made her better looking.
She still wouldn't be better looking than you, Mom.
Do you think this still hurts Alex?
His scar?
Oh, God... I sure hope not, honey.
That would just be the worst thing in the world...

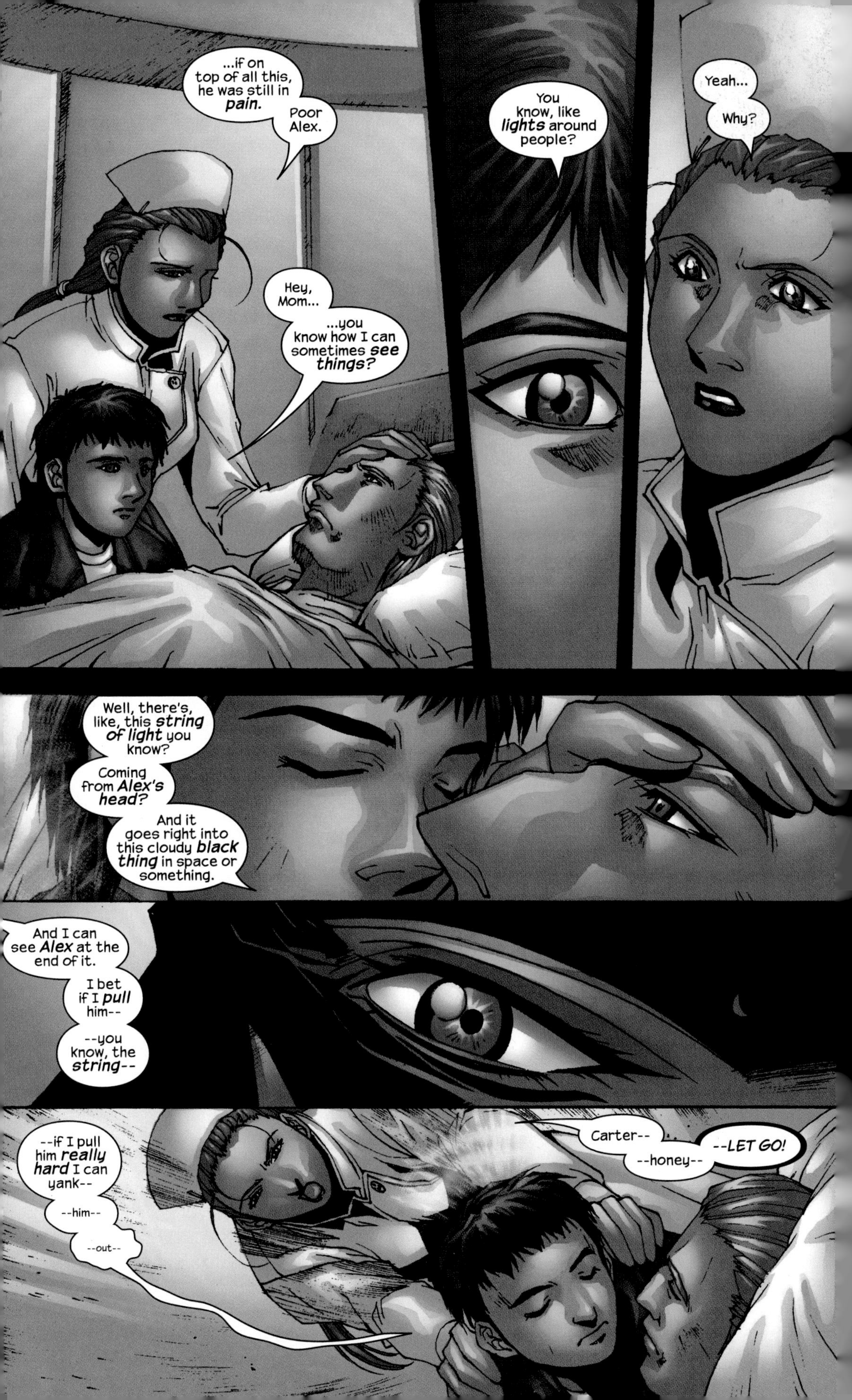
...if on top of all this, he was still in *pain.*
Poor Alex.
Hey, Mom...
...you know how I can sometimes *see things?*
You know, like *lights* around people?
Yeah...
Why?
Well, there's, like, this *string of light* you know?
Coming from *Alex's head?*
And it goes right into this cloudy *black thing* in space or something.
And I can see *Alex* at the end of it.
I bet if I *pull* him--
--you know, the *string*--
--if I pull him *really hard* I can yank--
--him--
--out--
Carter--
--honey--
--LET GO!

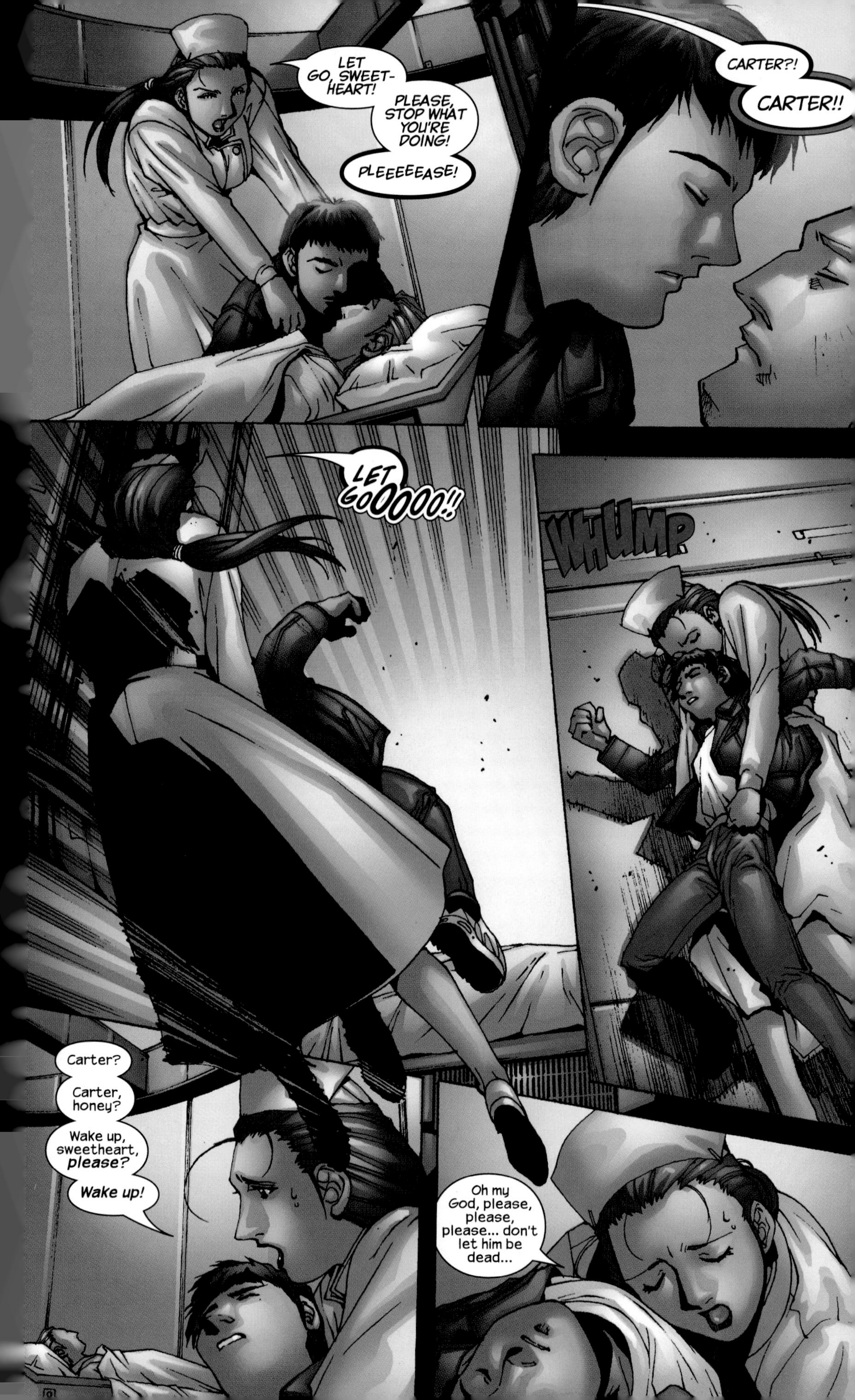
LET GO, SWEET-HEART!
PLEASE, STOP WHAT YOU'RE DOING!
PLEEEEEASE!
CARTER?!
CARTER!!
LET GOOOOO!!
WHUMP
Carter?
Carter, honey?
Wake up, sweetheart, *please?*
Wake up!
Oh my God, please, please, please... don't let him be dead...

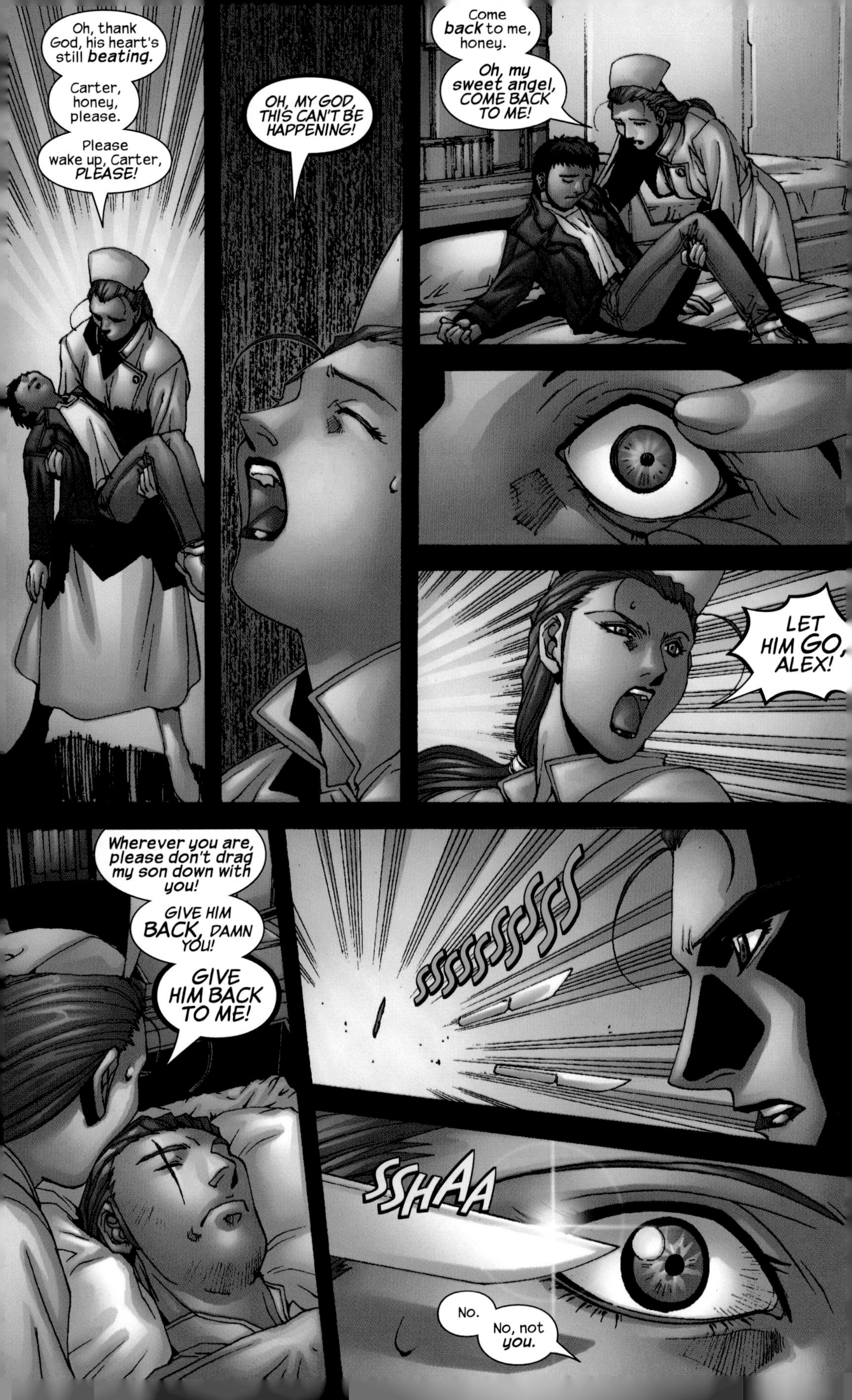
Oh, thank God, his heart's still beating.
Carter, honey, please.
Please wake up, Carter, PLEASE!
OH, MY GOD, THIS CAN'T BE HAPPENING!
Come back to me, honey.
Oh, my sweet angel, COME BACK TO ME!
LET HIM GO, ALEX!
Wherever you are, please don't drag my son down with you!
GIVE HIM BACK, DAMN YOU!
GIVE HIM BACK TO ME!
SSSSSSSSSS
SSHAA
No.
No, not you.

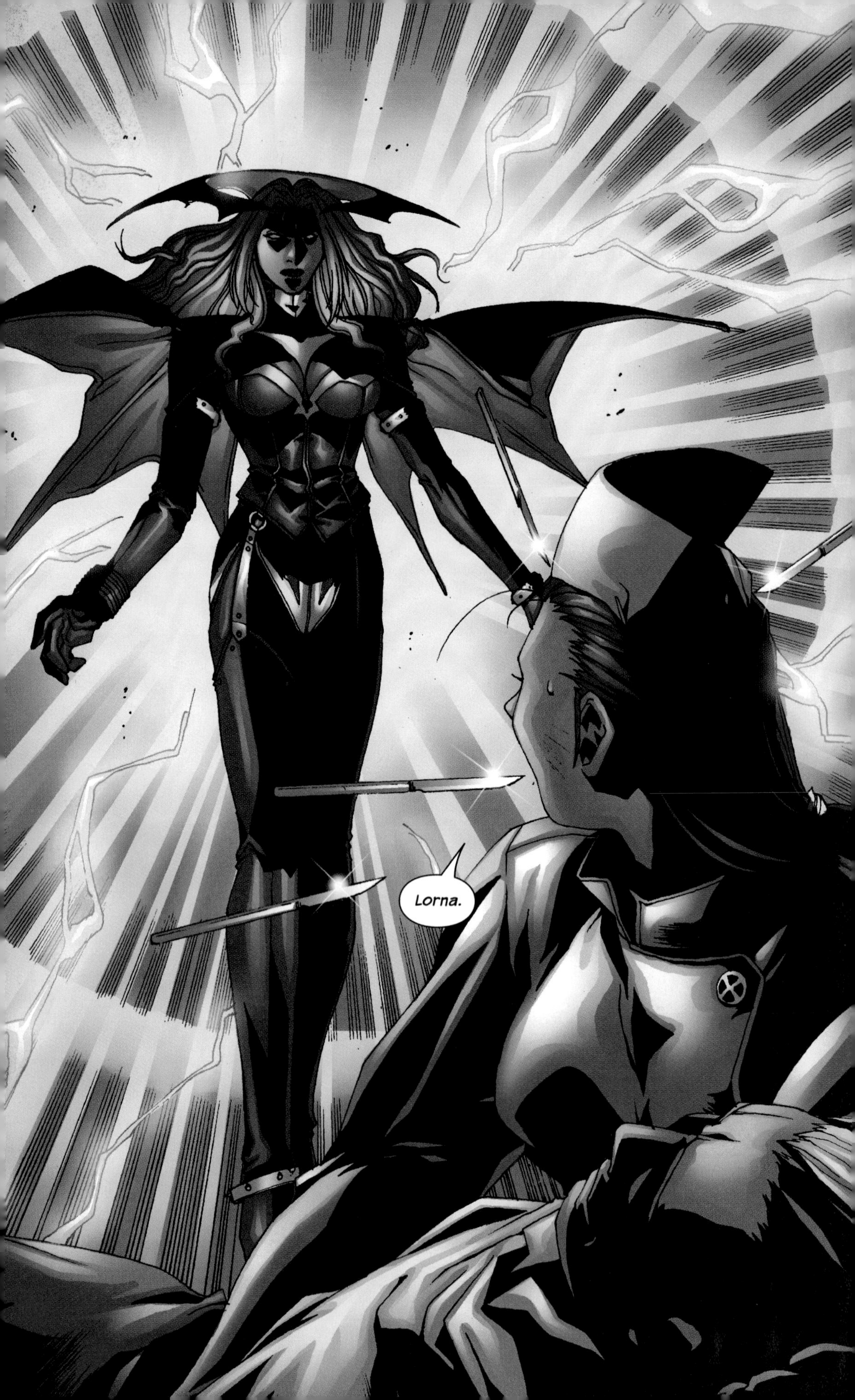
Lorna.

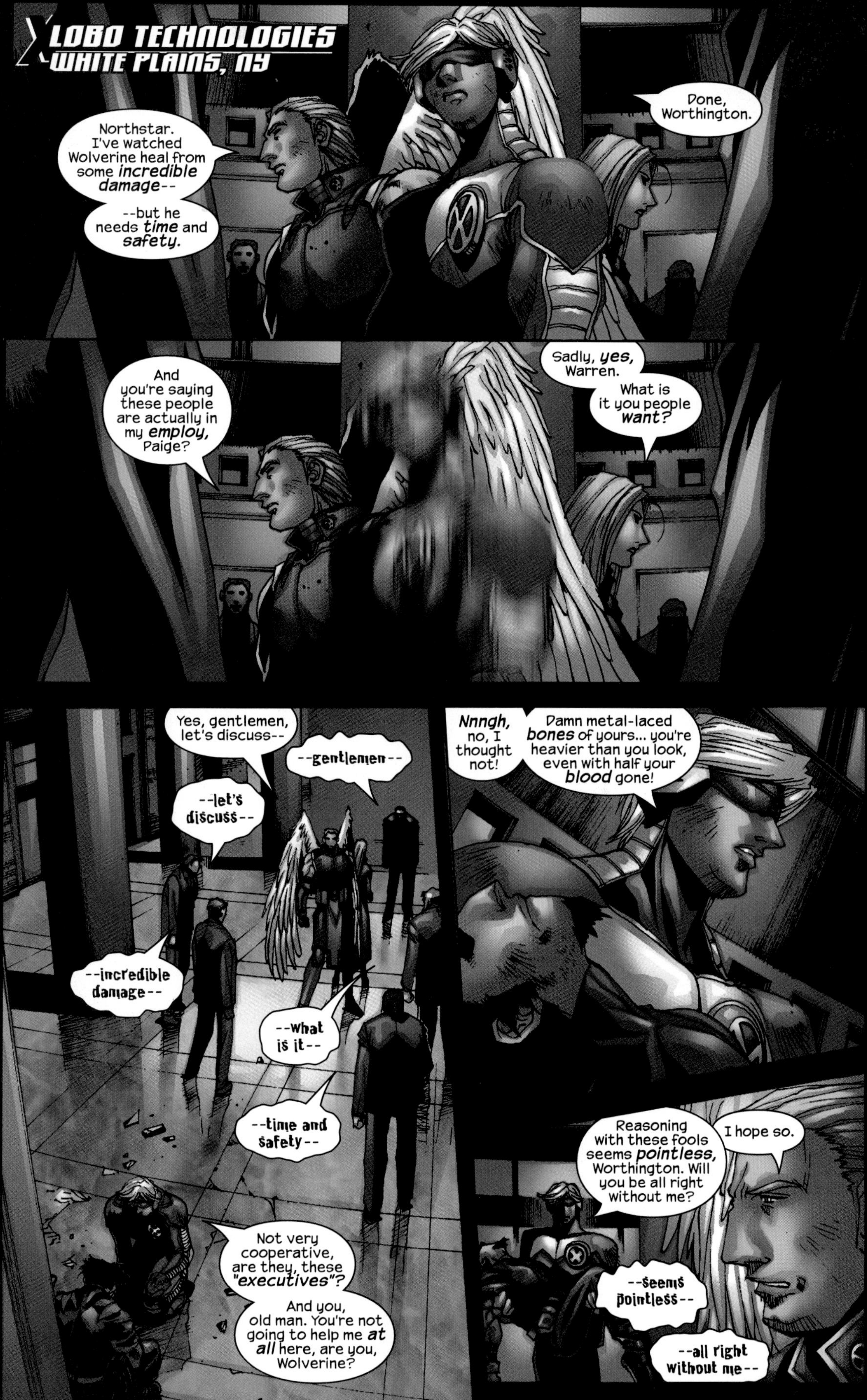
LOBO TECHNOLOGIES
WHITE PLAINS, NY
Northstar. I've watched Wolverine heal from some incredible damage--
--but he needs time and safety.
Done, Worthington.
And you're saying these people are actually in my employ, Paige?
Sadly, yes, Warren.
What is it you people want?
Yes, gentlemen, let's discuss--
--gentlemen--
--let's discuss--
--incredible damage--
--what is it--
--time and safety--
Not very cooperative, are they, these "executives"?
And you, old man. You're not going to help me at all here, are you, Wolverine?
Nnngh, no, I thought not!
Damn metal-laced bones of yours... you're heavier than you look, even with half your blood gone!
Reasoning with these fools seems pointless, Worthington. Will you be all right without me?
I hope so.
--seems pointless--
--all right without me--

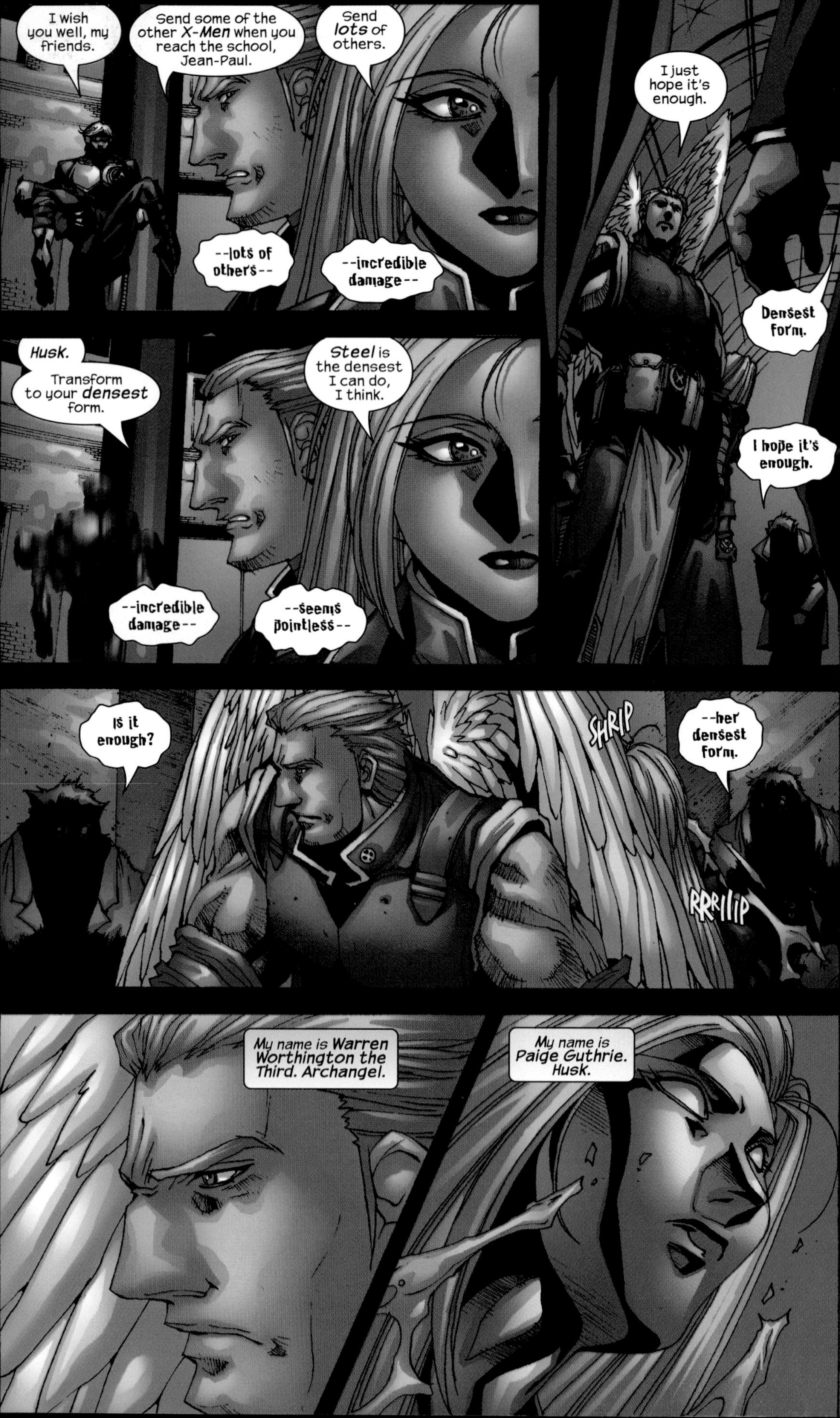
I wish you well, my friends.
Send some of the other X-Men when you reach the school, Jean-Paul.
Send lots of others.
--lots of others--
--incredible damage--
I just hope it's enough.
Husk.
Transform to your densest form.
Steel is the densest I can do, I think.
--incredible damage--
--seems pointless--
Densest form.
I hope it's enough.
Is it enough?
SHRIP
--her densest form.
RRRILIP
My name is Warren Worthington the Third. Archangel.
My name is Paige Guthrie. Husk.

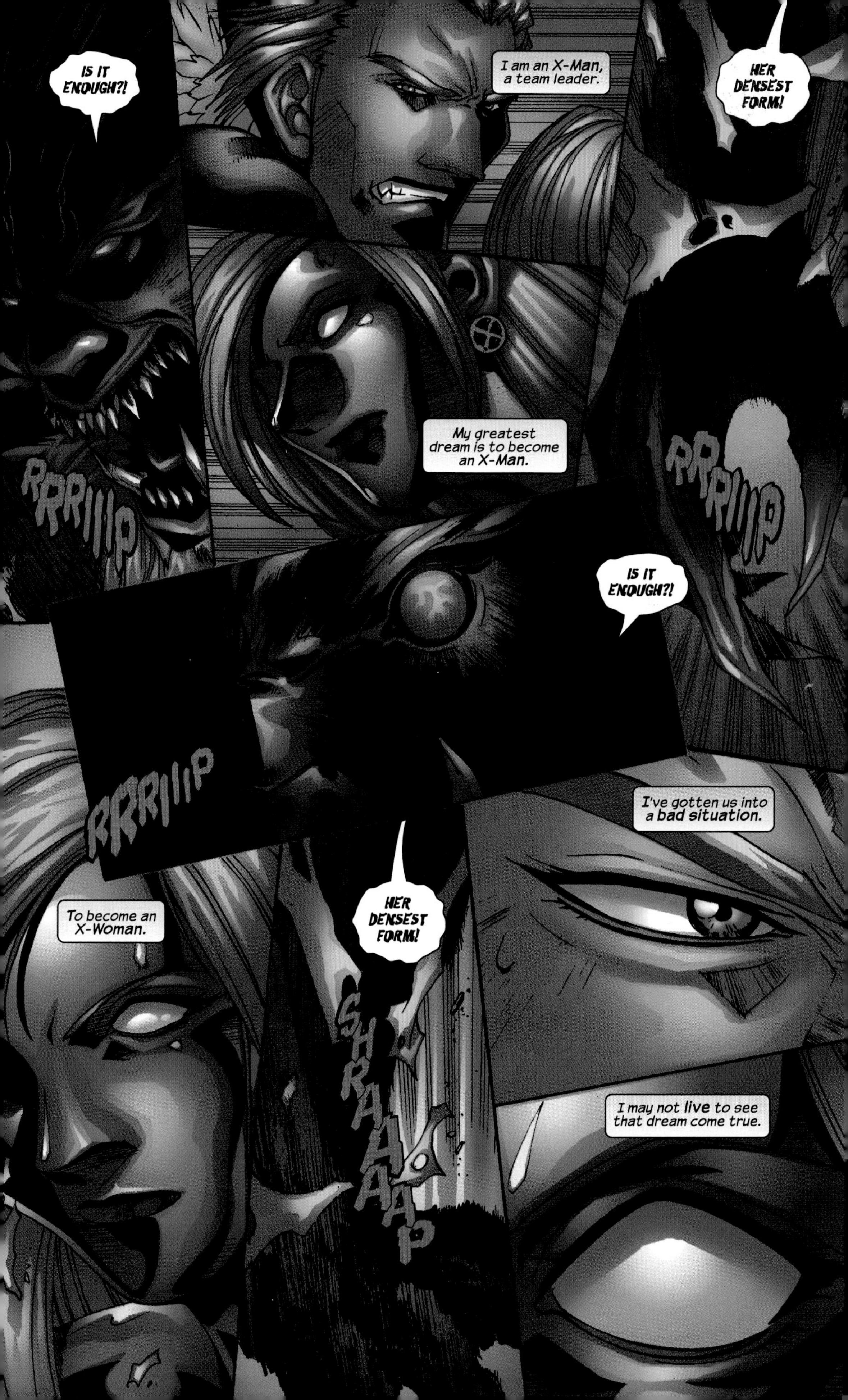
IS IT ENOUGH?!
I am an X-Man, a team leader.
HER DENSEST FORM!
RRRIIIP
My greatest dream is to become an X-Man.
RRRIIIP
IS IT ENOUGH?!
RRRIIIP
I've gotten us into a bad situation.
To become an X-Woman.
HER DENSEST FORM!
SHRAAAAP
I may not live to see that dream come true.

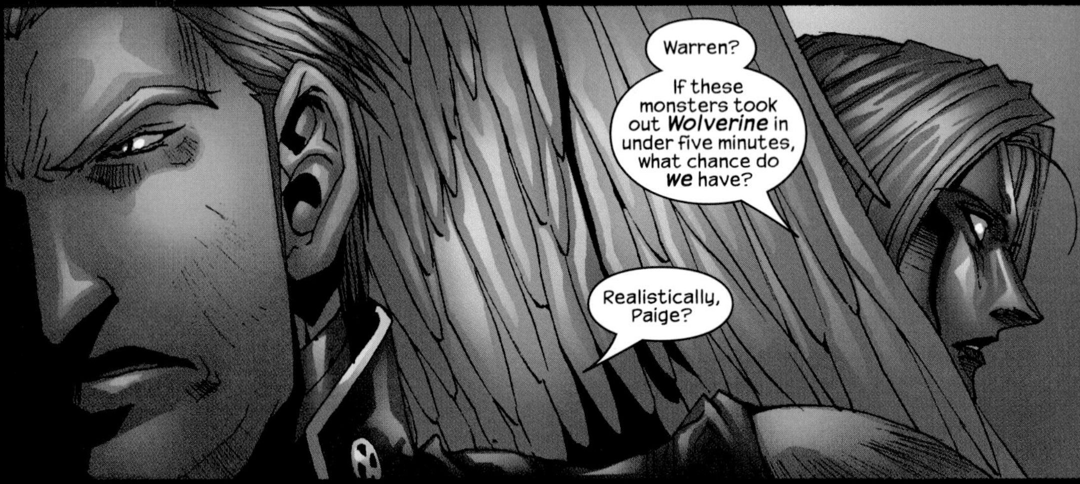
Warren?
If these monsters took out *Wolverine* in under five minutes, what chance do *we* have?
Realistically, Paige?

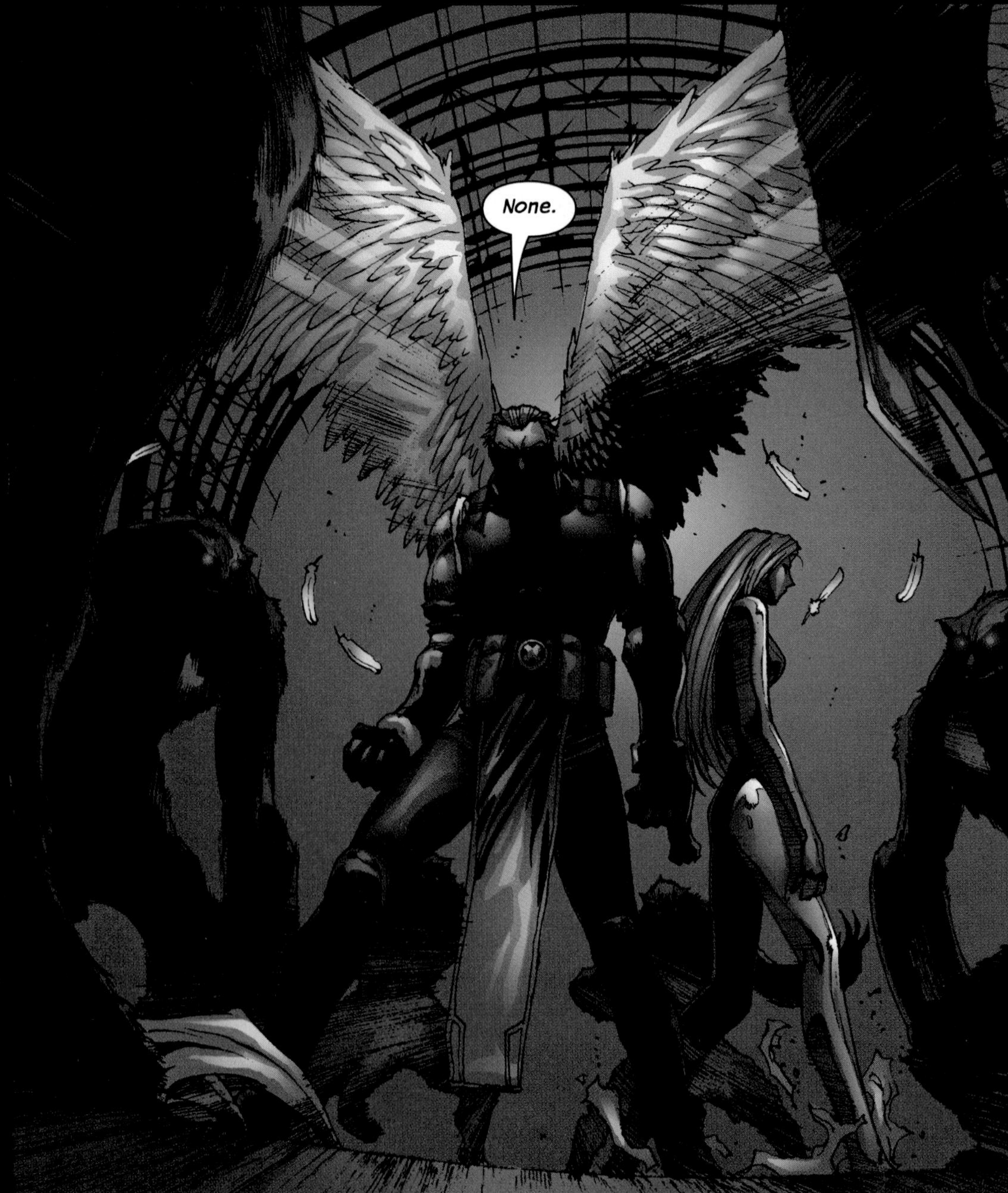
None.

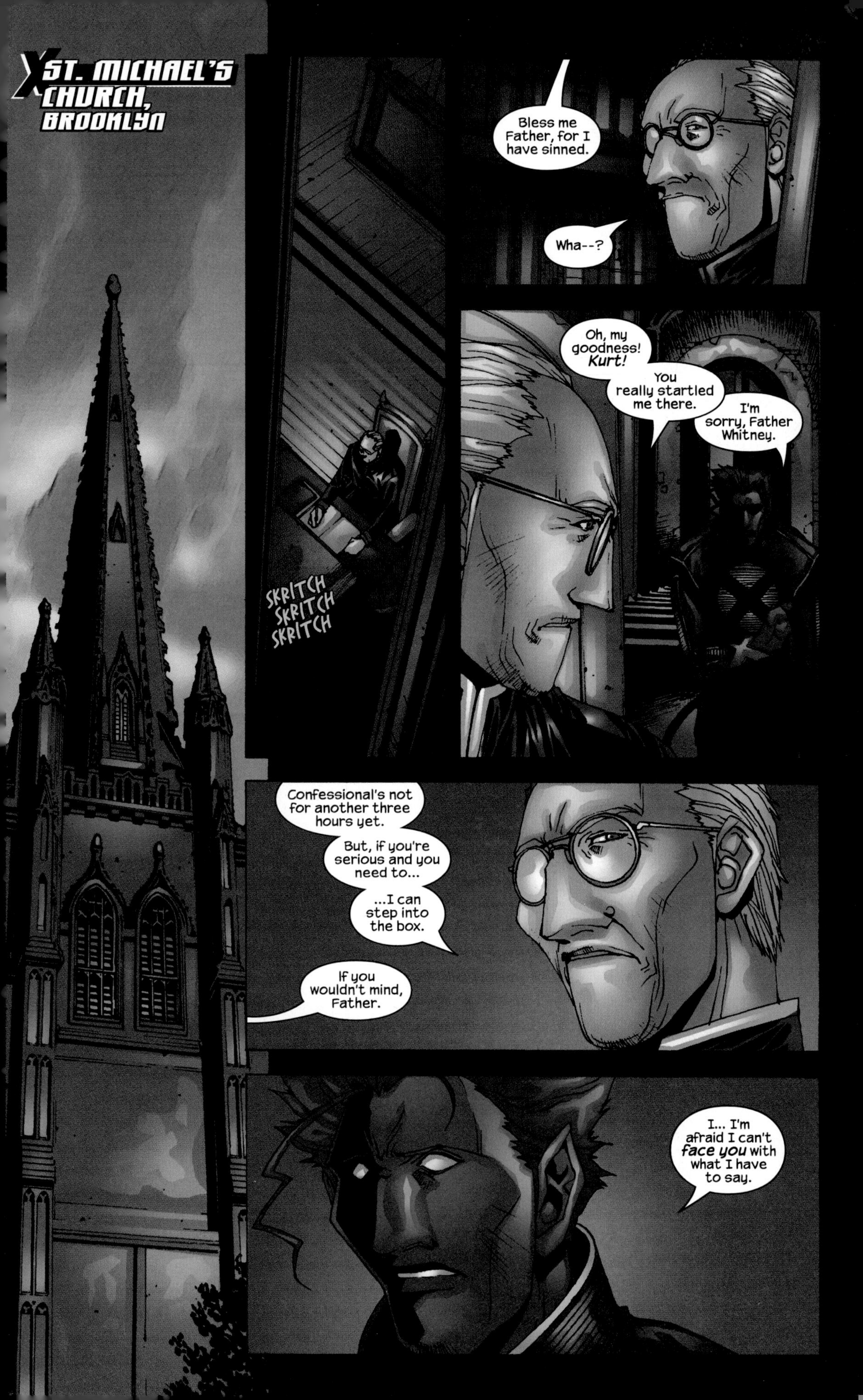
ST. MICHAEL'S CHURCH, BROOKLYN
Bless me Father, for I have sinned.
Wha--?
SKRITCH SKRITCH SKRITCH
Oh, my goodness! Kurt!
You really startled me there.
I'm sorry, Father Whitney.
Confessional's not for another three hours yet.
But, if you're serious and you need to...
...I can step into the box.
If you wouldn't mind, Father.
I... I'm afraid I can't face you with what I have to say.

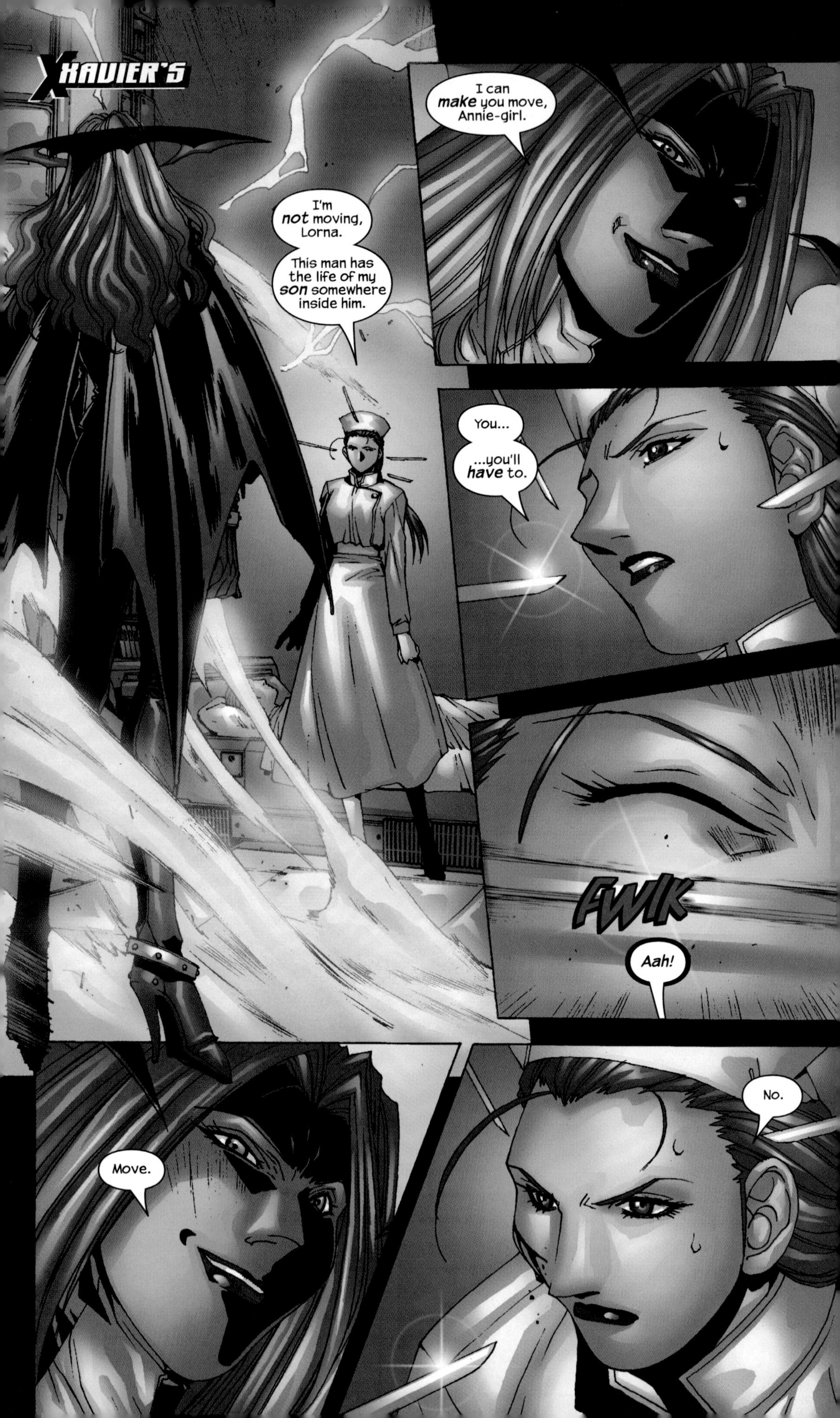

XAVIER'S
I'm not moving, Lorna.
This man has the life of my son somewhere inside him.
I can make you move, Annie-girl.
You...
...you'll have to.
FWIK
Aah!
Move.
No.

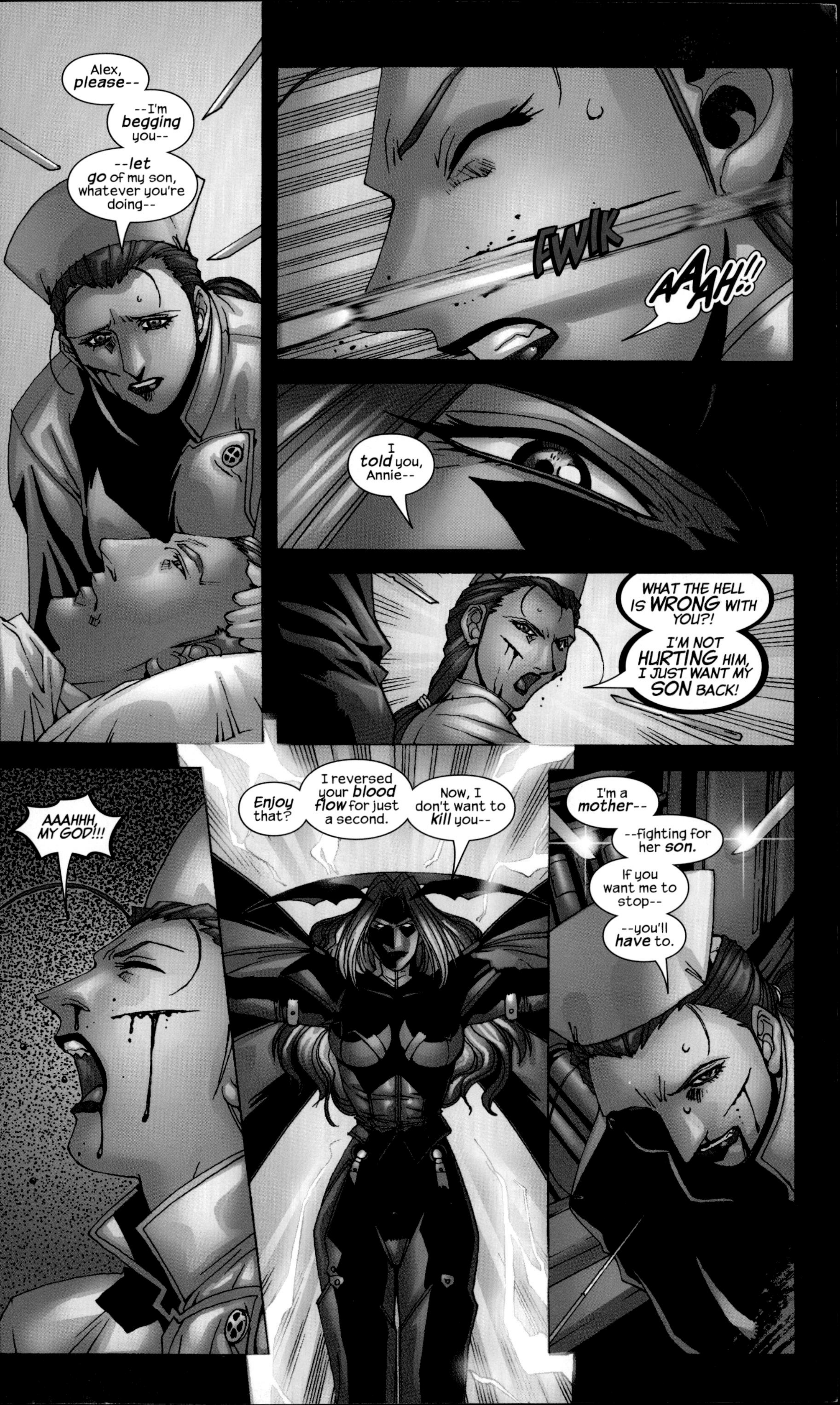
Alex, please--
--I'm begging you--
--let go of my son, whatever you're doing--
FWIK
AAAAH!!
I told you, Annie--
WHAT THE HELL IS WRONG WITH YOU?!
I'M NOT HURTING HIM, I JUST WANT MY SON BACK!
AAAHHH, MY GOD!!!
Enjoy that?
I reversed your blood flow for just a second.
Now, I don't want to kill you--
I'm a mother--
--fighting for her son.
If you want me to stop--
--you'll have to.

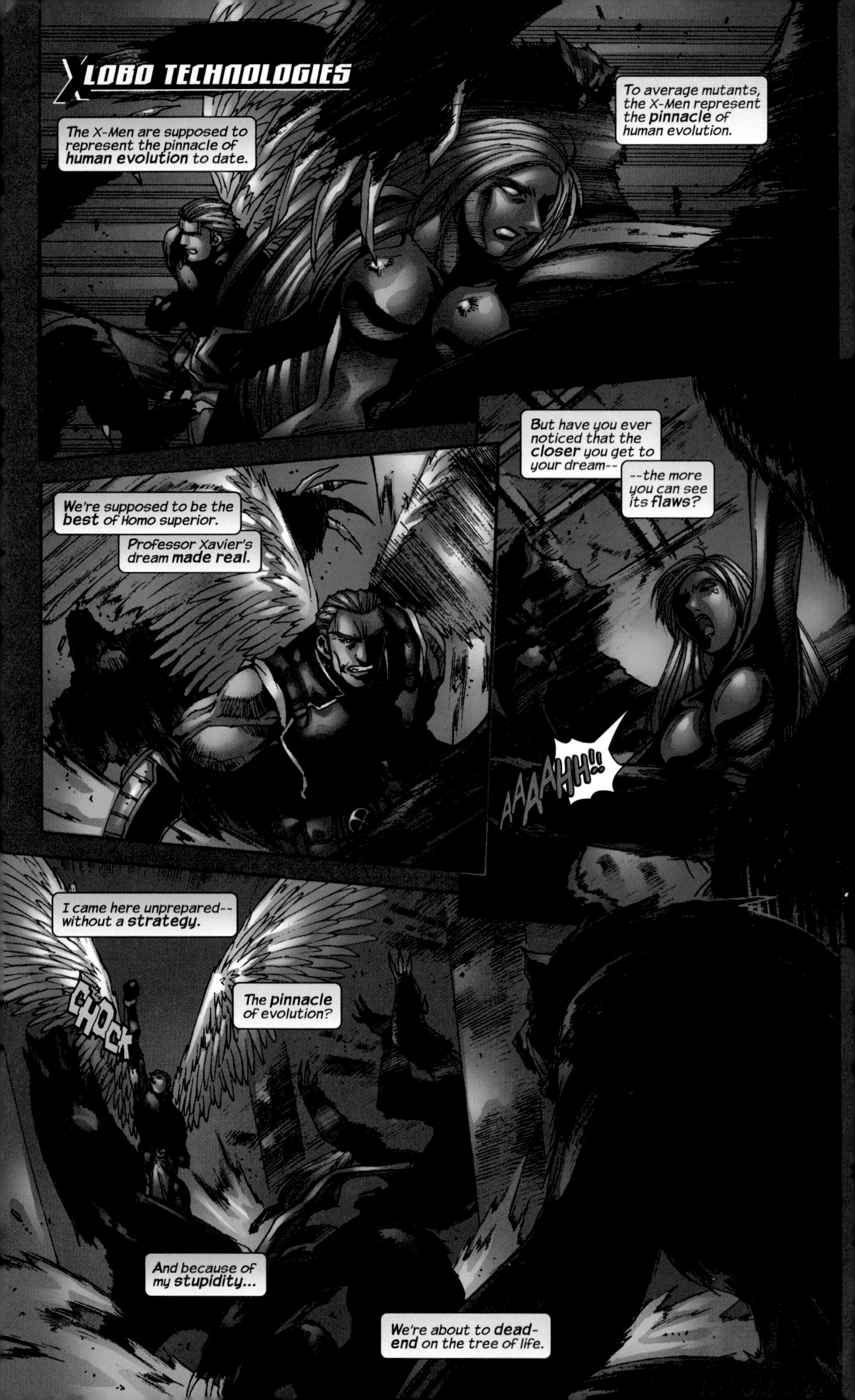

LOBO TECHNOLOGIES
The X-Men are supposed to represent the pinnacle of human evolution to date.
To average mutants, the X-Men represent the pinnacle of human evolution.
We're supposed to be the best of Homo superior.
Professor Xavier's dream made real.
But have you ever noticed that the closer you get to your dream--
--the more you can see its flaws?
AAAAHH!!
I came here unprepared--without a strategy.
CHOCK
The pinnacle of evolution?
And because of my stupidity...
We're about to dead-end on the tree of life.

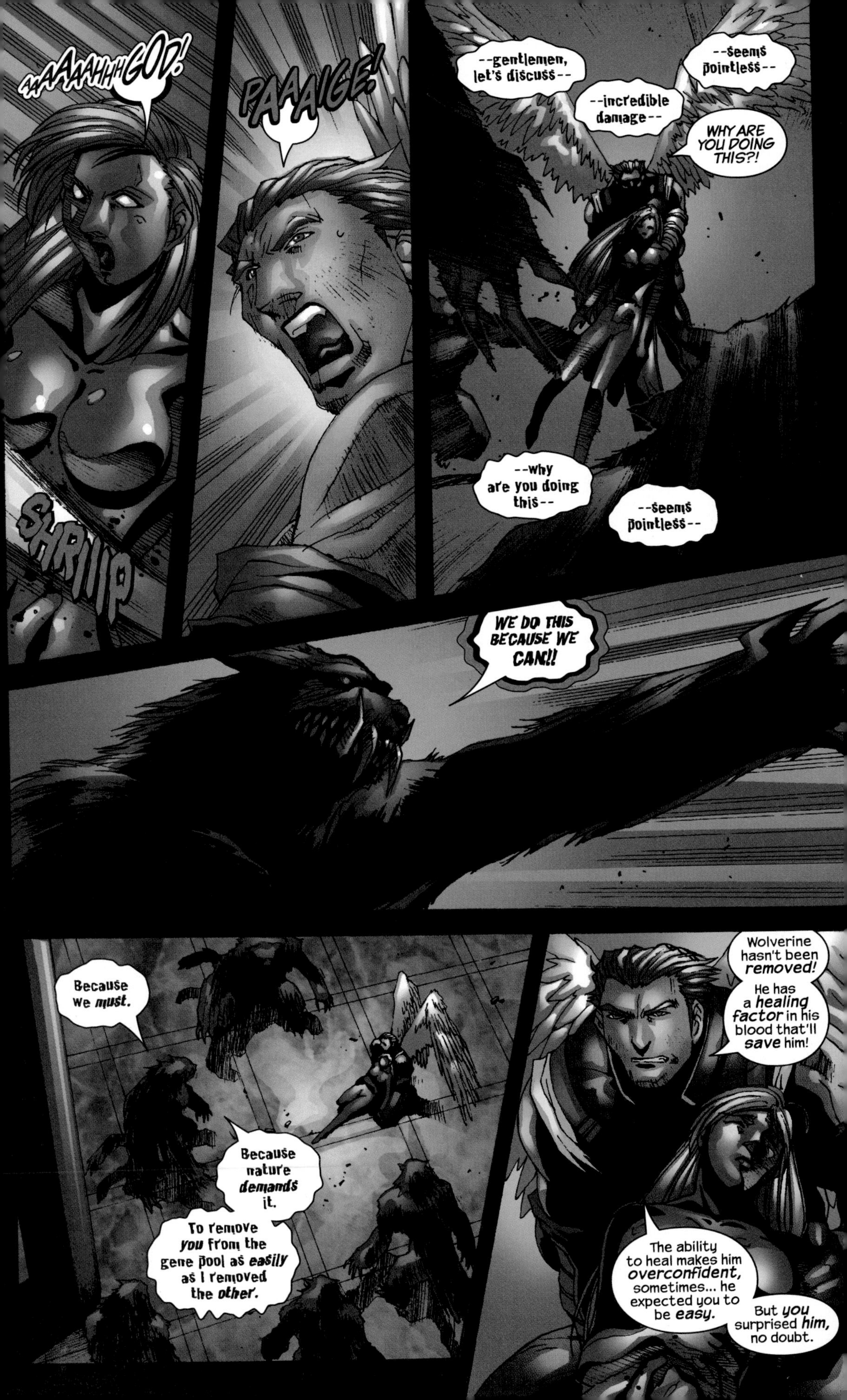

AAAAAAHH GOD!
SHRIIIP
PAAAIGE!
--gentlemen, let's discuss--
--incredible damage--
--seems pointless--
WHY ARE YOU DOING THIS?!
--why are you doing this--
--seems pointless--
WE DO THIS BECAUSE WE CAN!!
Because we must.
Because nature demands it.
To remove you from the gene pool as easily as I removed the other.
Wolverine hasn't been removed!
He has a healing factor in his blood that'll save him!
The ability to heal makes him overconfident, sometimes... he expected you to be easy.
But you surprised him, no doubt.

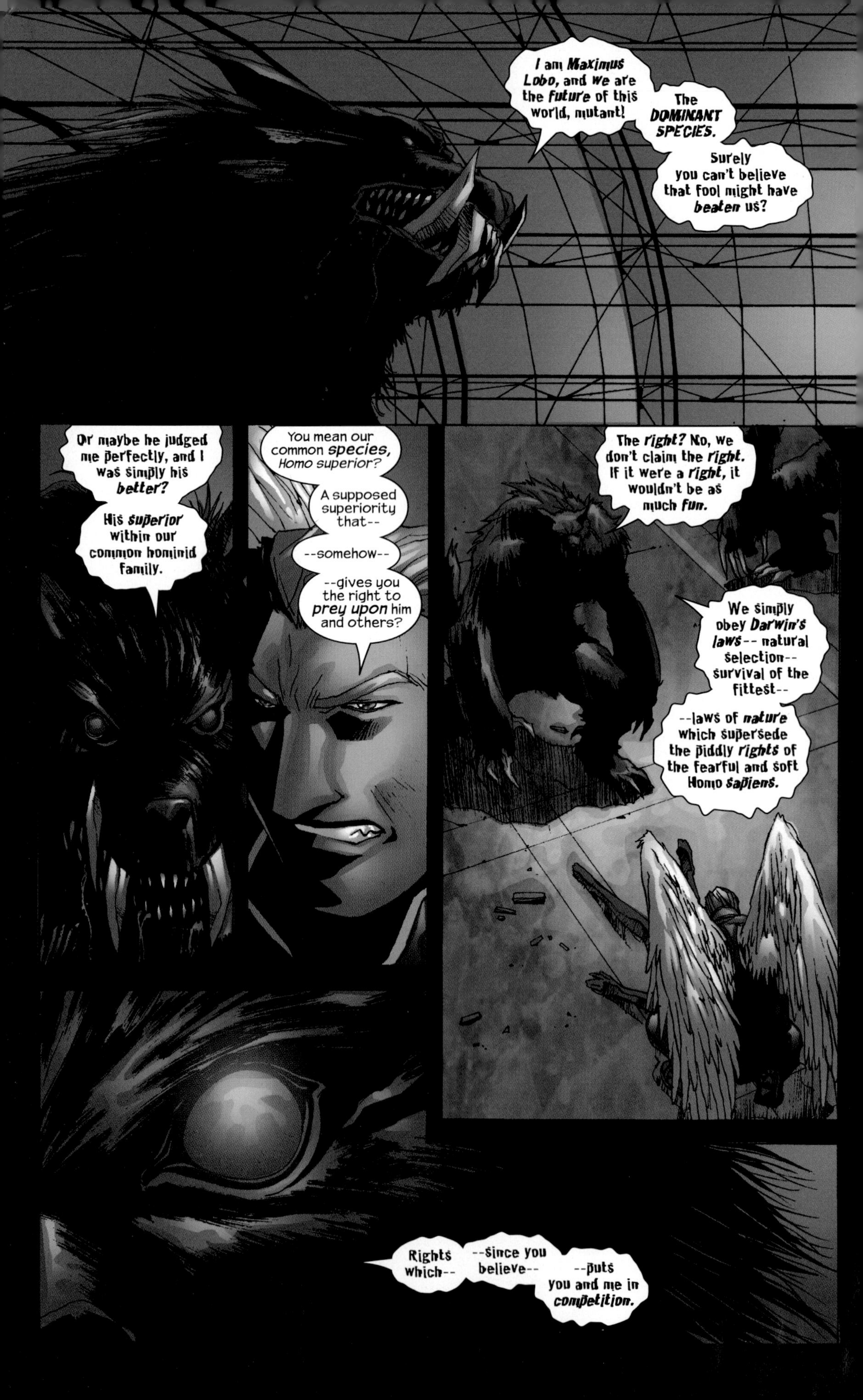
I am Maximus Lobo, and we are the future of this world, mutant!
The DOMINANT SPECIES.
Surely you can't believe that fool might have beaten us?
Or maybe he judged me perfectly, and I was simply his better?
His superior within our common hominid family.
You mean our common species, Homo superior?
A supposed superiority that--
--somehow--
--gives you the right to prey upon him and others?
The right? No, we don't claim the right. If it were a right, it wouldn't be as much fun.
We simply obey Darwin's laws-- natural selection-- survival of the fittest--
--laws of nature which supersede the piddly rights of the fearful and soft Homo sapiens.
Rights which--
--since you believe--
--puts you and me in competition.

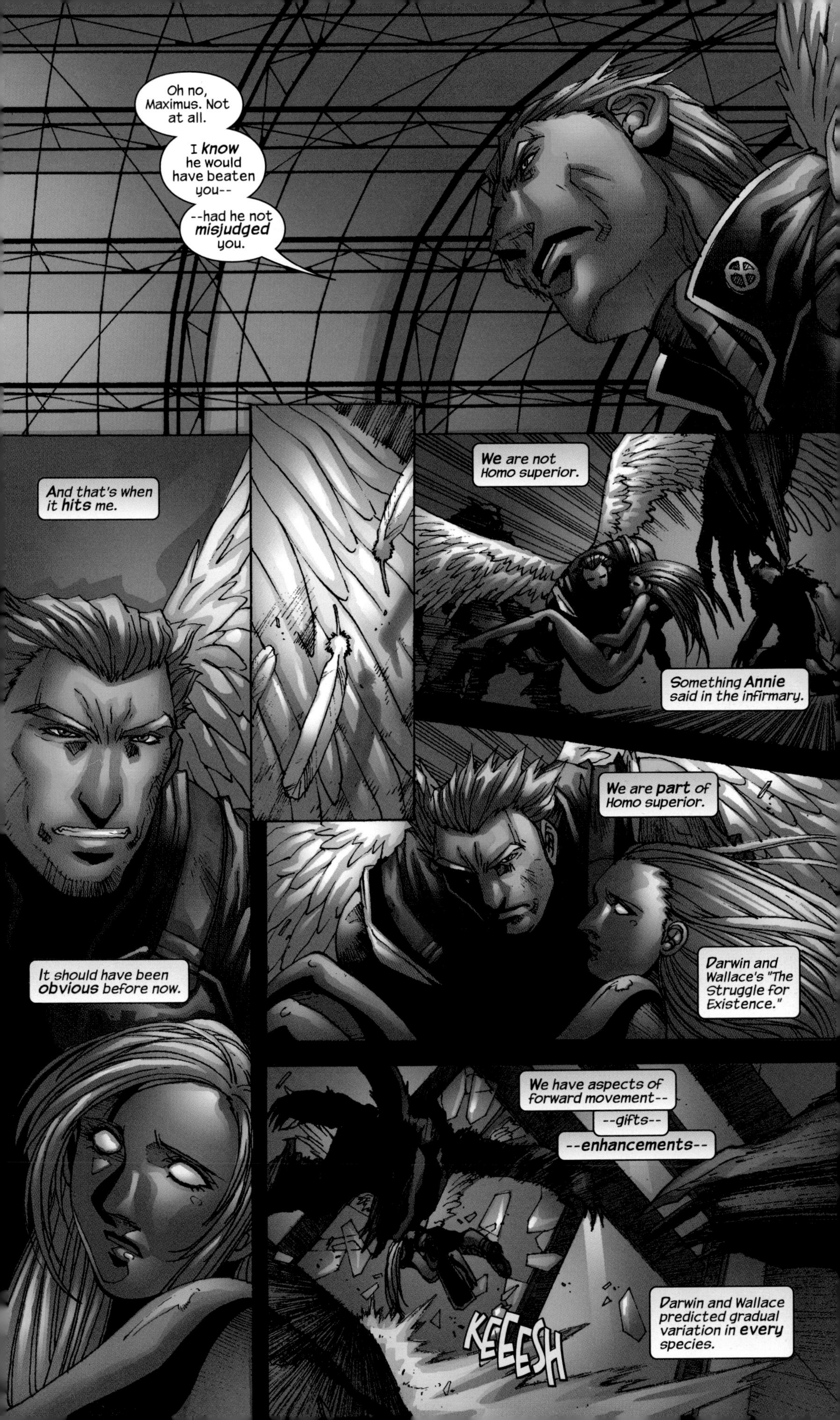

Oh no, Maximus. Not at all.
I *know* he would have beaten you--
--had he not *misjudged* you.
And that's when it **hits** me.
It should have been **obvious** before now.
We are not Homo superior.
Something **Annie** said in the infirmary.
We are **part** of Homo superior.
Darwin and Wallace's "The Struggle for Existence."
We have aspects of forward movement--
--gifts--
--**enhancements**--
KEEESH
Darwin and Wallace predicted gradual variation in **every** species.

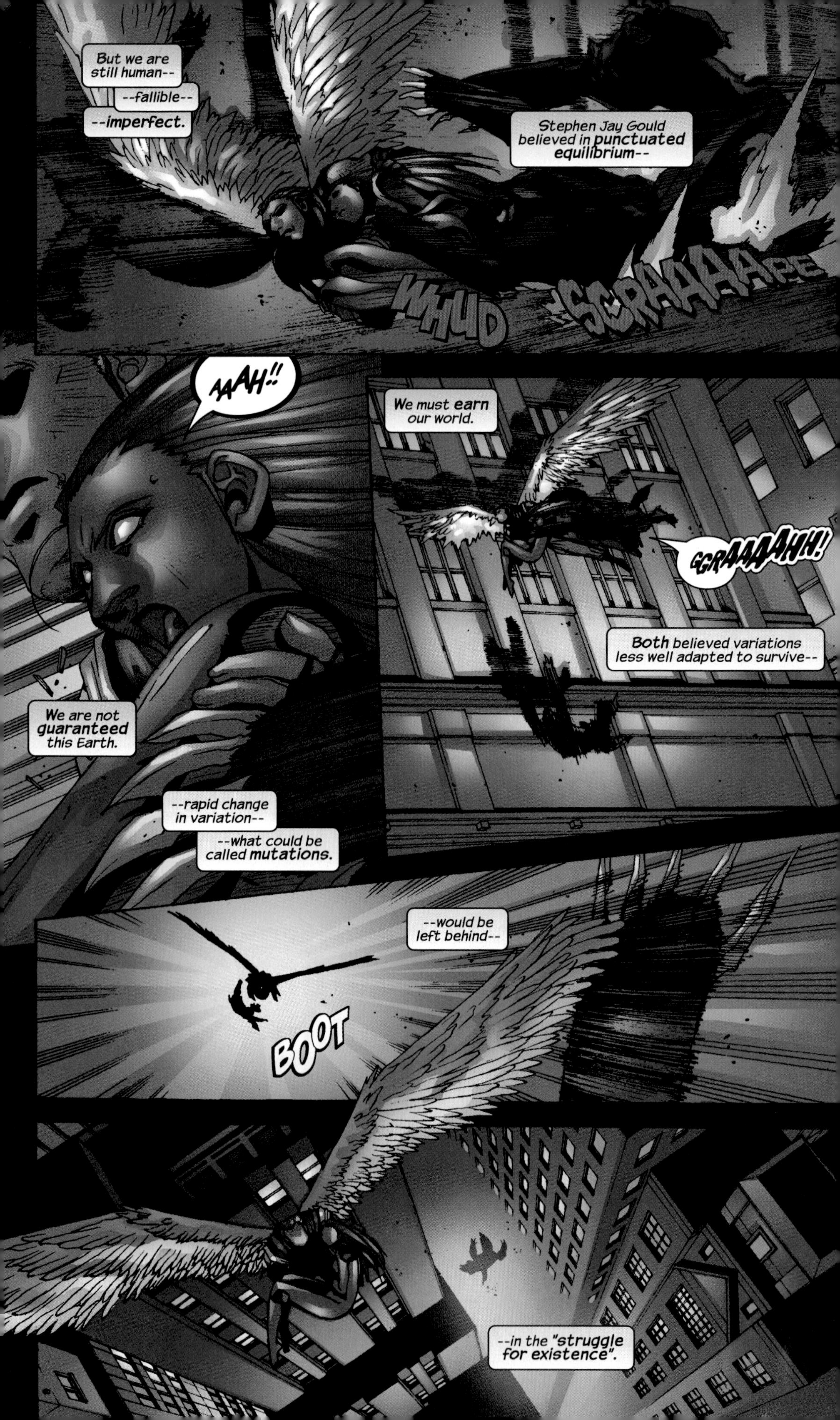

But we are still human--
--fallible--
--imperfect.
Stephen Jay Gould believed in punctuated equilibrium--
WHUD
SCRAAAAPE
AAAH!!
We are not guaranteed this Earth.
--rapid change in variation--
--what could be called mutations.
We must earn our world.
GGRAAAAAHH!
Both believed variations less well adapted to survive--
--would be left behind--
BOOT
--in the "struggle for existence".

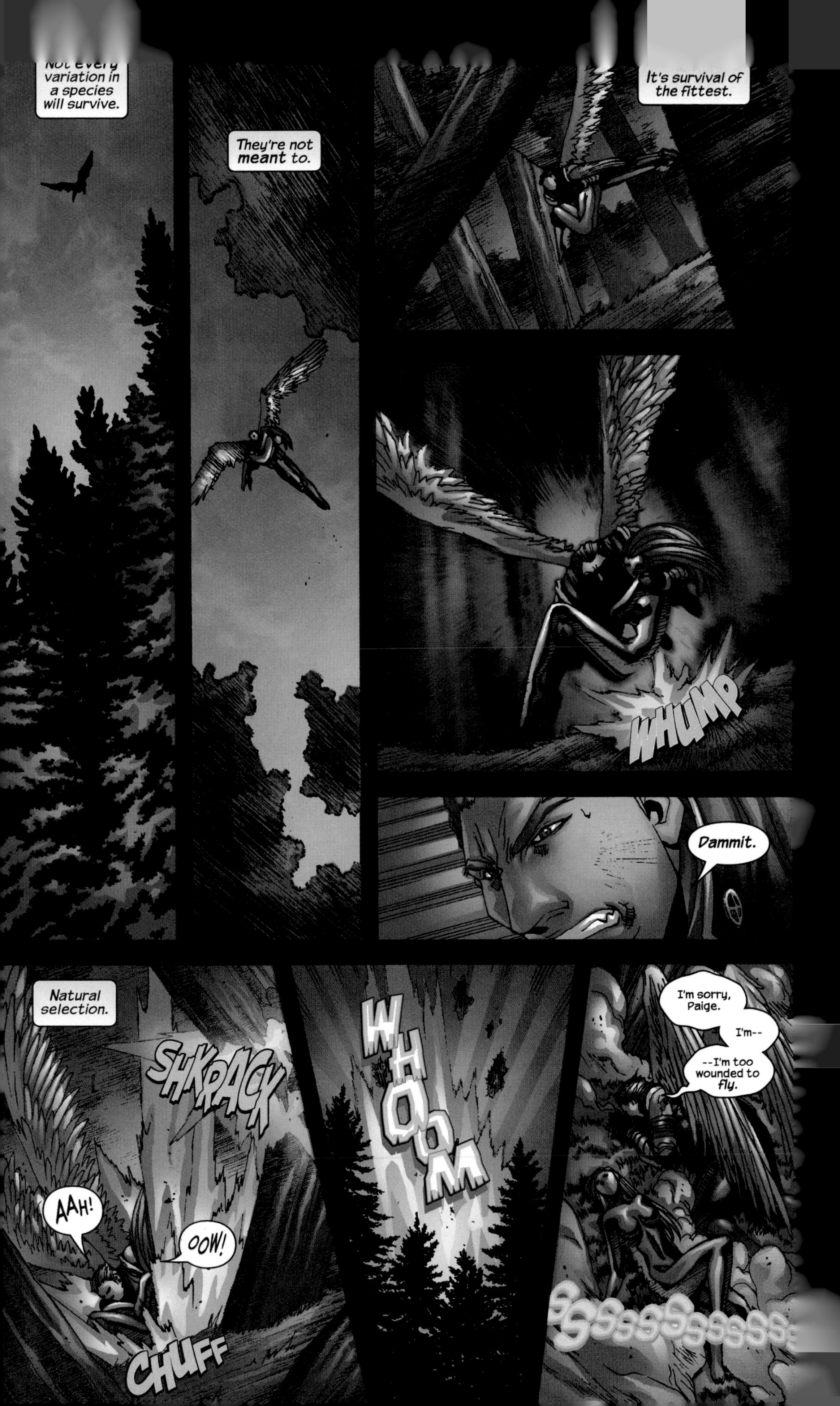
Not every variation in a species will survive.
They're not meant to.
It's survival of the fittest.
WHUMP
Dammit.
Natural selection.
SHKRACK
AAH!
OOW!
CHUFF
WHOOOM
I'm sorry, Paige.
I'm--
--I'm too wounded to fly.
SSSSSSSSSSSSS

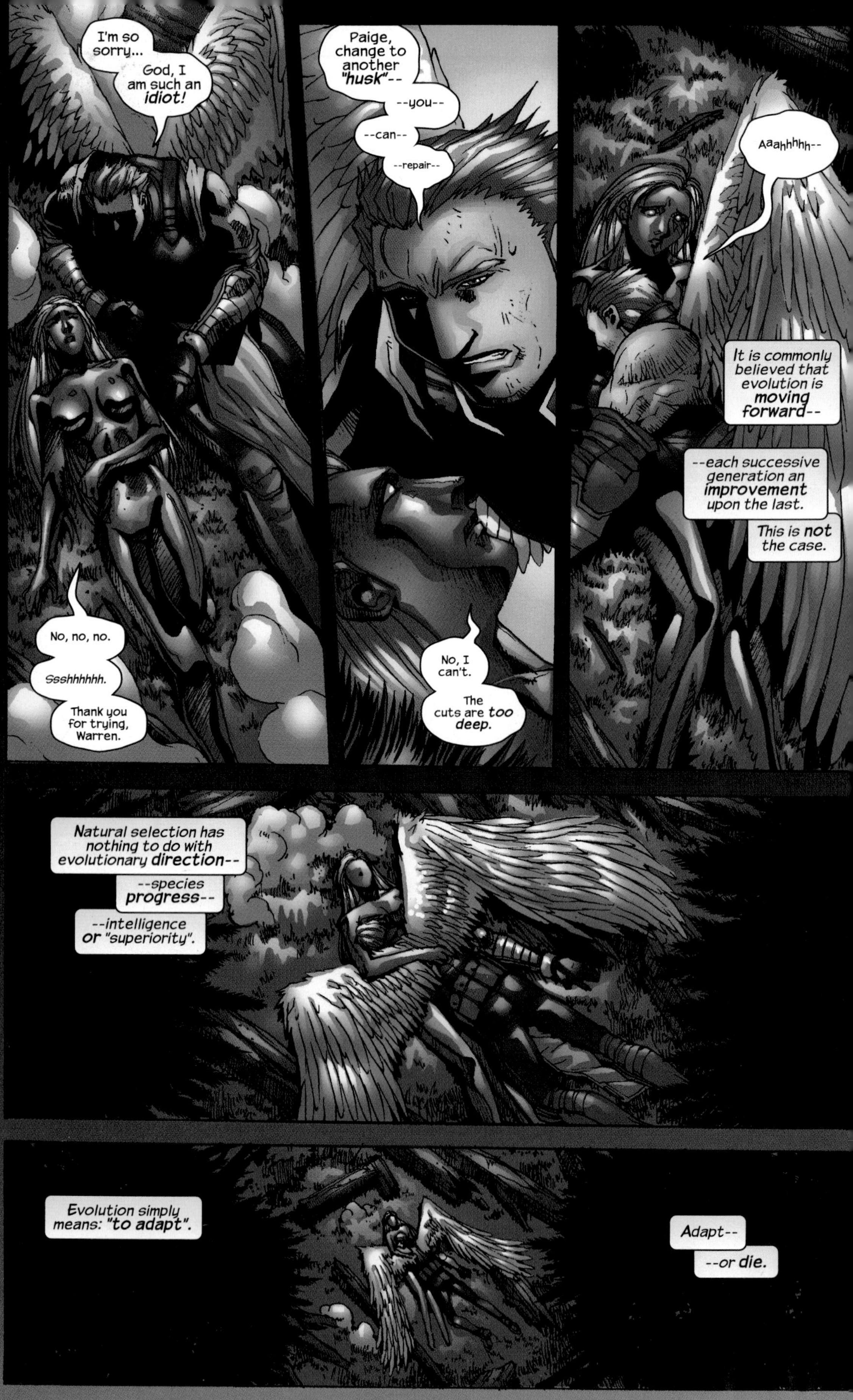

I'm so sorry...
God, I am such an idiot!
No, no, no.
Ssshhhhhh.
Thank you for trying, Warren.
Paige, change to another "husk"--
--you--
--can--
--repair--
No, I can't.
The cuts are too deep.
Aaahhhhh--
It is commonly believed that evolution is moving forward--
--each successive generation an improvement upon the last.
This is not the case.
Natural selection has nothing to do with evolutionary direction--
--species progress--
--intelligence or "superiority".
Evolution simply means: "to adapt".
Adapt--
--or die.

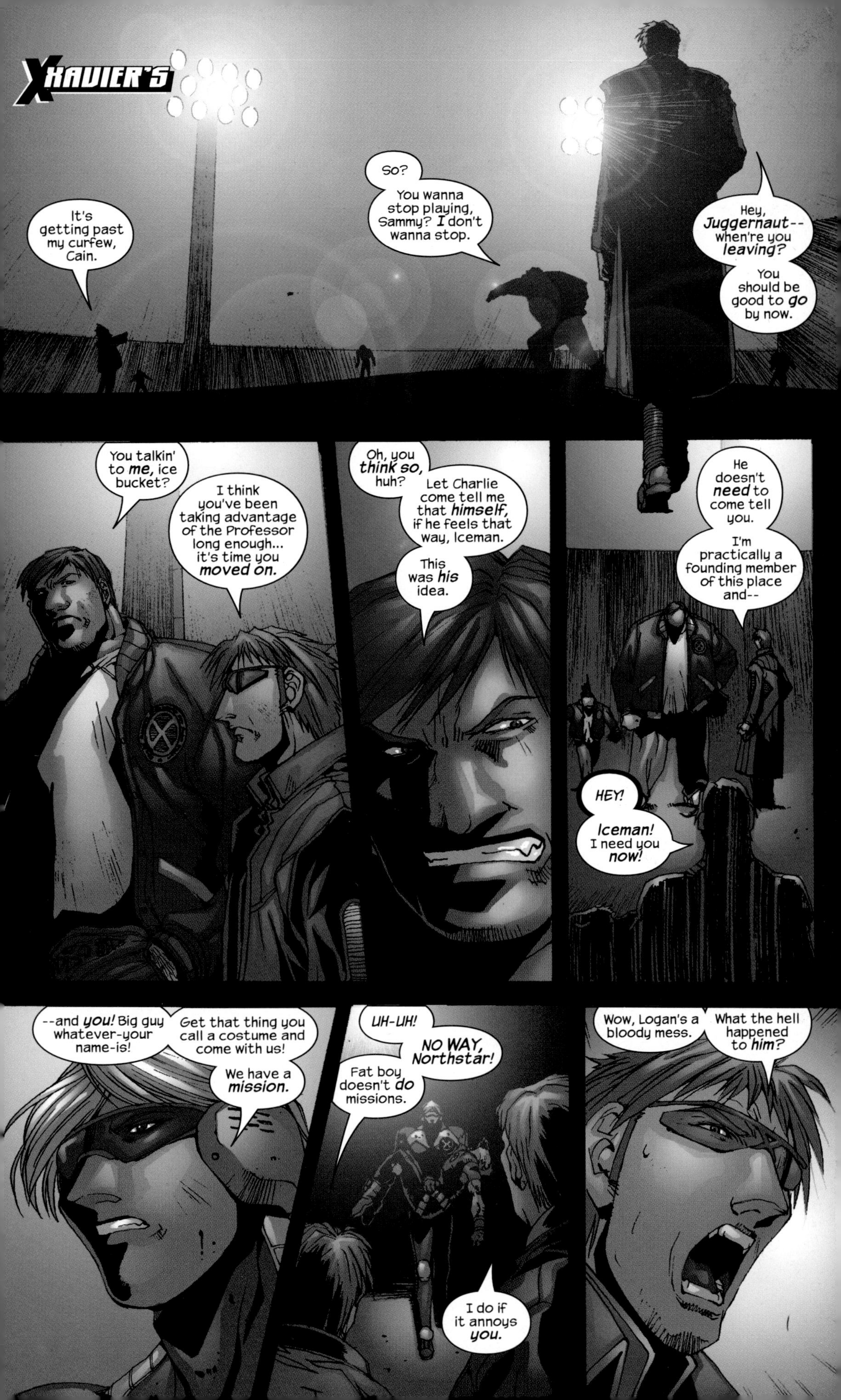
XAVIER'S
It's getting past my curfew, Cain.
So?
You wanna stop playing, Sammy? I don't wanna stop.
Hey, Juggernaut-- when're you leaving?
You should be good to go by now.
You talkin' to me, ice bucket?
I think you've been taking advantage of the Professor long enough... it's time you moved on.
Oh, you think so, huh?
Let Charlie come tell me that himself, if he feels that way, Iceman.
This was his idea.
He doesn't need to come tell you.
I'm practically a founding member of this place and--
HEY!
Iceman! I need you now!
--and you! Big guy whatever-your name-is!
Get that thing you call a costume and come with us!
We have a mission.
UH-UH!
NO WAY, Northstar!
Fat boy doesn't do missions.
I do if it annoys you.
Wow, Logan's a bloody mess.
What the hell happened to him?

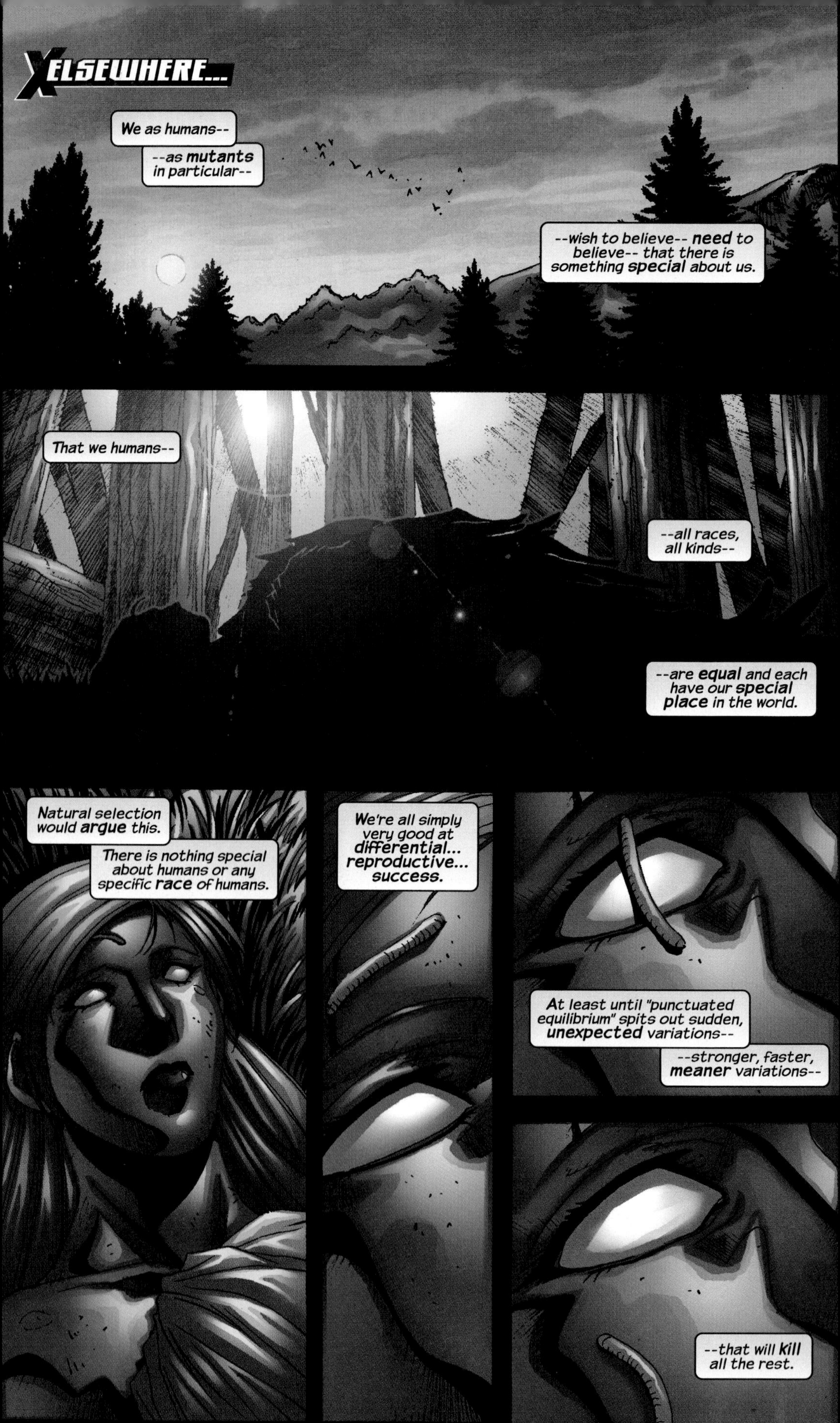

ELSEWHERE...
We as humans--
--as mutants in particular--
--wish to believe-- need to believe-- that there is something special about us.
That we humans--
--all races, all kinds--
--are equal and each have our special place in the world.
Natural selection would argue this.
There is nothing special about humans or any specific race of humans.
We're all simply very good at differential... reproductive... success.
At least until "punctuated equilibrium" spits out sudden, unexpected variations--
--stronger, faster, meaner variations--
--that will kill all the rest.

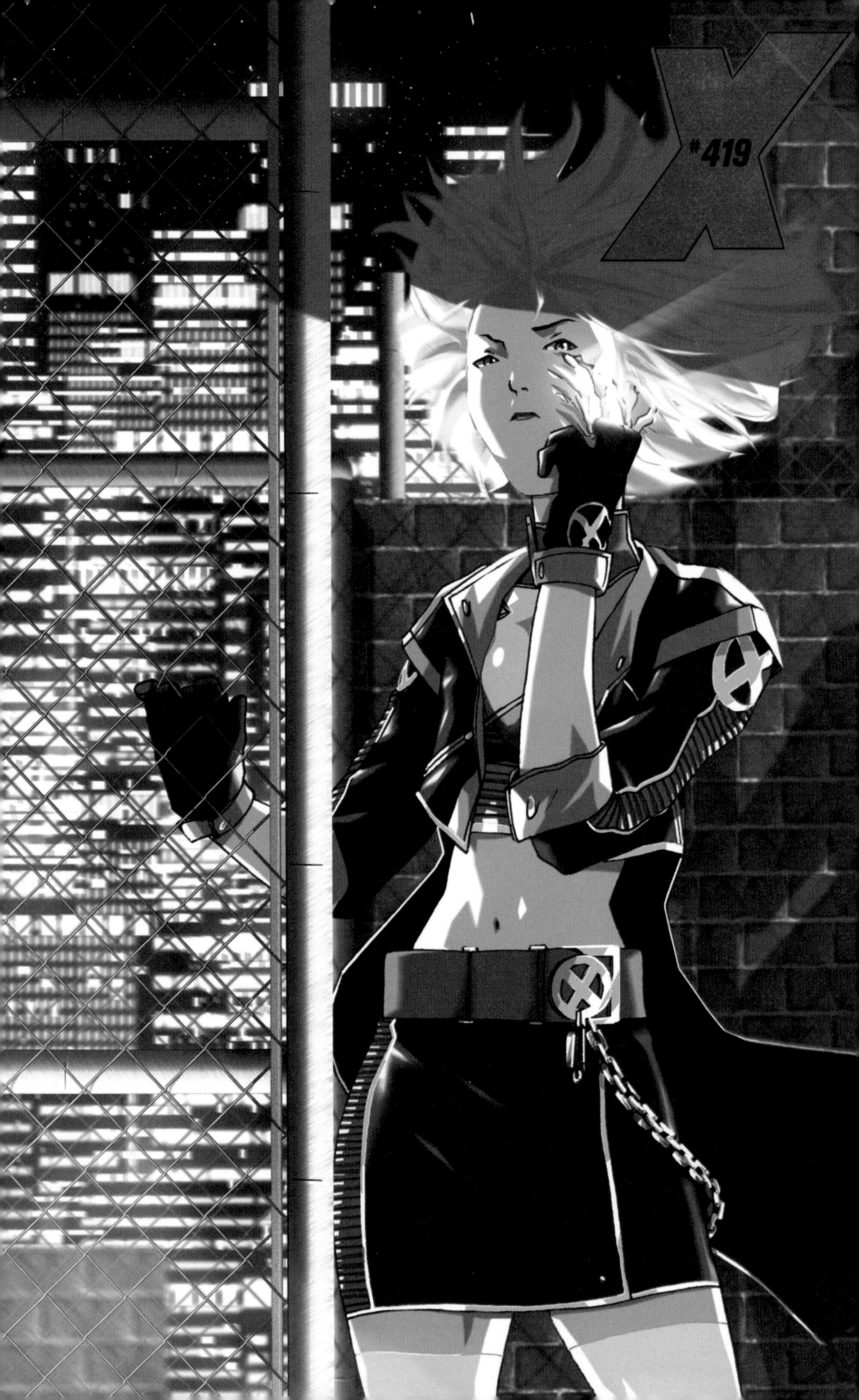
#419

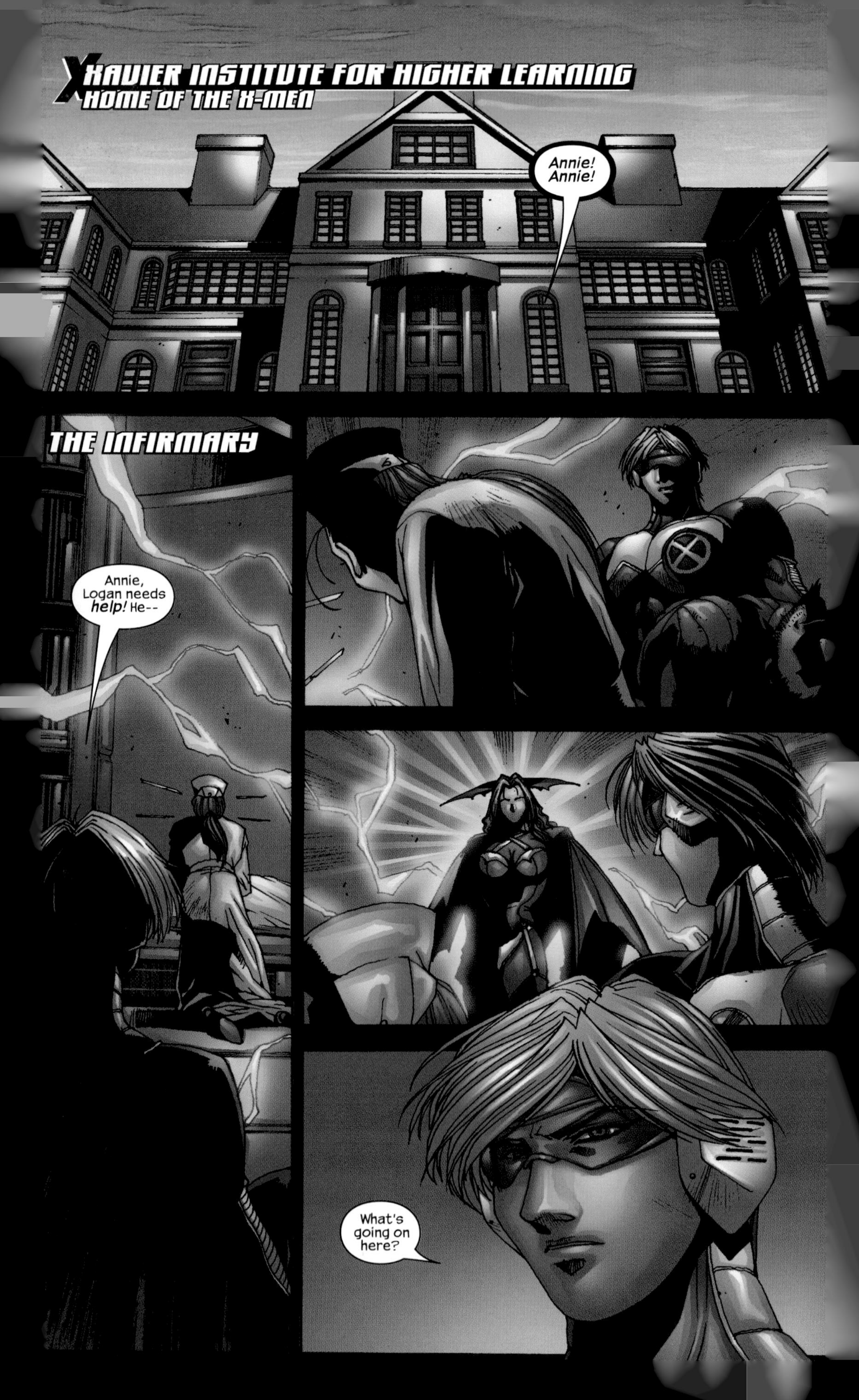
XAVIER INSTITUTE FOR HIGHER LEARNING
HOME OF THE X-MEN
Annie! Annie!
THE INFIRMARY
Annie, Logan needs help! He--
What's going on here?

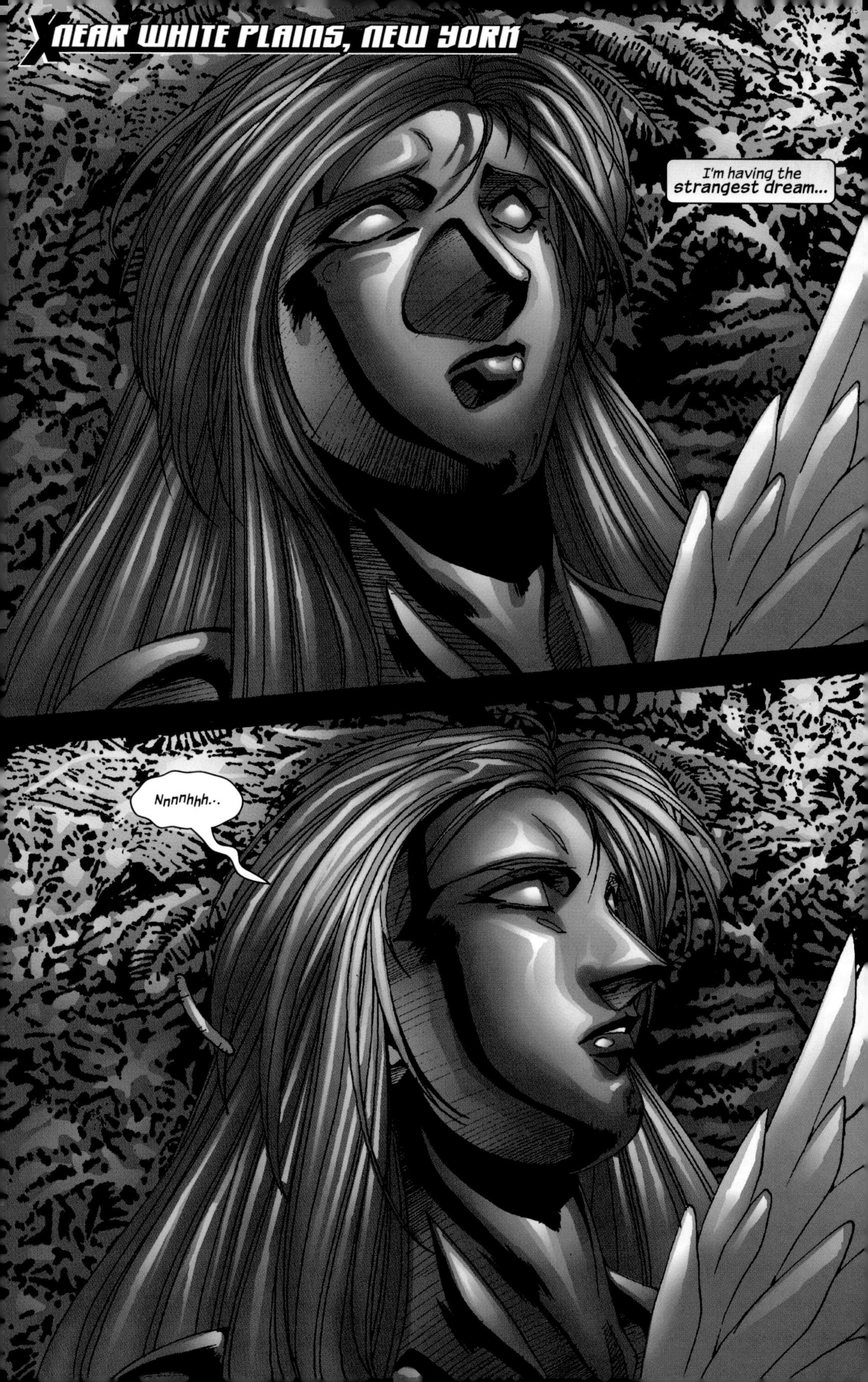
NEAR WHITE PLAINS, NEW YORK
I'm having the strangest dream...
Nnnnhhh...

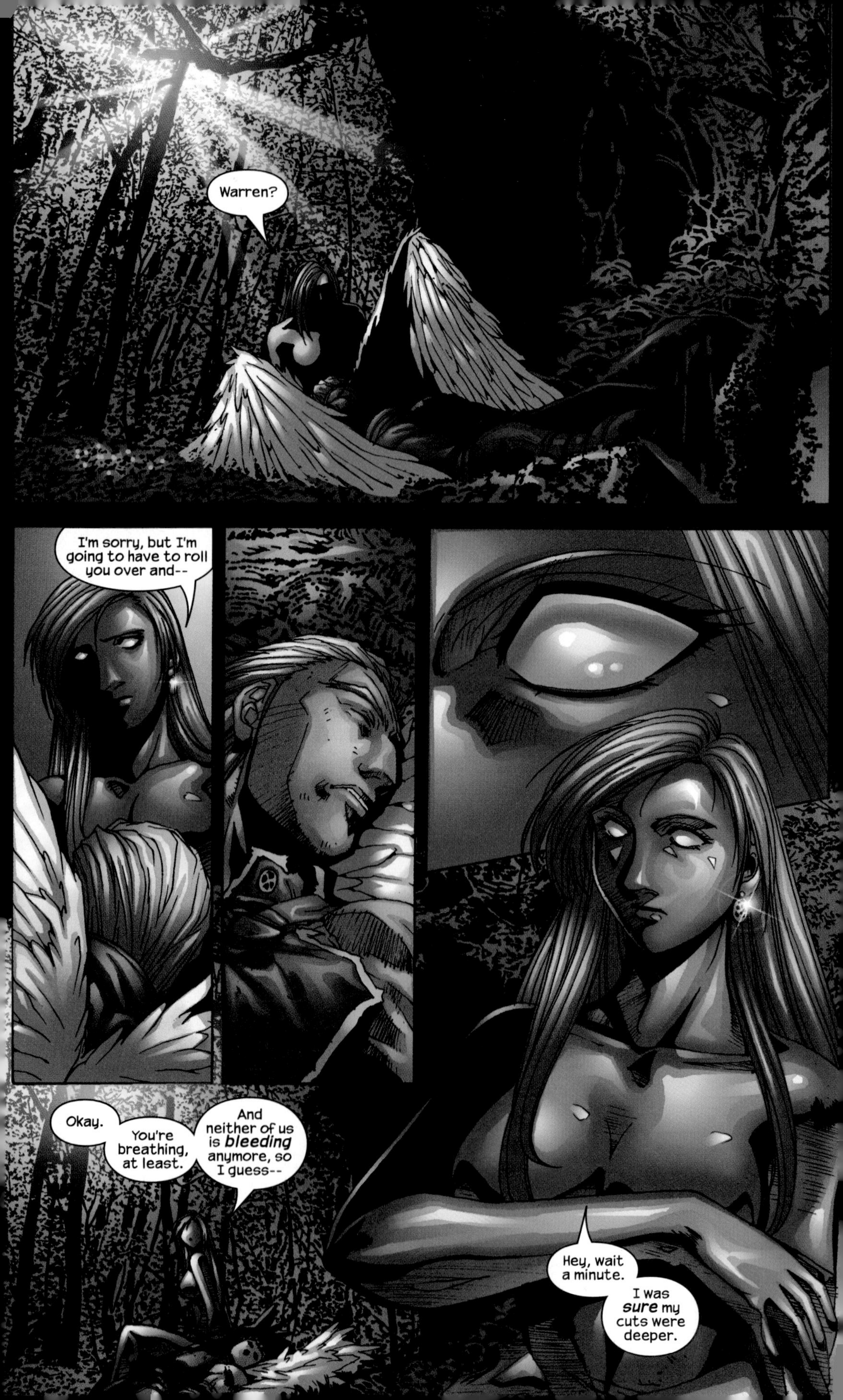
Warren?
I'm sorry, but I'm going to have to roll you over and--
Okay.
You're breathing, at least.
And neither of us is *bleeding* anymore, so I guess--
Hey, wait a minute.
I was *sure* my cuts were deeper.

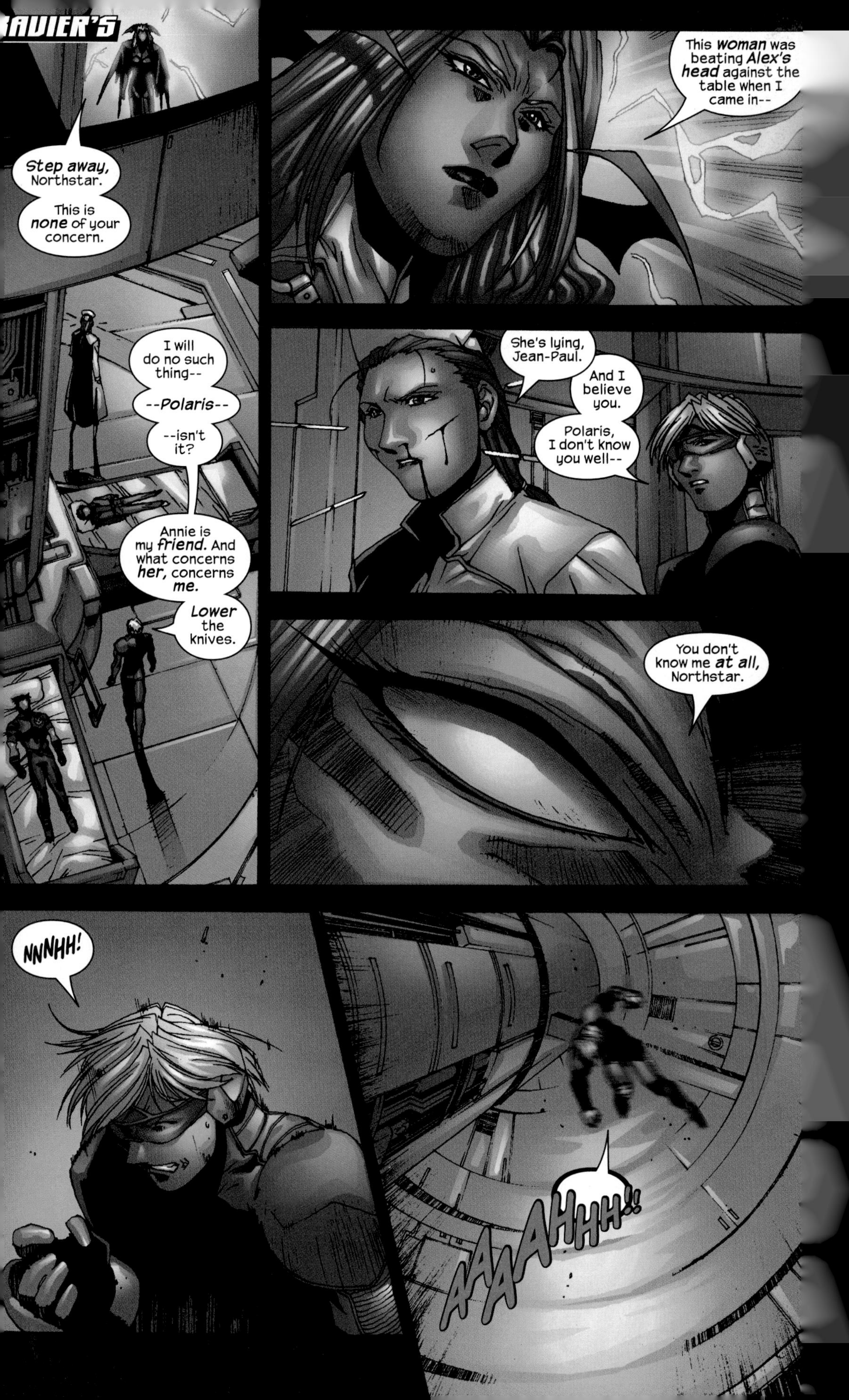

AVIER'S
Step away, Northstar.
This is none of your concern.
This woman was beating Alex's head against the table when I came in--
I will do no such thing--
--Polaris--
--isn't it?
Annie is my friend. And what concerns her, concerns me.
Lower the knives.
She's lying, Jean-Paul.
And I believe you.
Polaris, I don't know you well--
You don't know me at all, Northstar.
NNNHH!
AAAAHHH!!

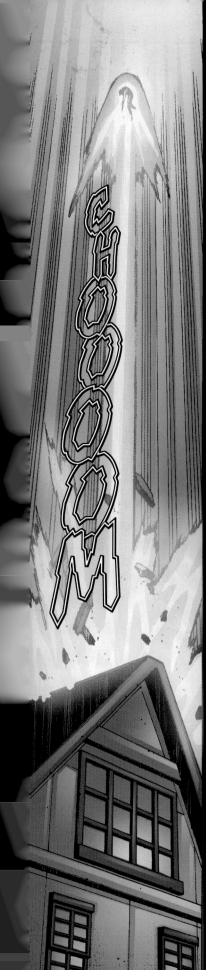

CHOOOOM

You accused me of *lying.*

I *really* don't appreciate being judged by a *lesser species.*

I can't believe Alex ever loved anyone like you...

HEY!

WHAT THE HELL DO YOU THINK YOU'RE DOING, LADY?

Lorna?

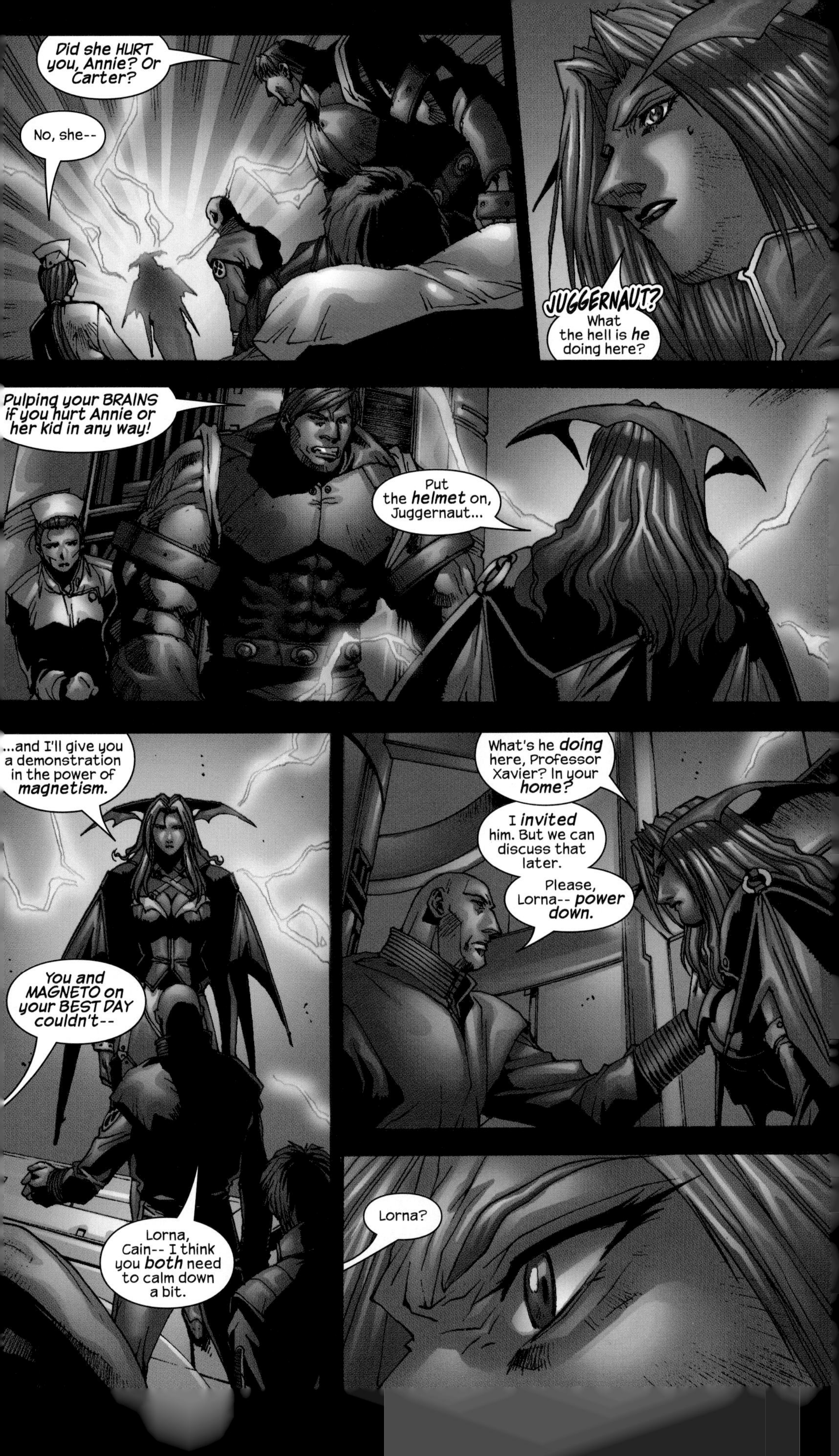

Did she HURT you, Annie? Or Carter?
No, she--
JUGGERNAUT? What the hell is he doing here?
Pulping your BRAINS if you hurt Annie or her kid in any way!
Put the helmet on, Juggernaut...
...and I'll give you a demonstration in the power of magnetism.
You and MAGNETO on your BEST DAY couldn't--
Lorna, Cain-- I think you both need to calm down a bit.
What's he doing here, Professor Xavier? In your home?
I invited him. But we can discuss that later.
Please, Lorna-- power down.
Lorna?

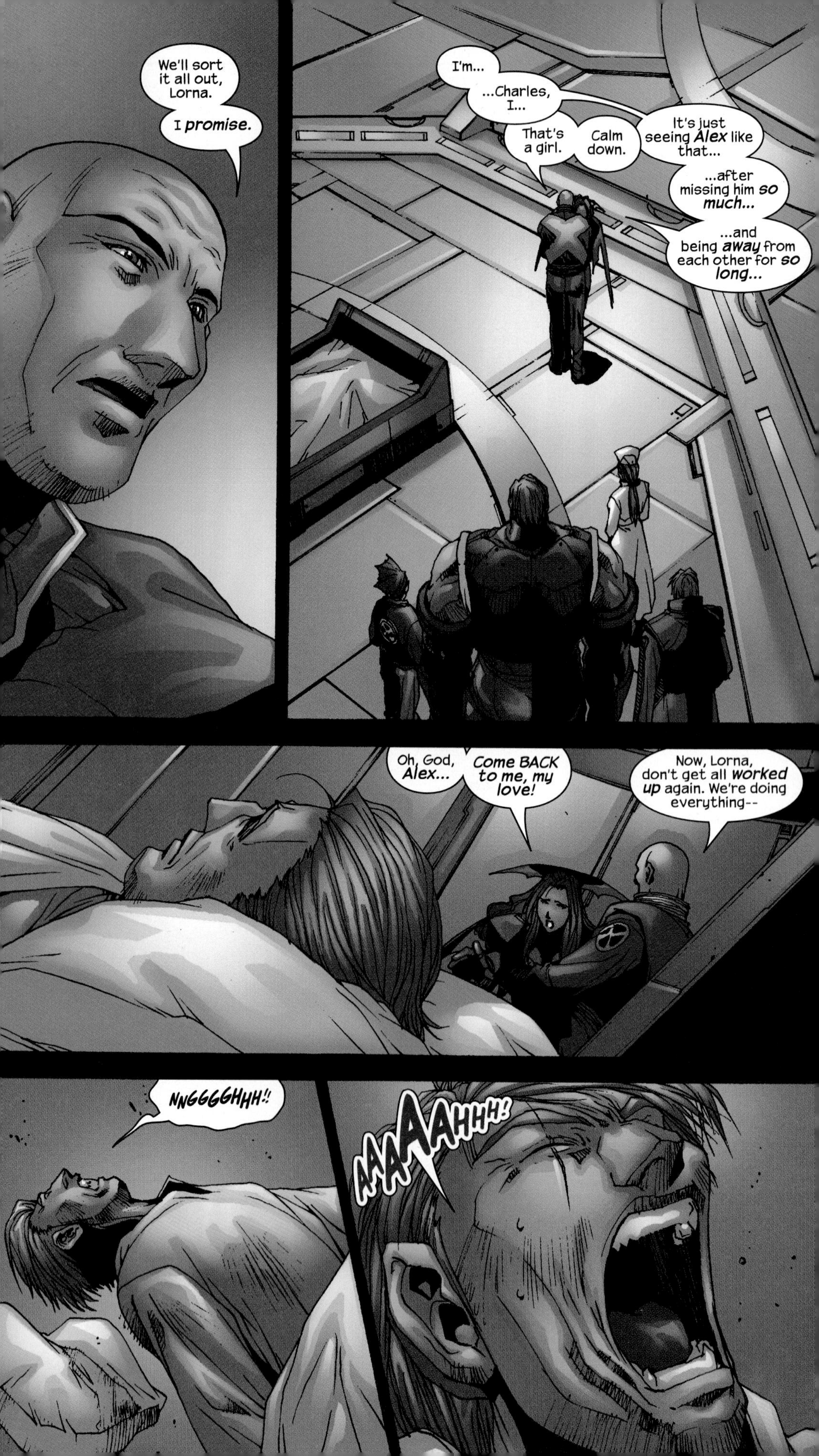

We'll sort it all out, Lorna.
I *promise.*
I'm...
...Charles, I...
That's a girl.
Calm down.
It's just seeing *Alex* like that...
...after missing him *so much...*
...and being *away* from each other for *so long...*
Oh, God, *Alex...*
Come BACK to me, my love!
Now, Lorna, don't get all *worked up* again. We're doing everything--
NNGGGGHHH!!
AAAAAAHHH!

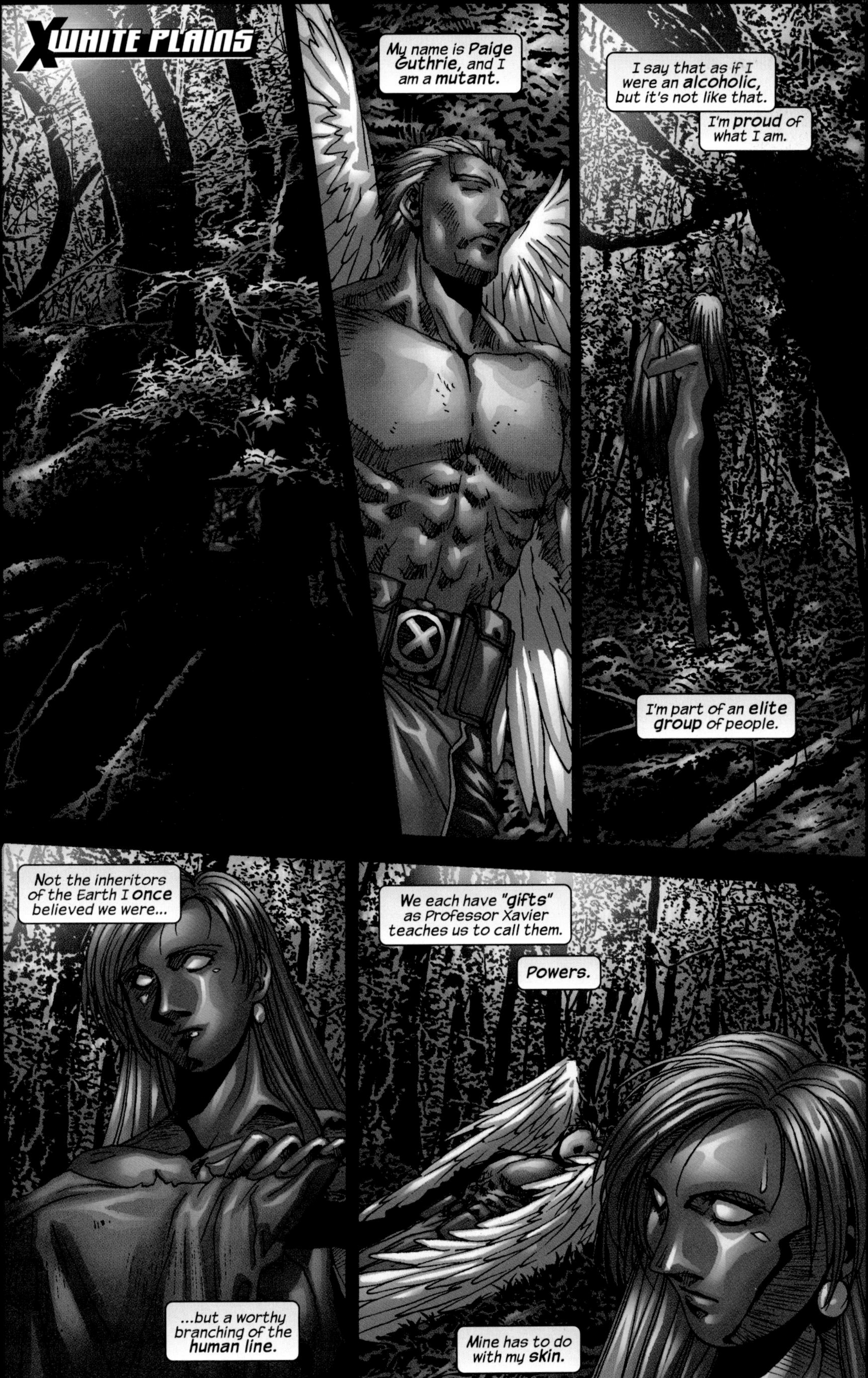
WHITE PLAINS
My name is Paige Guthrie, and I am a mutant.
I say that as if I were an alcoholic, but it's not like that.
I'm proud of what I am.
I'm part of an elite group of people.
Not the inheritors of the Earth I once believed we were...
...but a worthy branching of the human line.
We each have "gifts" as Professor Xavier teaches us to call them.
Powers.
Mine has to do with my skin.

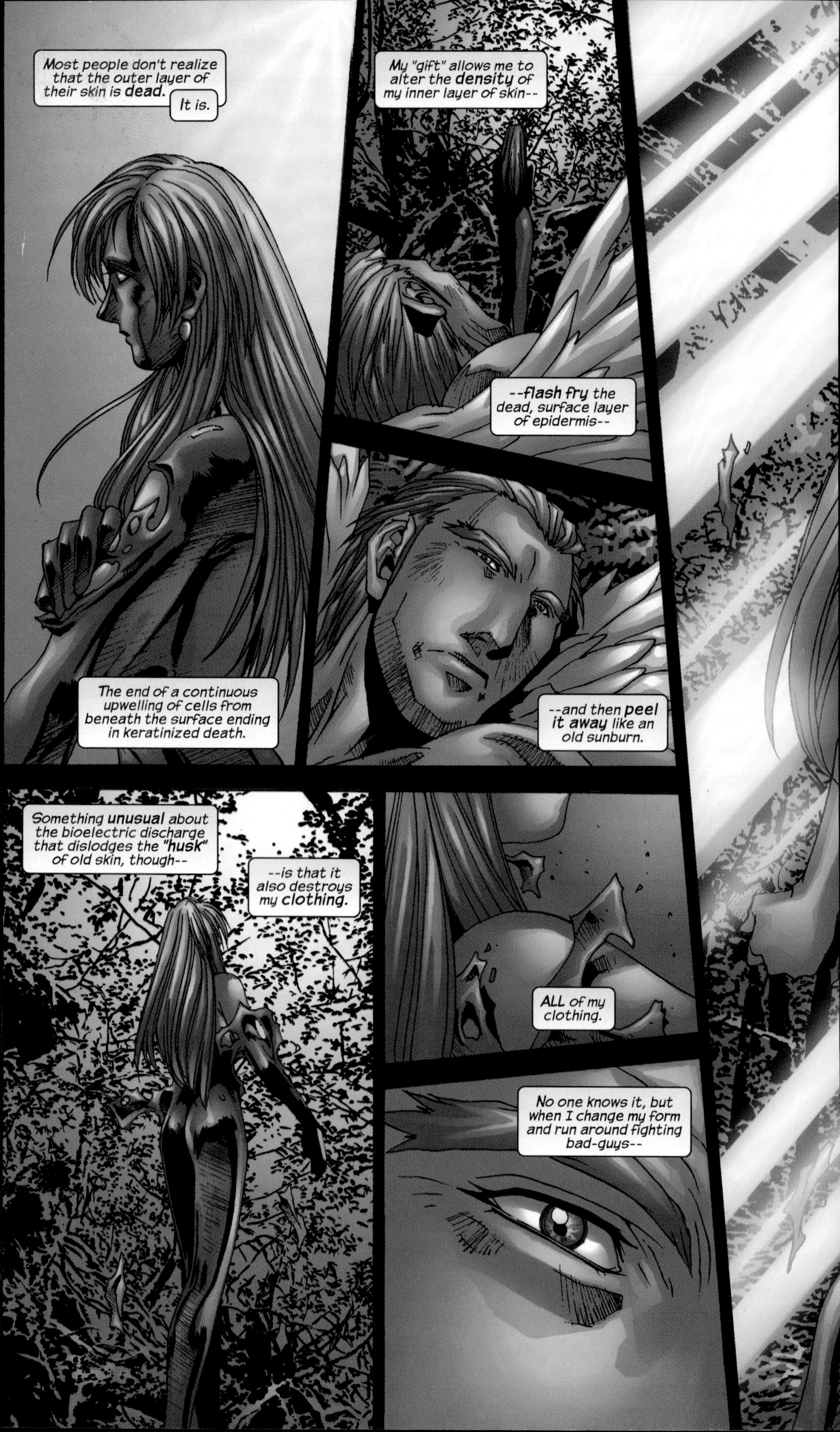
Most people don't realize that the outer layer of their skin is dead.
It is.
The end of a continuous upwelling of cells from beneath the surface ending in keratinized death.
My "gift" allows me to alter the density of my inner layer of skin--
--flash fry the dead, surface layer of epidermis--
--and then peel it away like an old sunburn.
Something unusual about the bioelectric discharge that dislodges the "husk" of old skin, though--
--is that it also destroys my clothing.
ALL of my clothing.
No one knows it, but when I change my form and run around fighting bad-guys--

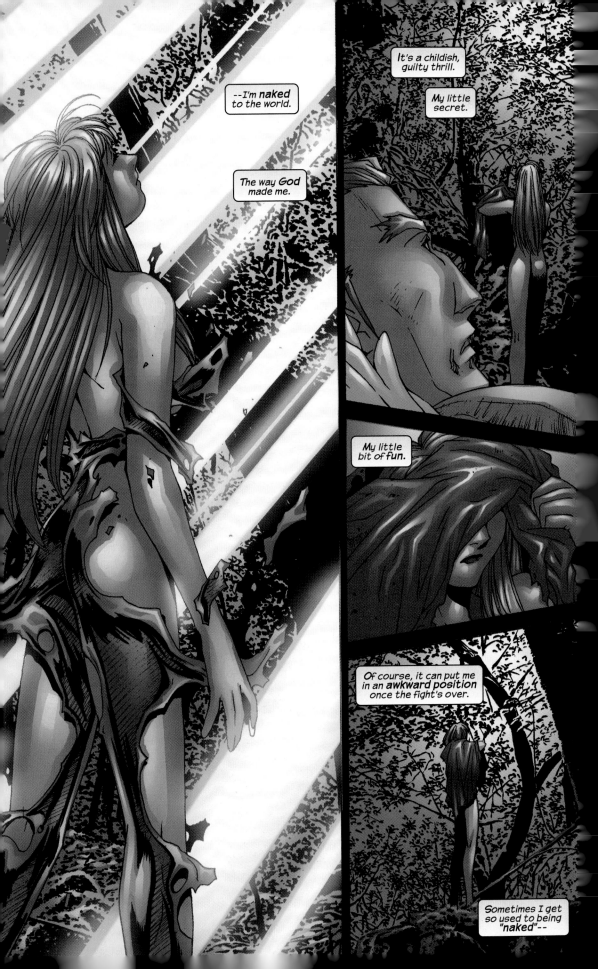

--I'm **naked** to the world.

The way God made me.

It's a childish, guilty thrill.

My little secret.

My little bit of **fun**.

Of course, it can put me in an **awkward position** once the fight's over.

Sometimes I get so used to being "**naked**"--

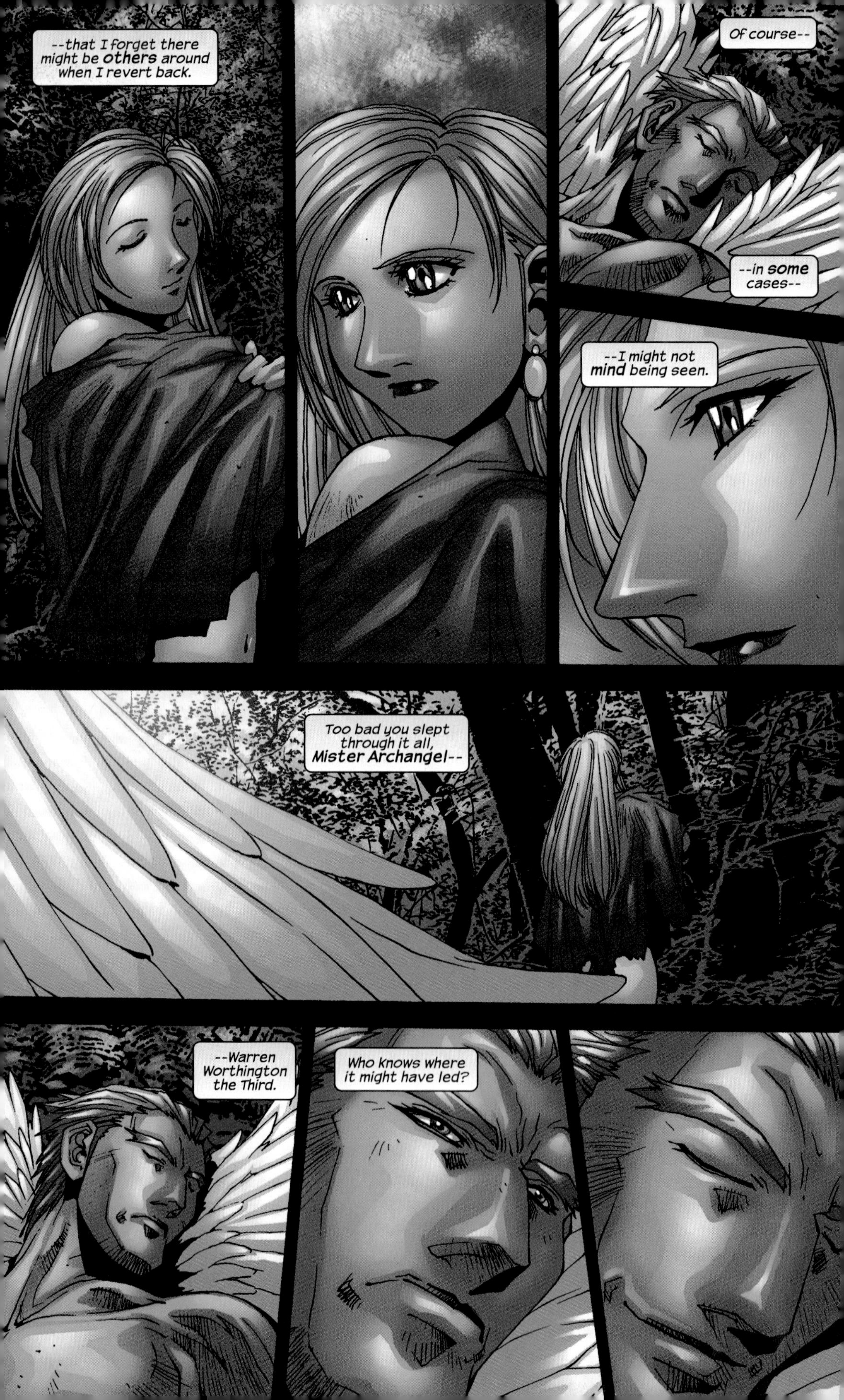
--that I forget there might be **others** around when I revert back.
Of course--
--in **some** cases--
--I might not **mind** being seen.
Too bad you slept through it all, **Mister Archangel**--
--Warren Worthington the Third.
Who knows where it might have led?

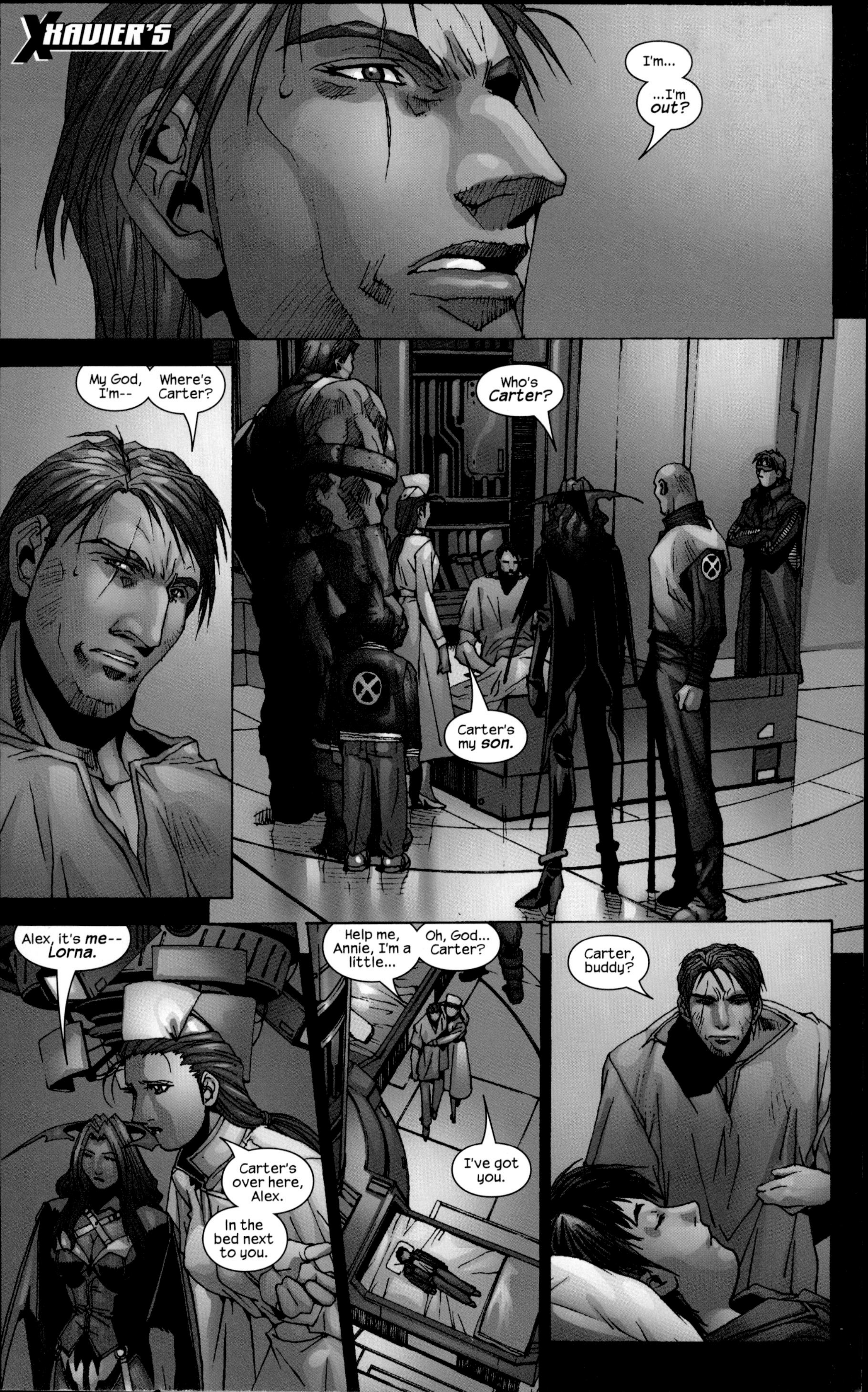
XAVIER'S
I'm...
...I'm out?
My God, I'm--
Where's Carter?
Who's Carter?
Carter's my son.
Alex, it's me-- Lorna.
Carter's over here, Alex.
In the bed next to you.
Help me, Annie, I'm a little...
Oh, God... Carter?
I've got you.
Carter, buddy?

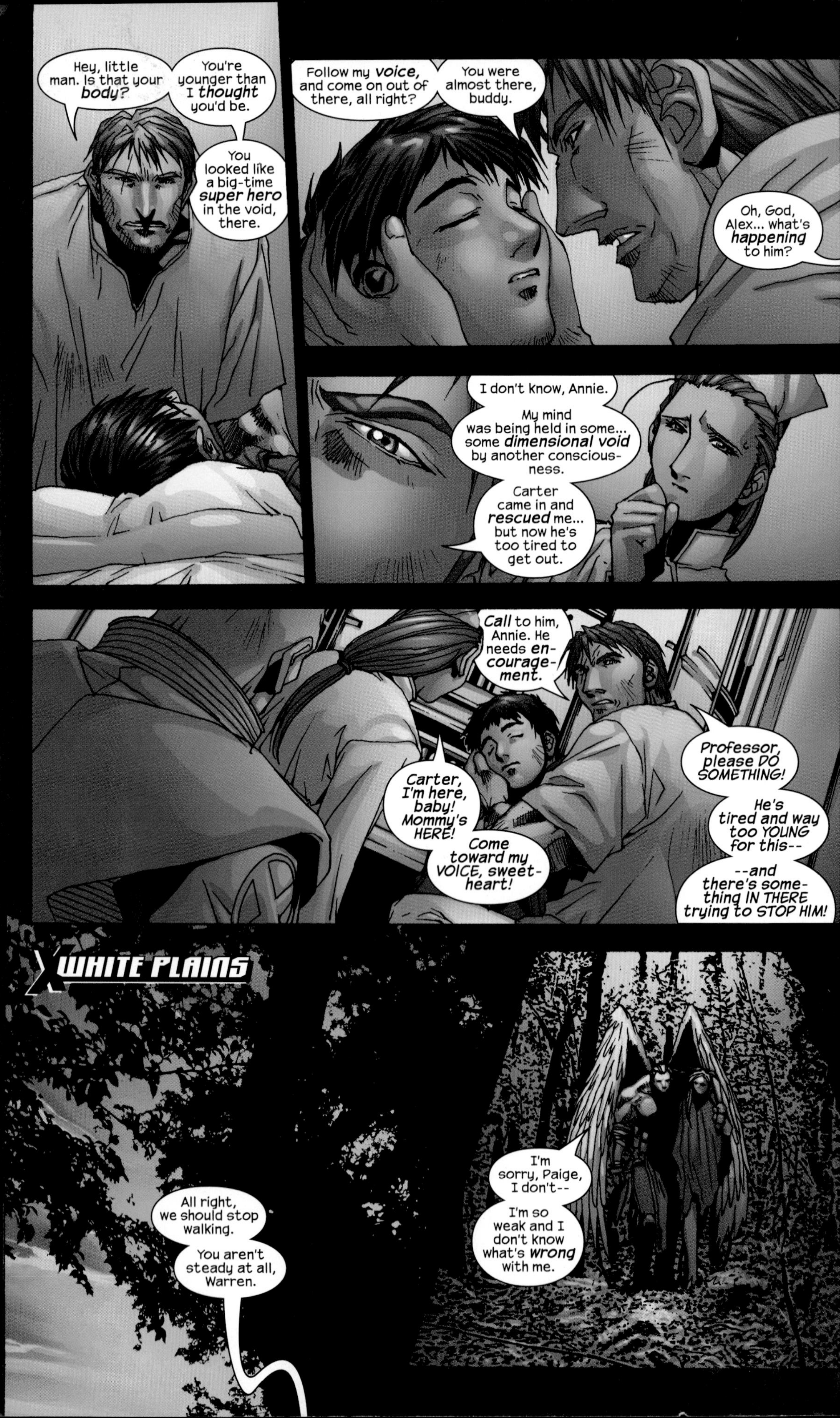
Hey, little man. Is that your *body?*
You're younger than I *thought* you'd be.
You looked like a big-time *super hero* in the void, there.
Follow my *voice,* and come on out of there, all right?
You were almost there, buddy.
Oh, God, Alex... what's *happening* to him?
I don't know, Annie.
My mind was being held in some... some *dimensional void* by another conscious-ness.
Carter came in and *rescued* me... but now he's too tired to get out.
Call to him, Annie. He needs *en-courage-ment.*
Carter, I'm here, baby! Mommy's HERE!
Come toward my VOICE, sweet-heart!
Professor, please DO SOMETHING!
He's tired and way too YOUNG for this--
--and there's some-thing IN THERE trying to STOP HIM!
WHITE PLAINS
All right, we should stop walking.
You aren't steady at all, Warren.
I'm sorry, Paige, I don't--
I'm so weak and I don't know what's *wrong* with me.

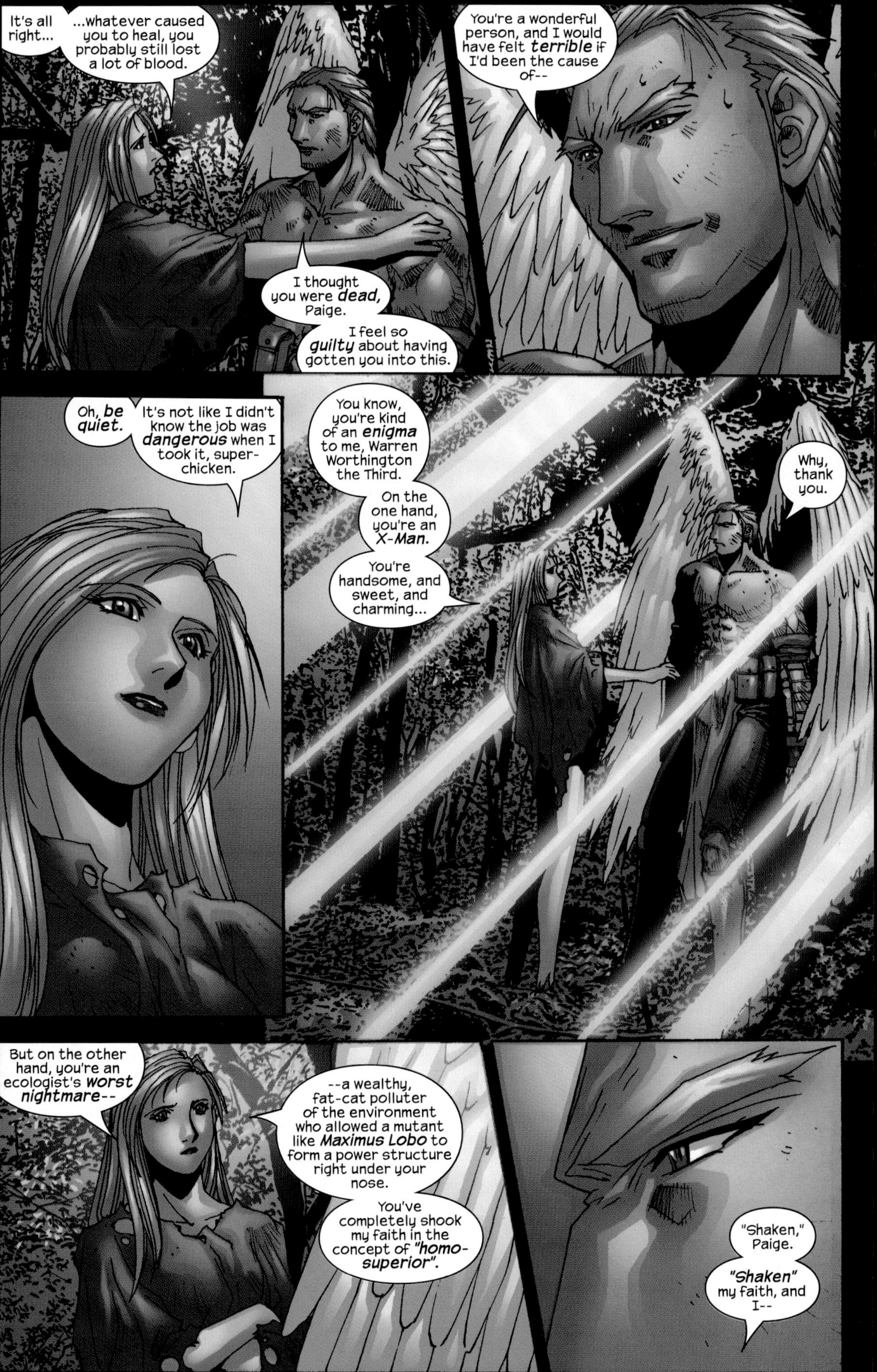
It's all right...
...whatever caused you to heal, you probably still lost a lot of blood.
I thought you were dead, Paige.
I feel so guilty about having gotten you into this.
You're a wonderful person, and I would have felt terrible if I'd been the cause of--
Oh, be quiet.
It's not like I didn't know the job was dangerous when I took it, super-chicken.
You know, you're kind of an enigma to me, Warren Worthington the Third.
On the one hand, you're an X-Man.
You're handsome, and sweet, and charming...
Why, thank you.
But on the other hand, you're an ecologist's worst nightmare--
--a wealthy, fat-cat polluter of the environment who allowed a mutant like Maximus Lobo to form a power structure right under your nose.
You've completely shook my faith in the concept of "homo-superior".
"Shaken," Paige.
"Shaken" my faith, and I--

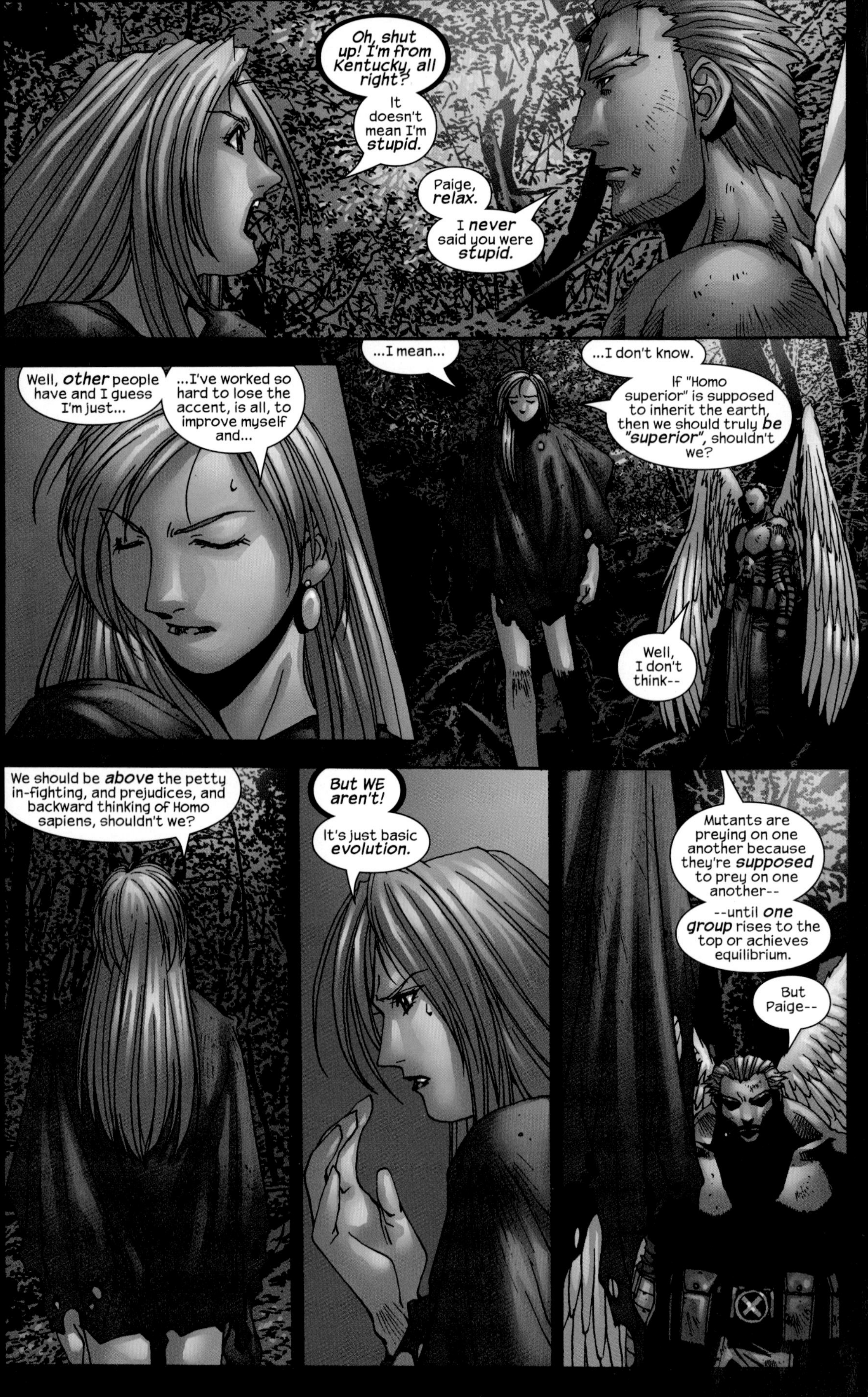
Oh, shut up! I'm from Kentucky, all right?
It doesn't mean I'm stupid.
Paige, relax.
I never said you were stupid.
Well, other people have and I guess I'm just...
...I've worked so hard to lose the accent, is all, to improve myself and...
...I mean...
...I don't know.
If "Homo superior" is supposed to inherit the earth, then we should truly be "superior", shouldn't we?
Well, I don't think--
We should be above the petty in-fighting, and prejudices, and backward thinking of Homo sapiens, shouldn't we?
But WE aren't!
It's just basic evolution.
Mutants are preying on one another because they're supposed to prey on one another--
--until one group rises to the top or achieves equilibrium.
But Paige--

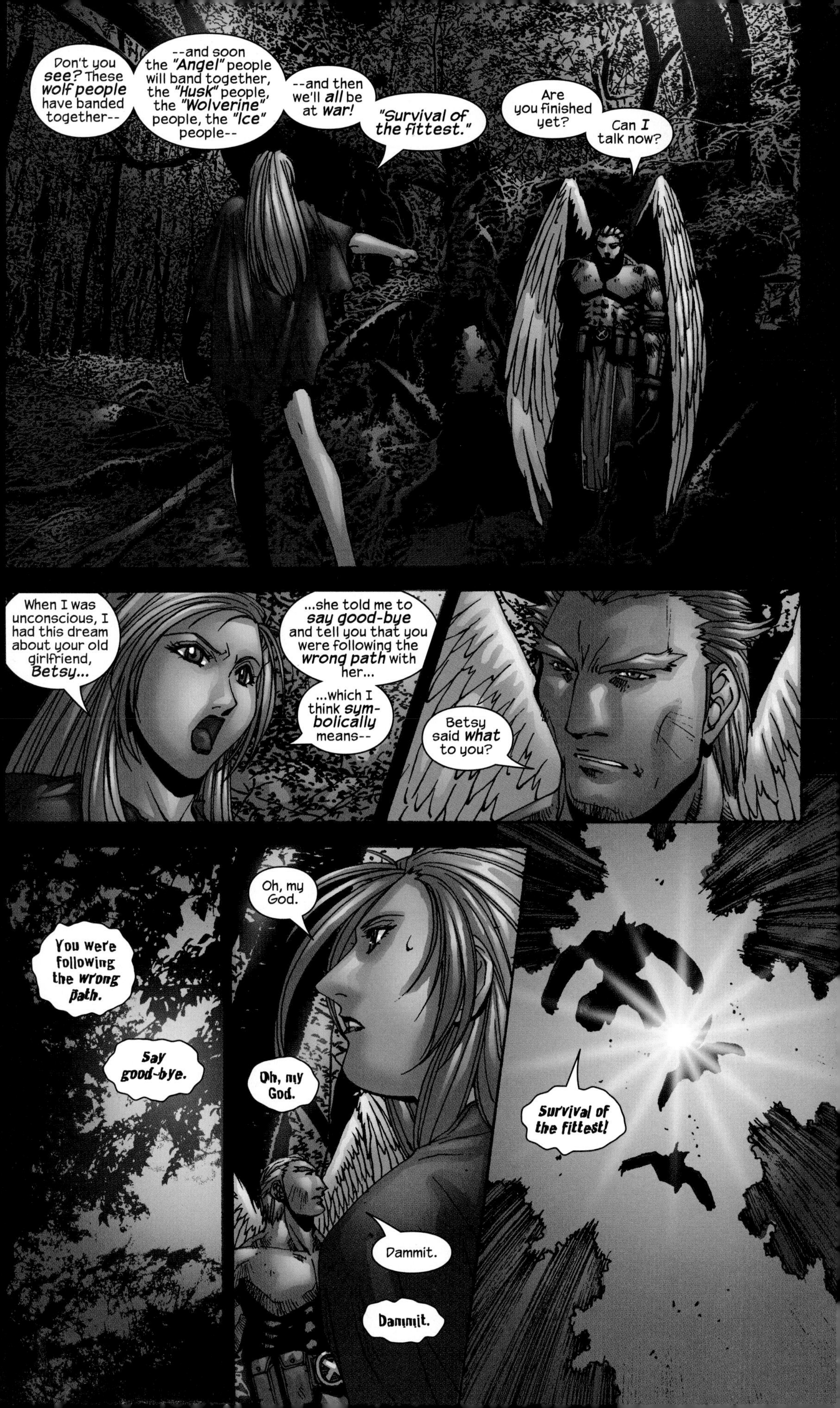
Don't you see? These wolf people have banded together--
--and soon the "Angel" people will band together, the "Husk" people, the "Wolverine" people, the "Ice" people--
--and then we'll all be at war!
"Survival of the fittest."
Are you finished yet?
Can I talk now?
When I was unconscious, I had this dream about your old girlfriend, Betsy...
...she told me to say good-bye and tell you that you were following the wrong path with her...
...which I think symbolically means--
Betsy said what to you?
You were following the wrong path.
Say good-bye.
Oh, my God.
Oh, my God.
Dammit.
Dammit.
Survival of the fittest!

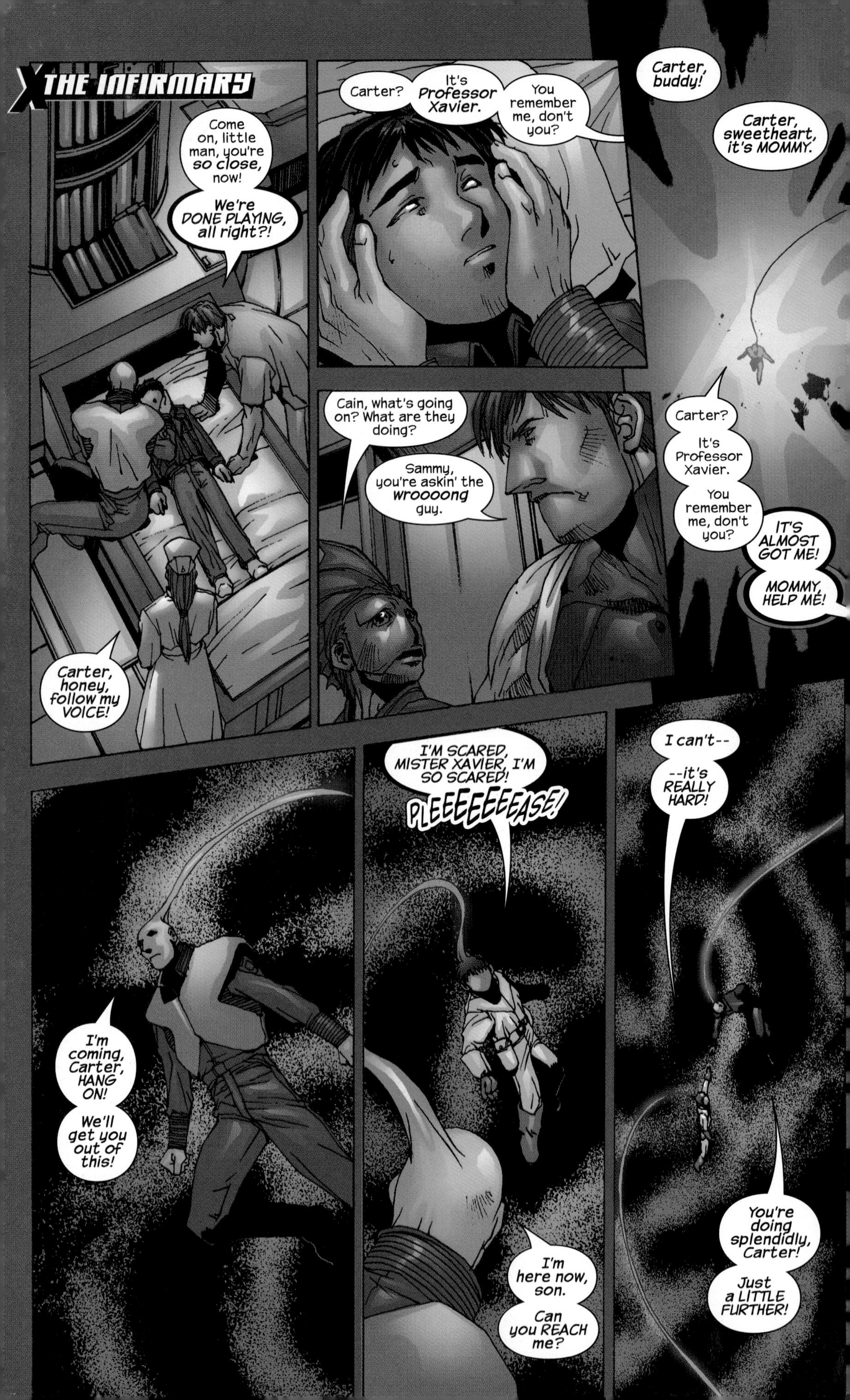
THE INFIRMARY
Come on, little man, you're so close, now!
We're DONE PLAYING, all right?!
Carter, honey, follow my VOICE!
Carter?
It's Professor Xavier.
You remember me, don't you?
Cain, what's going on? What are they doing?
Sammy, you're askin' the wroooong guy.
Carter, buddy!
Carter, sweetheart, it's MOMMY.
Carter?
It's Professor Xavier.
You remember me, don't you?
IT'S ALMOST GOT ME!
MOMMY, HELP ME!
I'm coming, Carter, HANG ON!
We'll get you out of this!
I'M SCARED, MISTER XAVIER, I'M SO SCARED!
PLEEEEEEEASE!
I'm here now, son.
Can you REACH me?
I can't--
--it's REALLY HARD!
You're doing splendidly, Carter!
Just a LITTLE FURTHER!

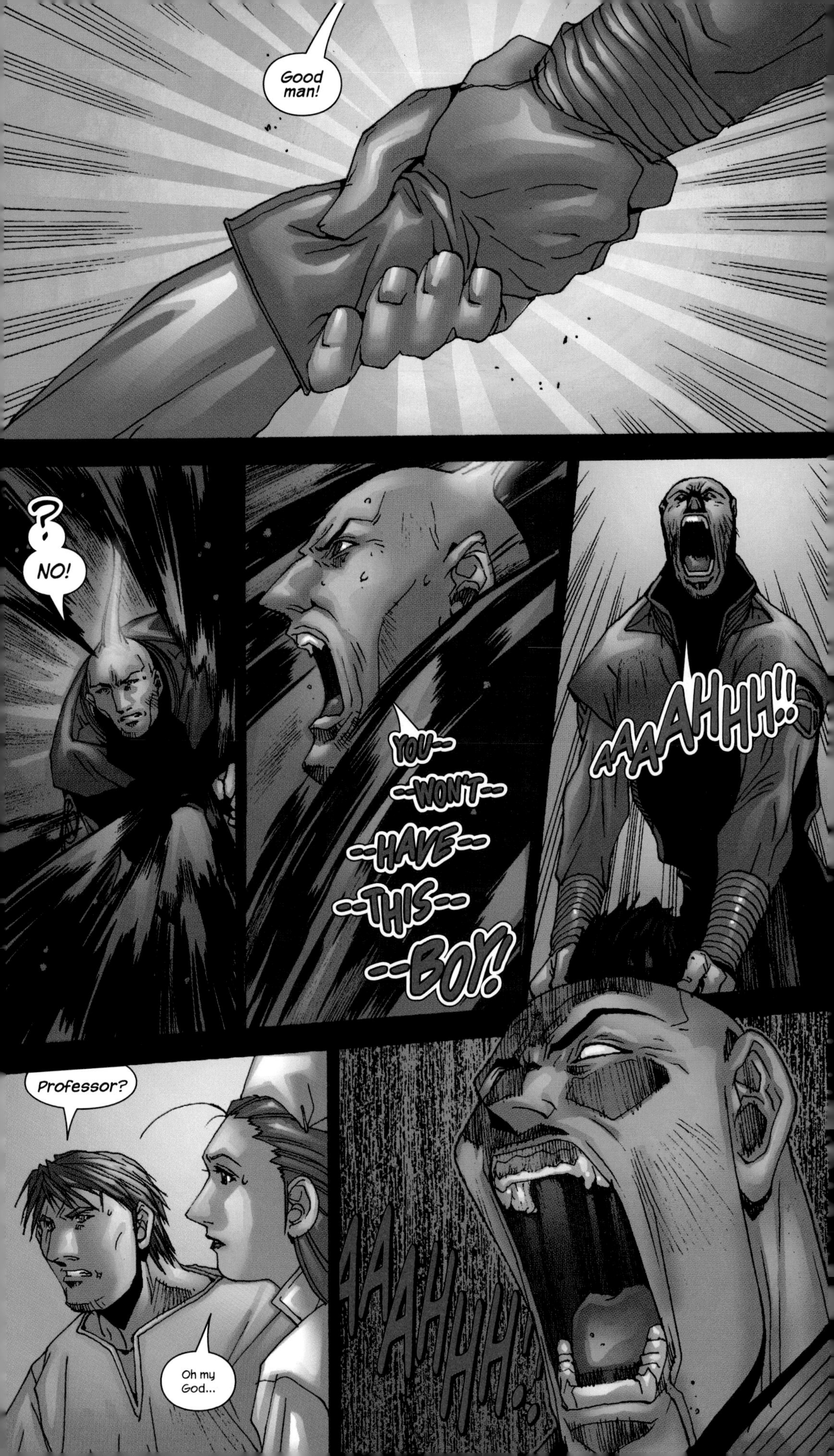

Good man!
?
NO!
YOU-- --WON'T-- --HAVE-- --THIS-- --BOY!
AAAAHHHH!!
Professor?
Oh my God...
AAAHHHH!!

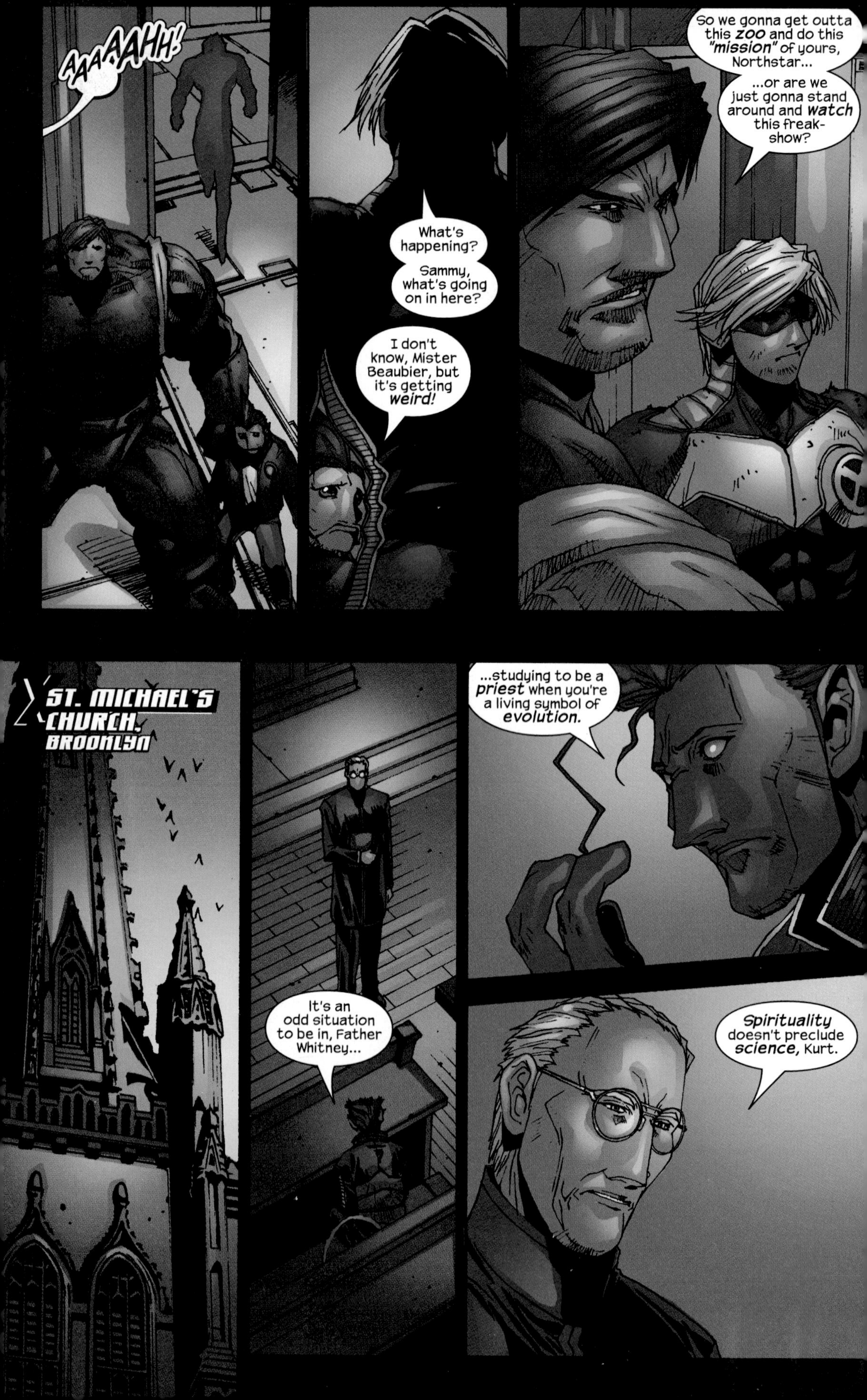
AAAAAHH!
What's happening?
Sammy, what's going on in here?
I don't know, Mister Beaubier, but it's getting *weird!*
So we gonna get outta this *zoo* and do this *"mission"* of yours, Northstar...
...or are we just gonna stand around and *watch* this freak-show?
ST. MICHAEL'S CHURCH, BROOKLYN
It's an odd situation to be in, Father Whitney...
...studying to be a *priest* when you're a living symbol of *evolution.*
Spirituality doesn't preclude *science,* Kurt.

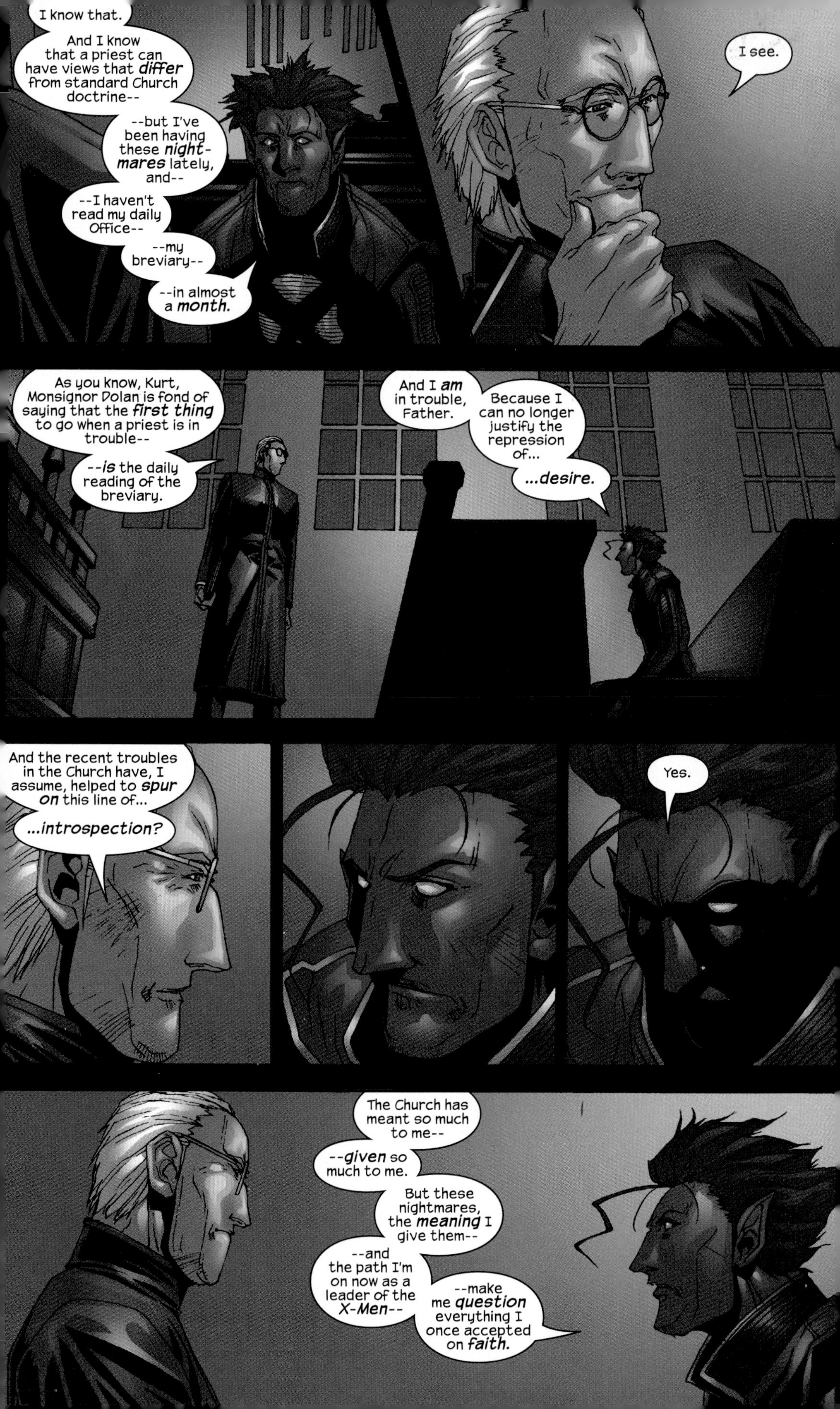
I know that.
And I know that a priest can have views that *differ* from standard Church doctrine--
--but I've been having these *night-mares* lately, and--
--I haven't read my daily Office--
--my breviary--
--in almost a *month.*
I see.
As you know, Kurt, Monsignor Dolan is fond of saying that the *first thing* to go when a priest is in trouble--
--*is* the daily reading of the breviary.
And I *am* in trouble, Father.
Because I can no longer justify the repression of...
...desire.
And the recent troubles in the Church have, I assume, helped to *spur on* this line of...
...introspection?
Yes.
The Church has meant so much to me--
--*given* so much to me.
But these nightmares, the *meaning* I give them--
--and the path I'm on now as a leader of the *X-Men*--
--make me *question* everything I once accepted on *faith.*

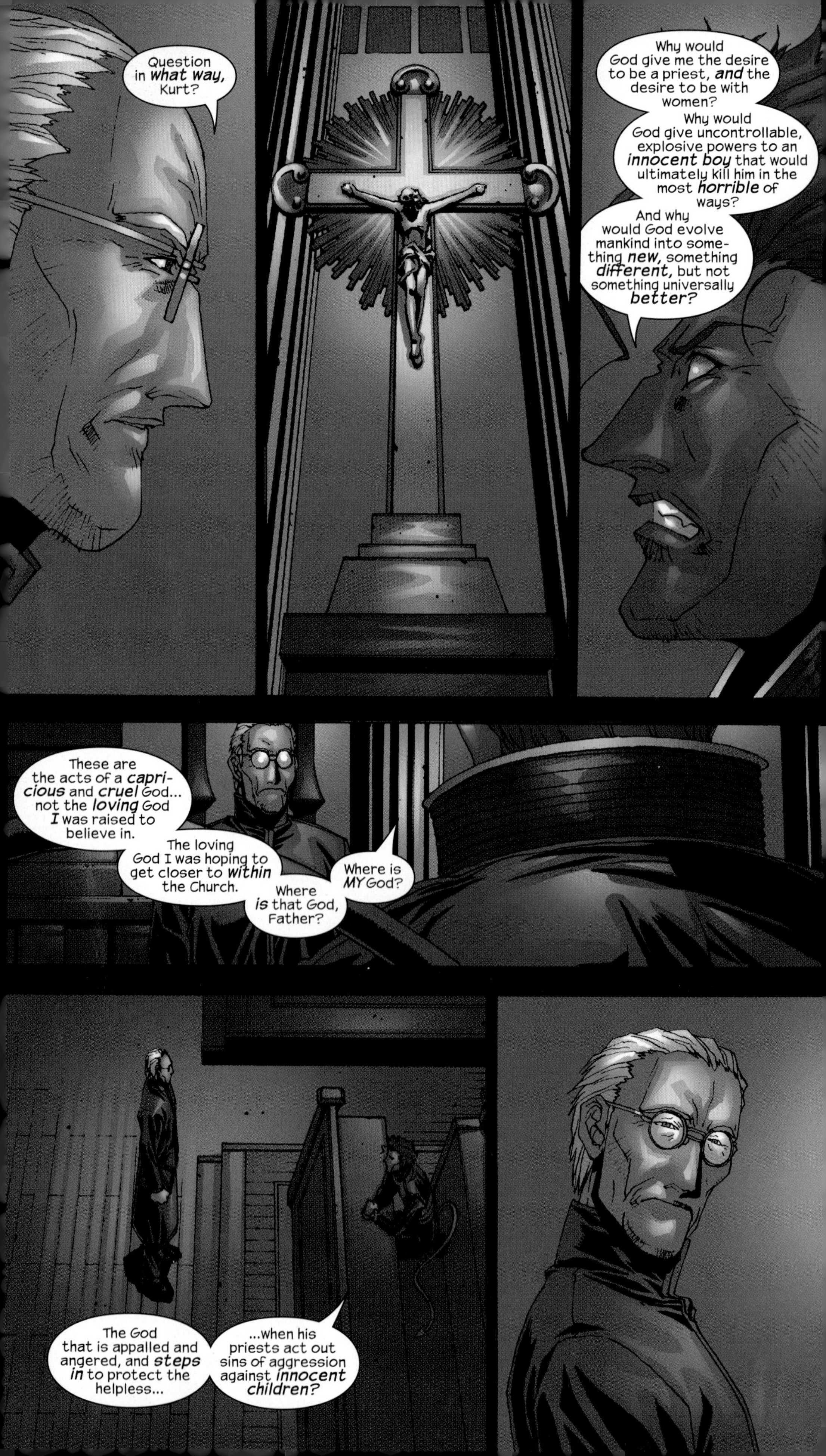
Question in *what way,* Kurt?
Why would God give me the desire to be a priest, *and* the desire to be with women?
Why would God give uncontrollable, explosive powers to an *innocent boy* that would ultimately kill him in the most *horrible* of ways?
And why would God evolve mankind into something *new,* something *different,* but not something universally *better?*
These are the acts of a *capricious* and *cruel* God... not the *loving* God *I* was raised to believe in.
The loving God I was hoping to get closer to *within* the Church.
Where *is* that God, Father?
Where is *MY* God?
The God that is appalled and angered, and *steps in* to protect the helpless...
...when his priests act out sins of aggression against *innocent children?*

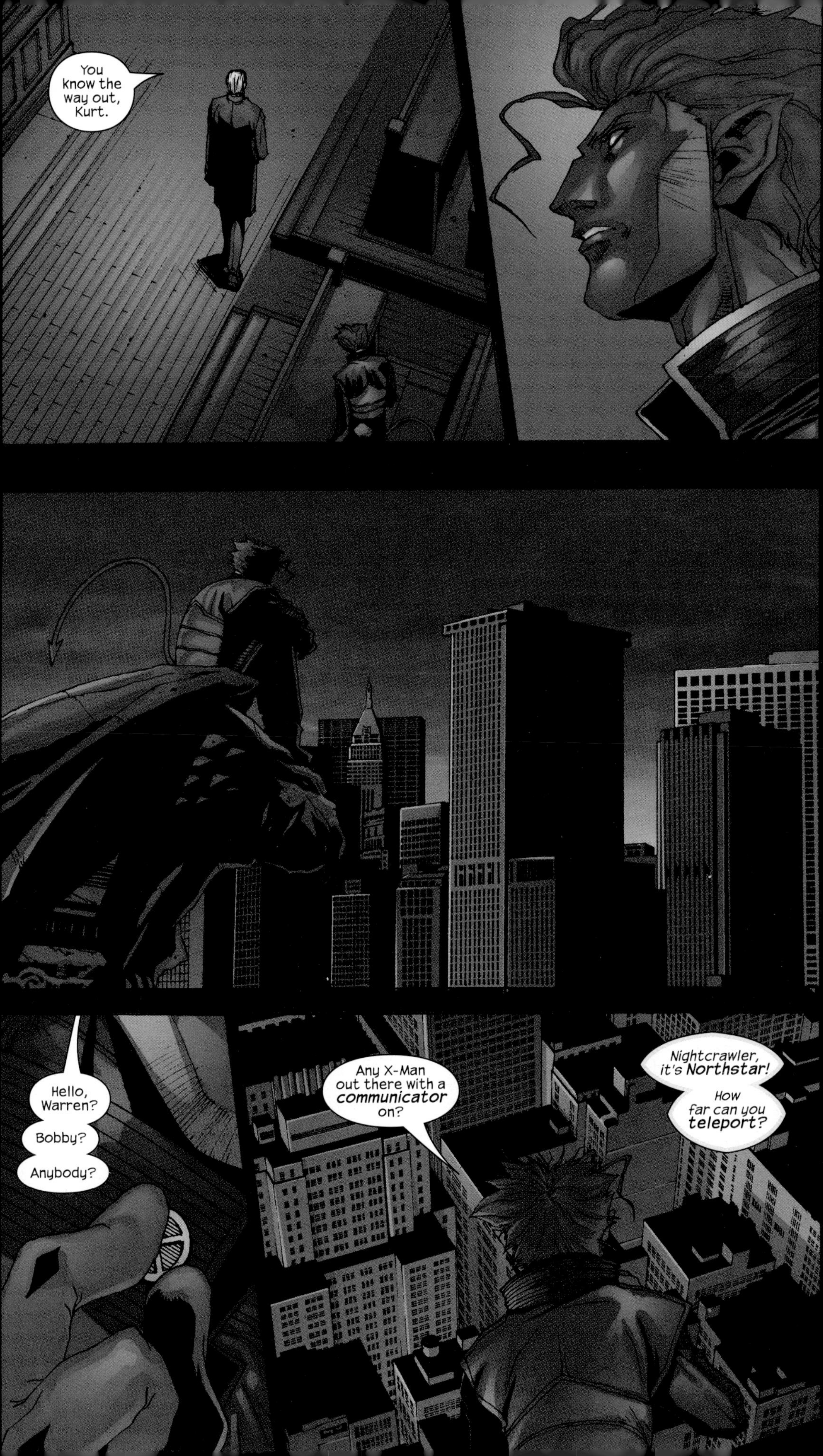
You know the way out, Kurt.
Hello, Warren?
Bobby?
Anybody?
Any X-Man out there with a communicator on?
Nightcrawler, it's Northstar!
How far can you teleport?

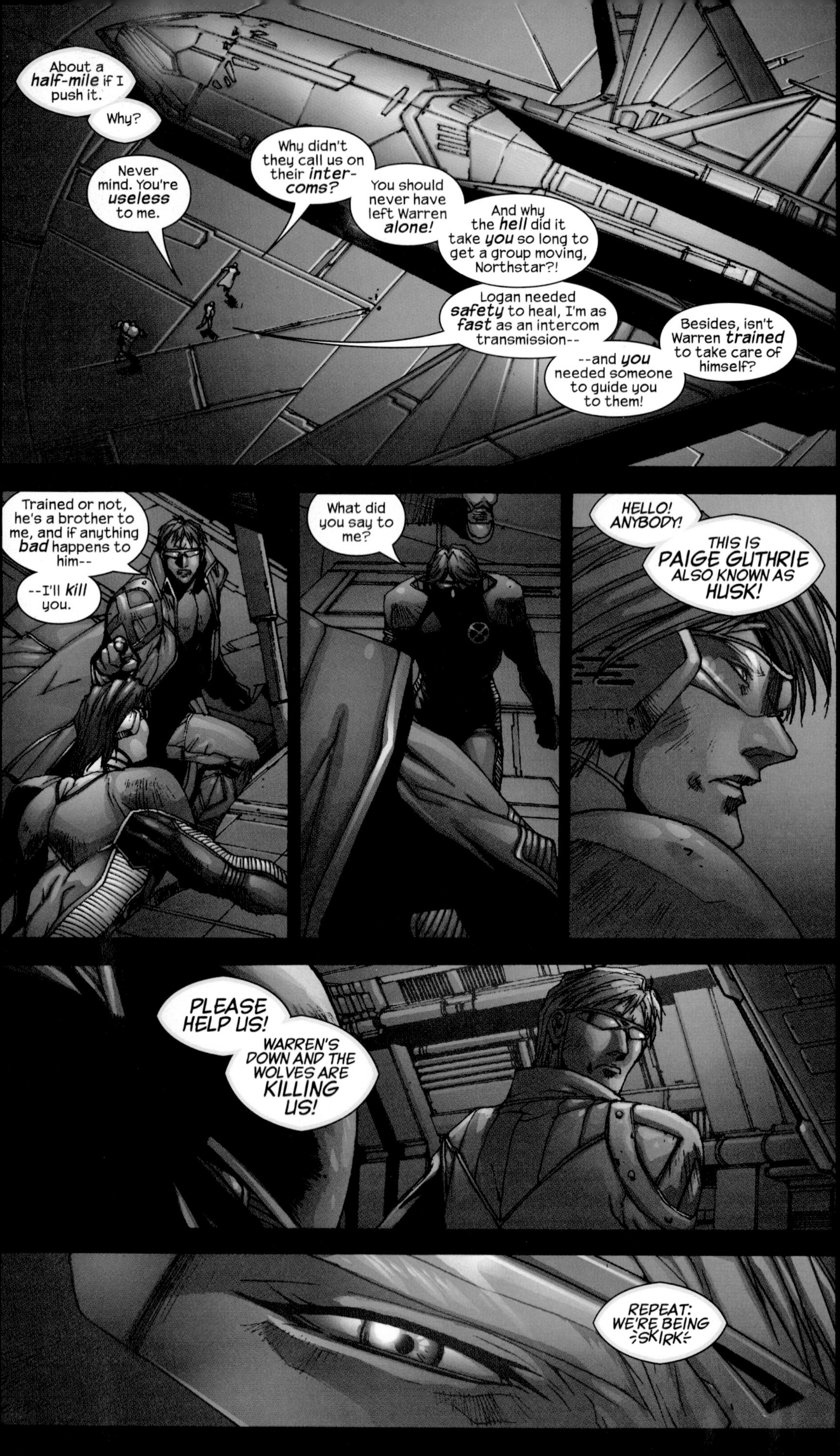
About a half-mile if I push it.
Why?
Never mind. You're useless to me.
Why didn't they call us on their inter-coms?
You should never have left Warren alone!
And why the hell did it take you so long to get a group moving, Northstar?!
Logan needed safety to heal, I'm as fast as an intercom transmission--
--and you needed someone to guide you to them!
Besides, isn't Warren trained to take care of himself?
Trained or not, he's a brother to me, and if anything bad happens to him--
--I'll kill you.
What did you say to me?
HELLO! ANYBODY!
THIS IS PAIGE GUTHRIE ALSO KNOWN AS HUSK!
PLEASE HELP US!
WARREN'S DOWN AND THE WOLVES ARE KILLING US!
REPEAT: WE'RE BEING
SKIRK

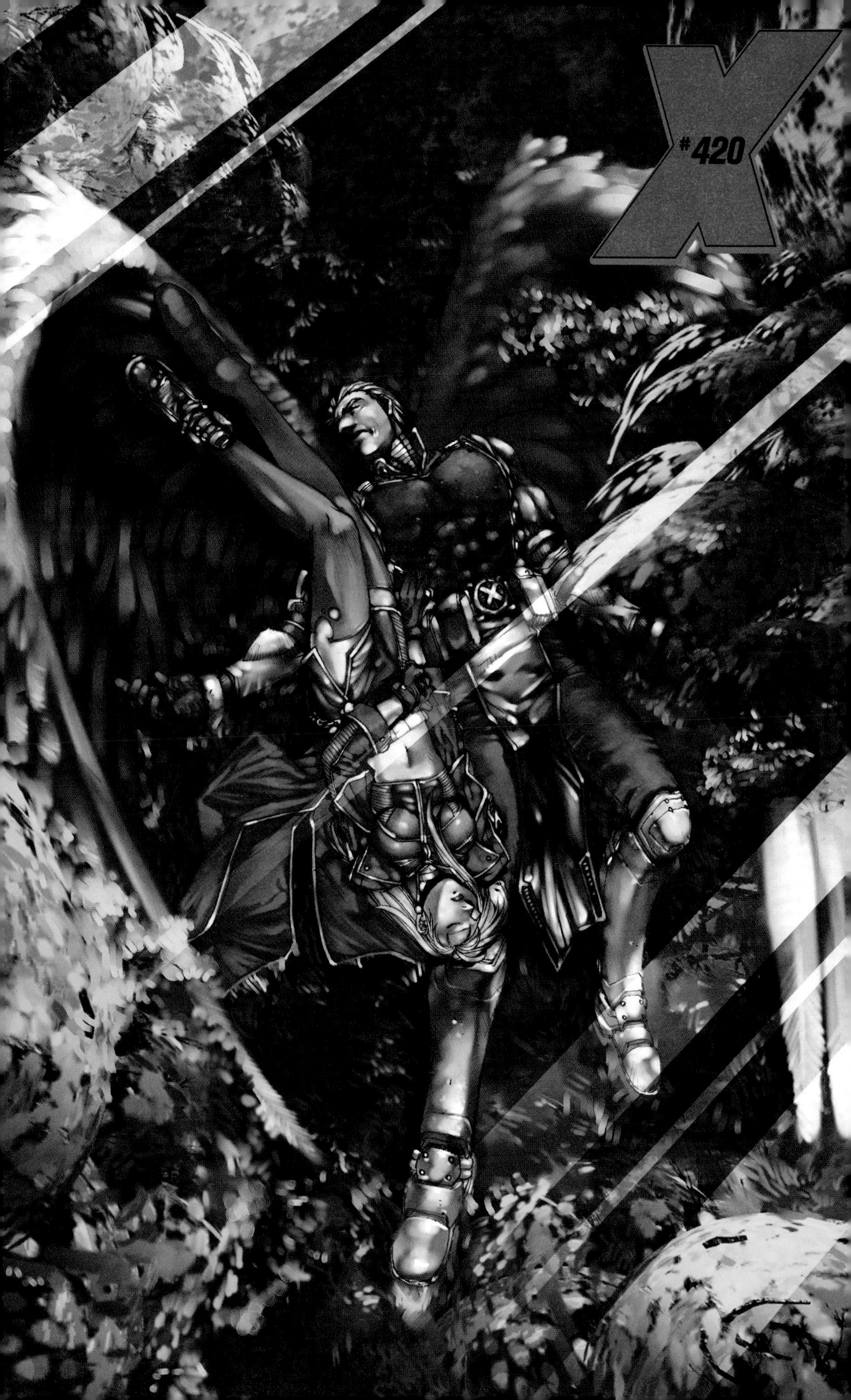
#420

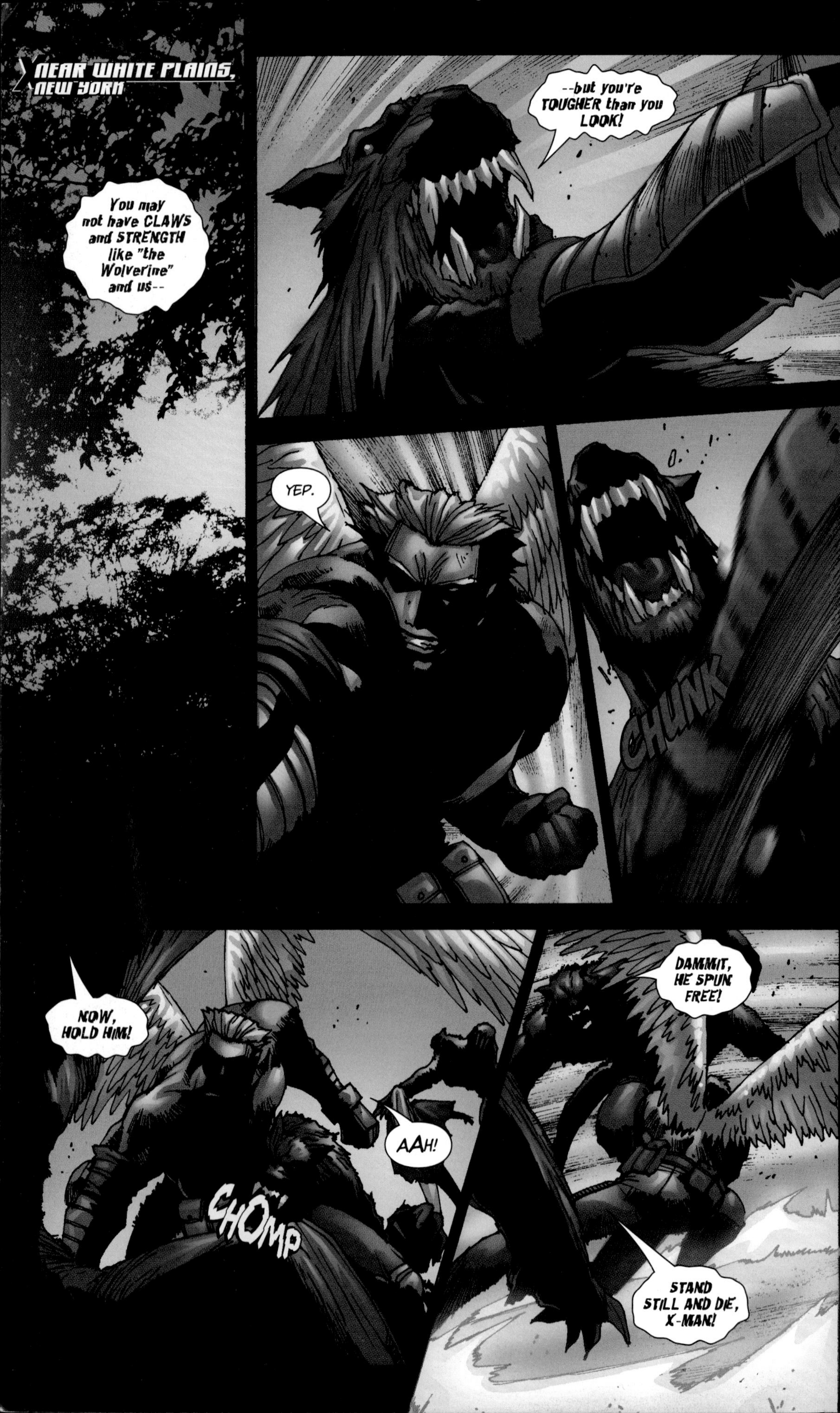
NEAR WHITE PLAINS, NEW YORK
You may not have CLAWS and STRENGTH like "the Wolverine" and us--
--but you're TOUGHER than you LOOK!
YEP.
CHUNK
NOW, HOLD HIM!
AAH!
CHOMP
DAMMIT, HE SPUN FREE!
STAND STILL AND DIE, X-MAN!

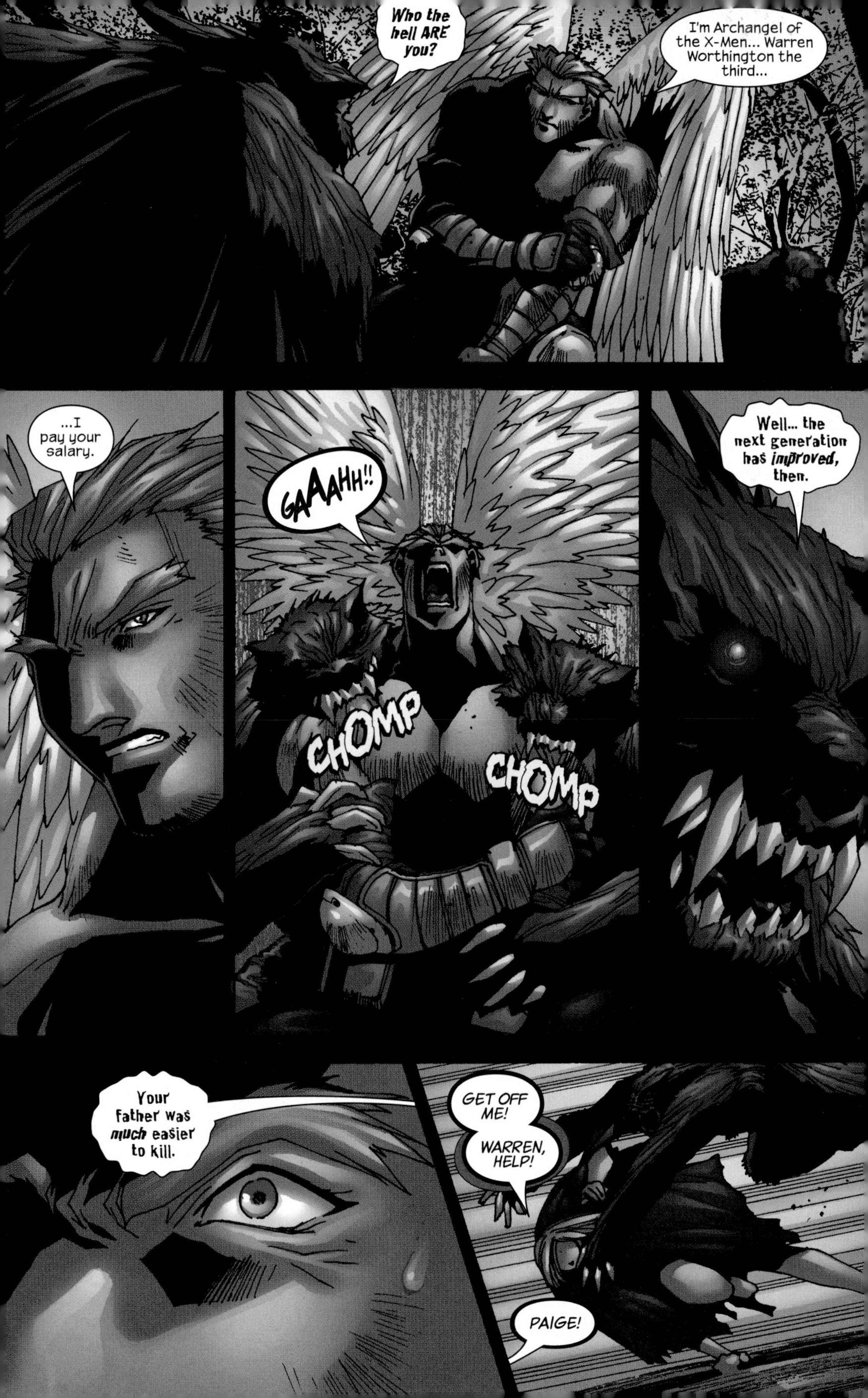
Who the hell ARE you?
I'm Archangel of the X-Men... Warren Worthington the third...
...I pay your salary.
GAAAHH!!
CHOMP
CHOMP
Well... the next generation has improved, then.
Your father was much easier to kill.
GET OFF ME!
WARREN, HELP!
PAIGE!

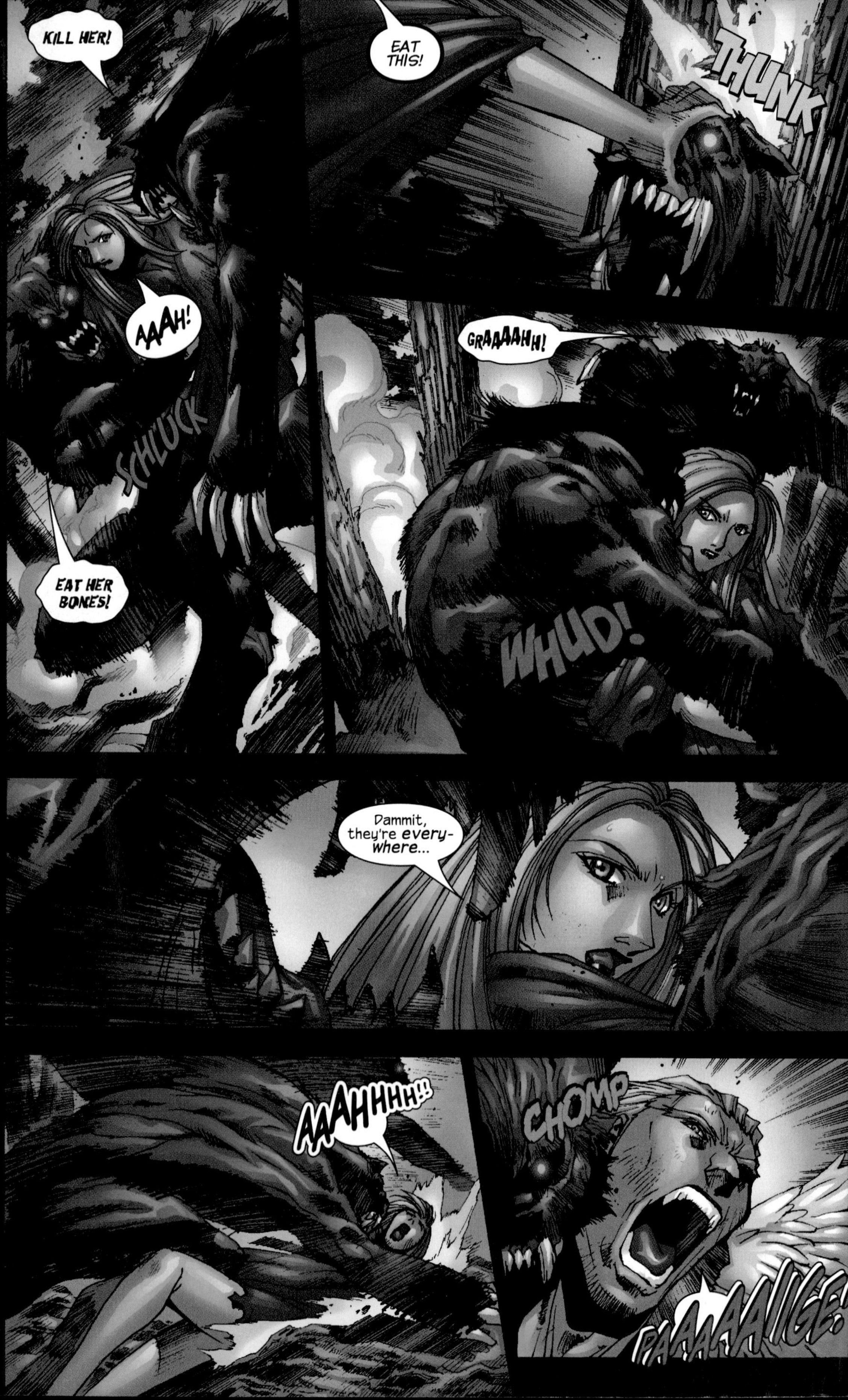
KILL HER!
EAT THIS!
THUNK
AAAH!
SCHLUCK
EAT HER BONES!
GRAAAAHH!
WHUD!
Dammit, they're every-where...
AAAHHHH!!
CHOMP
PAAAAAIGE!

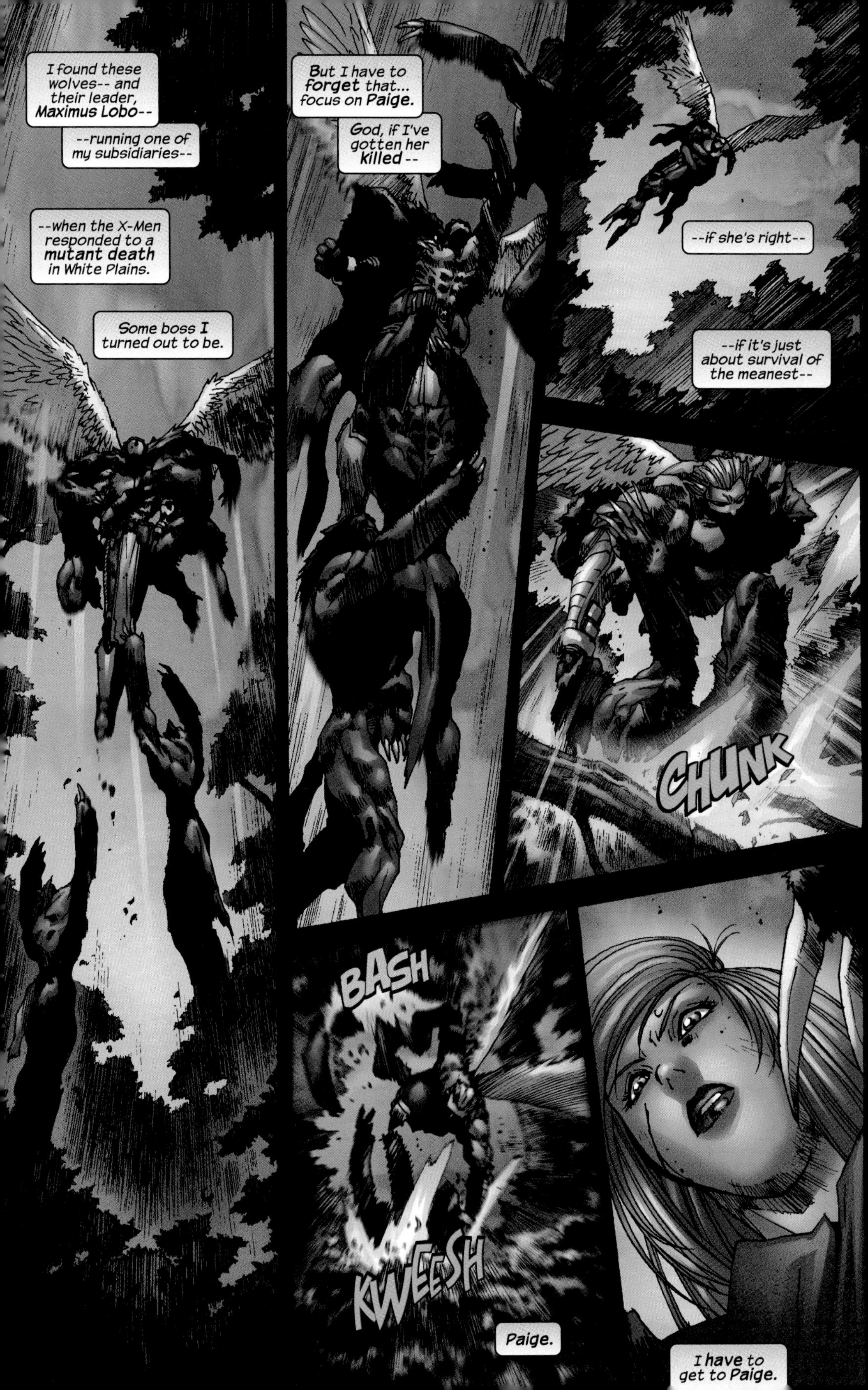
I found these wolves-- and their leader, Maximus Lobo--
--running one of my subsidiaries--
--when the X-Men responded to a mutant death in White Plains.
Some boss I turned out to be.
But I have to forget that... focus on Paige.
God, if I've gotten her killed--
--if she's right--
--if it's just about survival of the meanest--
CHUNK
BASH
KWEESH
Paige.
I have to get to Paige.

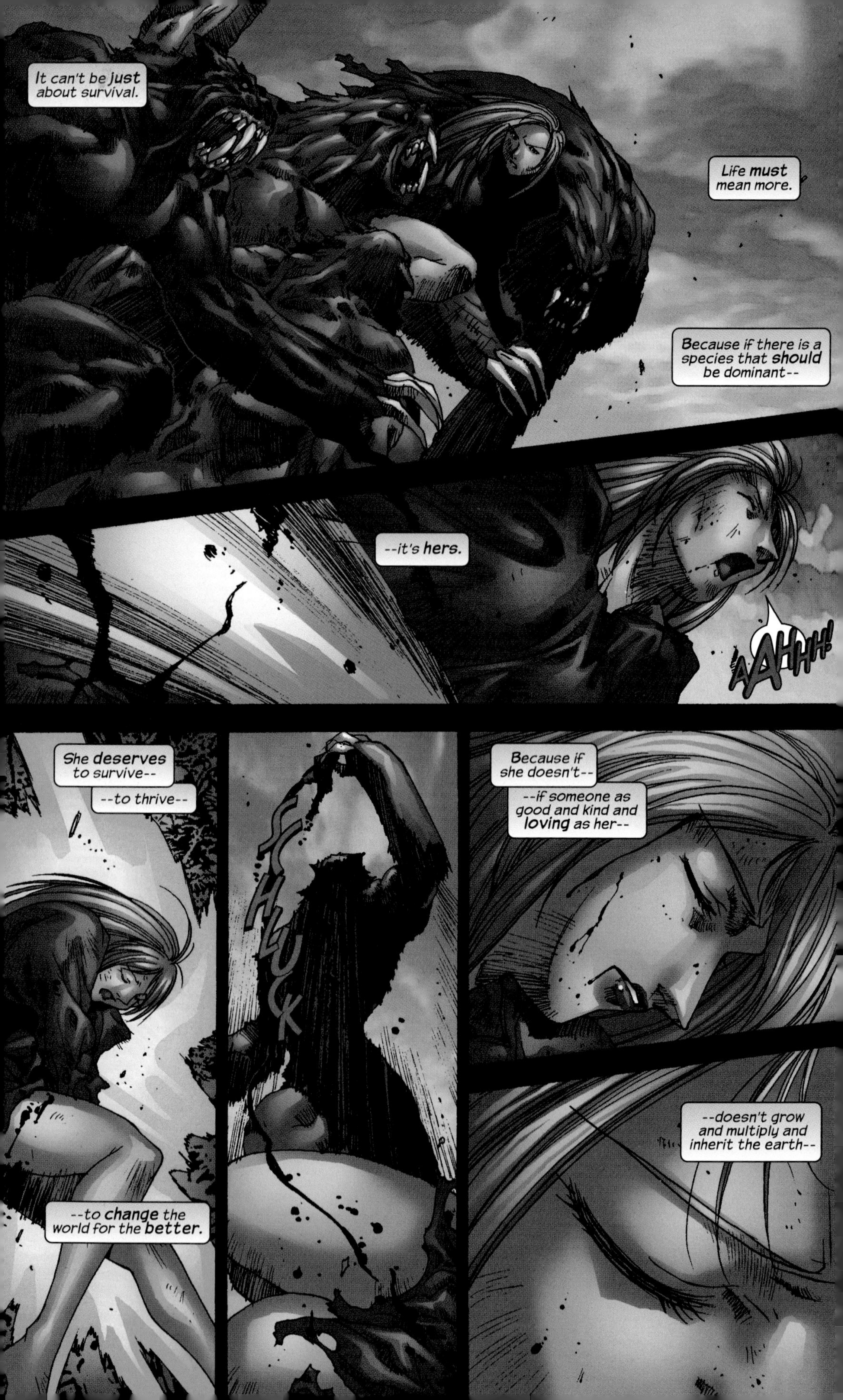
It can't be just about survival.
Life must mean more.
Because if there is a species that should be dominant--
--it's hers.
AAHHH!
She deserves to survive--
--to thrive--
--to change the world for the better.
HLUCK
Because if she doesn't--
--if someone as good and kind and loving as her--
--doesn't grow and multiply and inherit the earth--

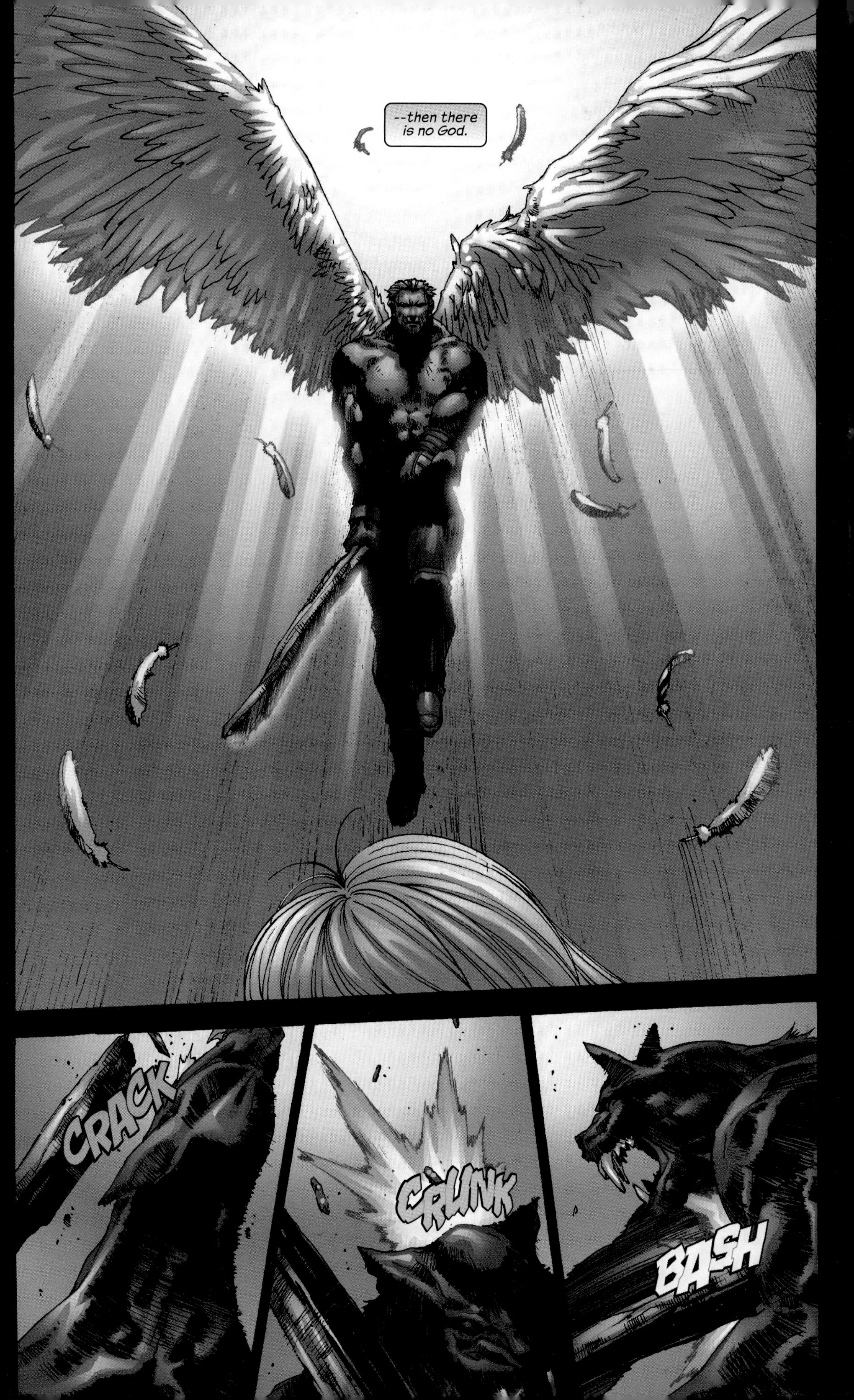
--then there is no God.
CRACK
CRUNK
BASH

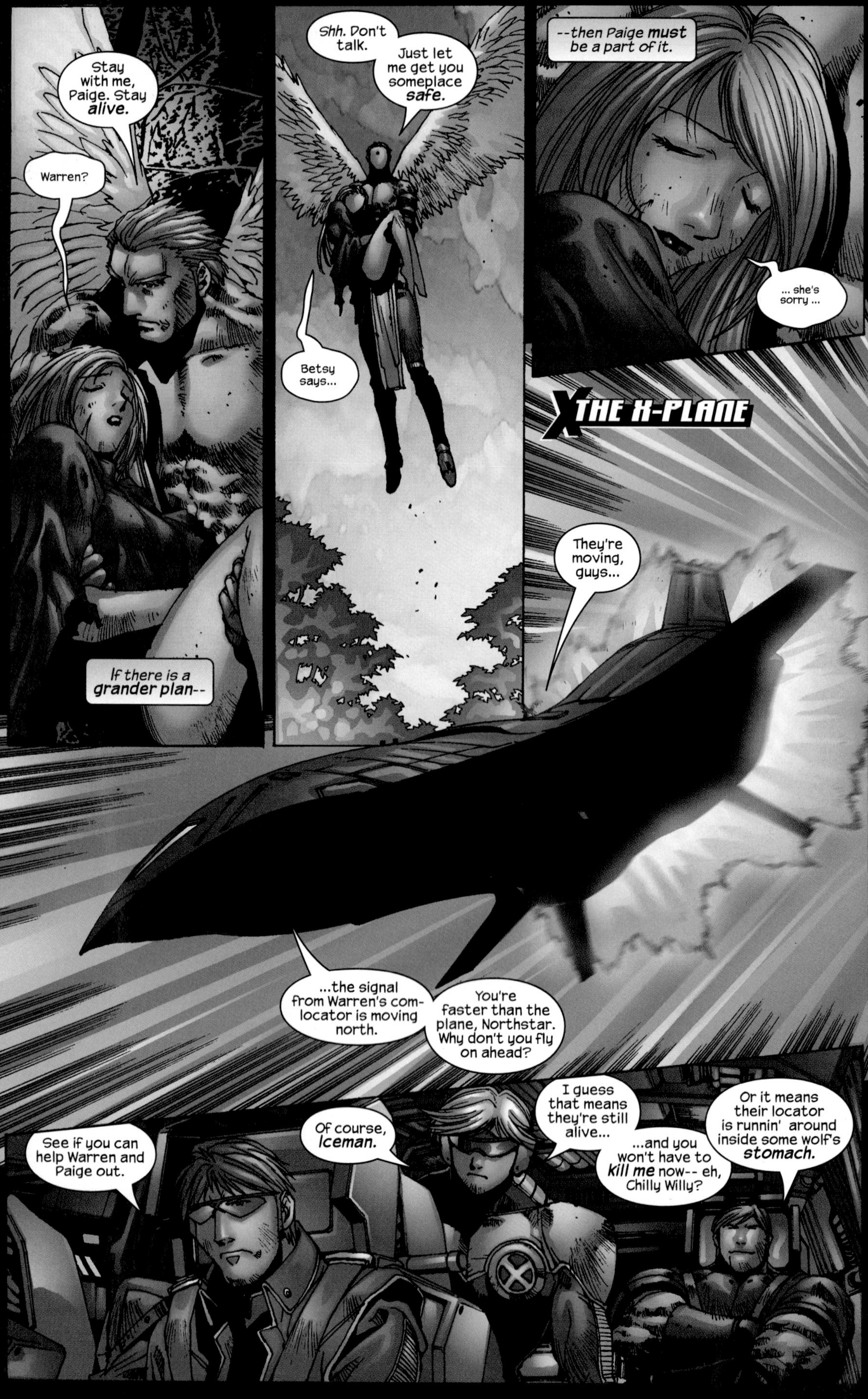
Stay with me, Paige. Stay *alive.*
Warren?
If there is a **grander plan**--
Shh. Don't talk.
Just let me get you someplace *safe.*
Betsy says...
--then Paige **must** be a part of it.
... she's sorry ...
THE X-PLANE
They're moving, guys...
...the signal from Warren's com-locator is moving north.
You're faster than the plane, Northstar. Why don't you fly on ahead?
See if you can help Warren and Paige out.
Of course, *Iceman.*
I guess that means they're still alive...
...and you won't have to *kill me* now-- eh, Chilly Willy?
Or it means their locator is runnin' around inside some wolf's *stomach.*

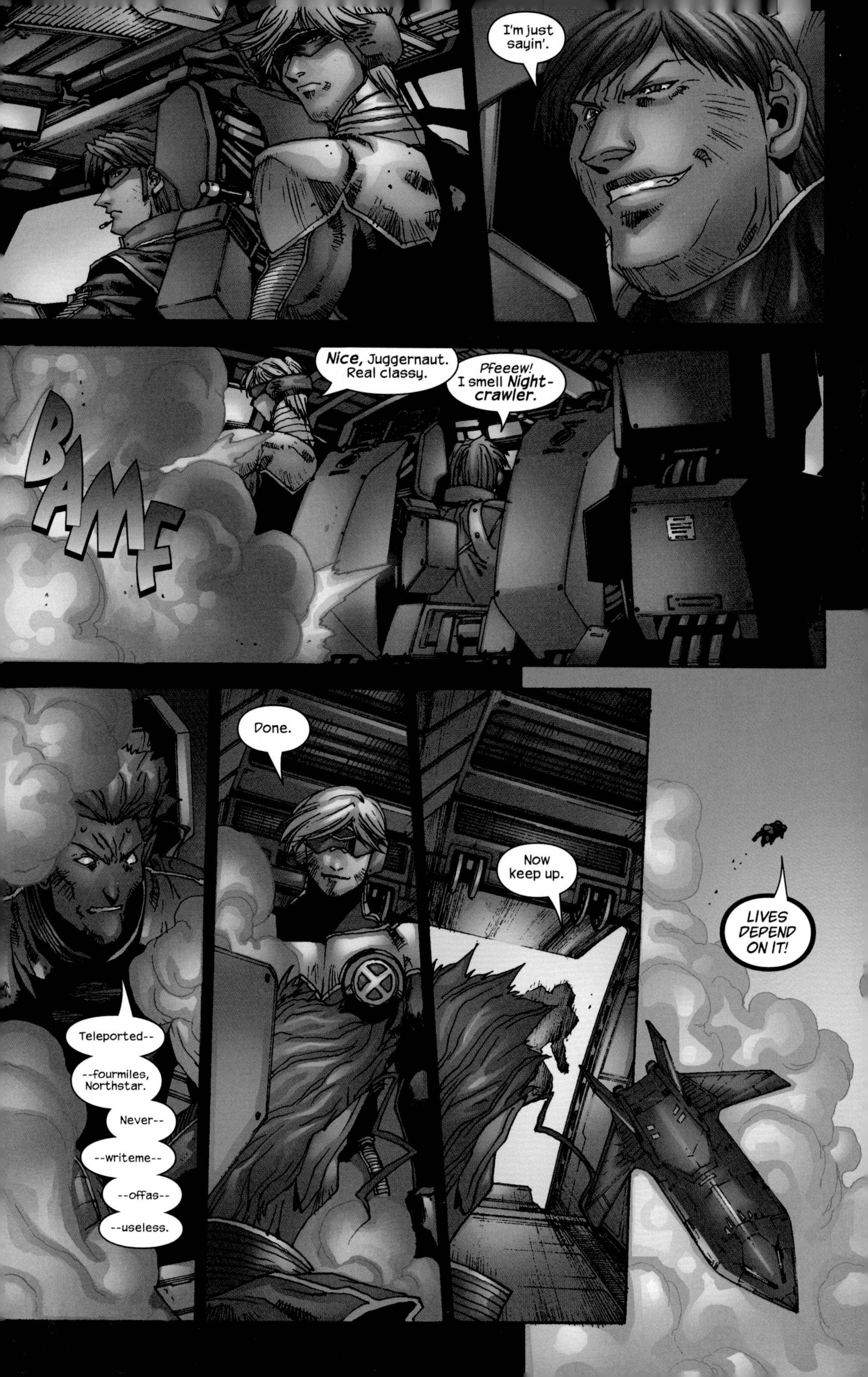
I'm just sayin'.
Nice, Juggernaut. Real classy.
Pfeeew! I smell Night-crawler.
BAMF
Teleported--
--fourmiles, Northstar.
Never--
--writeme--
--offas--
--useless.
Done.
Now keep up.
LIVES DEPEND ON IT!

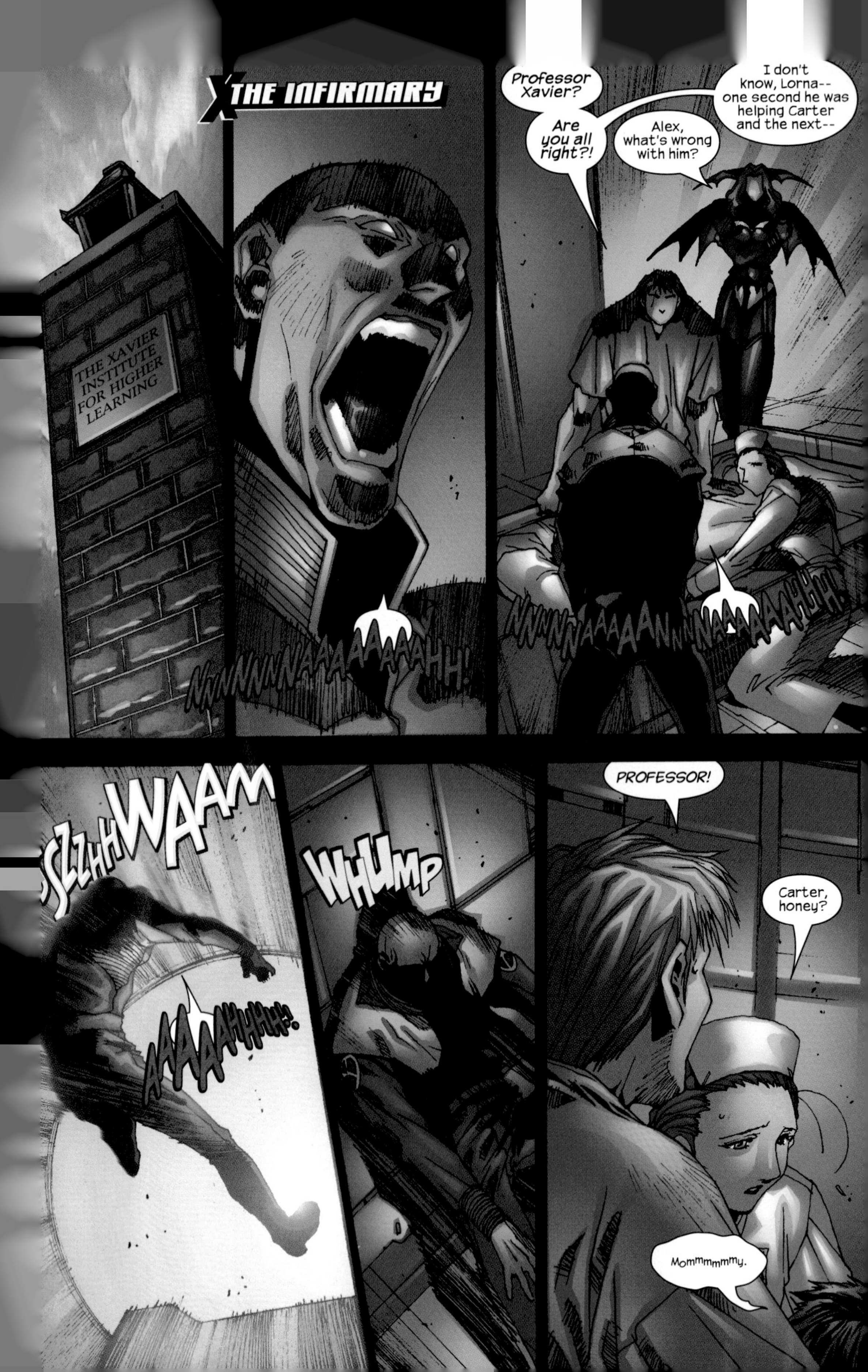
THE INFIRMARY
THE XAVIER INSTITUTE FOR HIGHER LEARNING
NNNNNNAAAAAAAAAHH!
Professor Xavier?
Are you all right?!
Alex, what's wrong with him?
I don't know, Lorna-- one second he was helping Carter and the next--
NNNNNAAAAANNNNAAAAAAHHH!
SZZHHWAAM
AAAAAHHHH!
WHUMP
PROFESSOR!
Carter, honey?
Mommmmmmy.

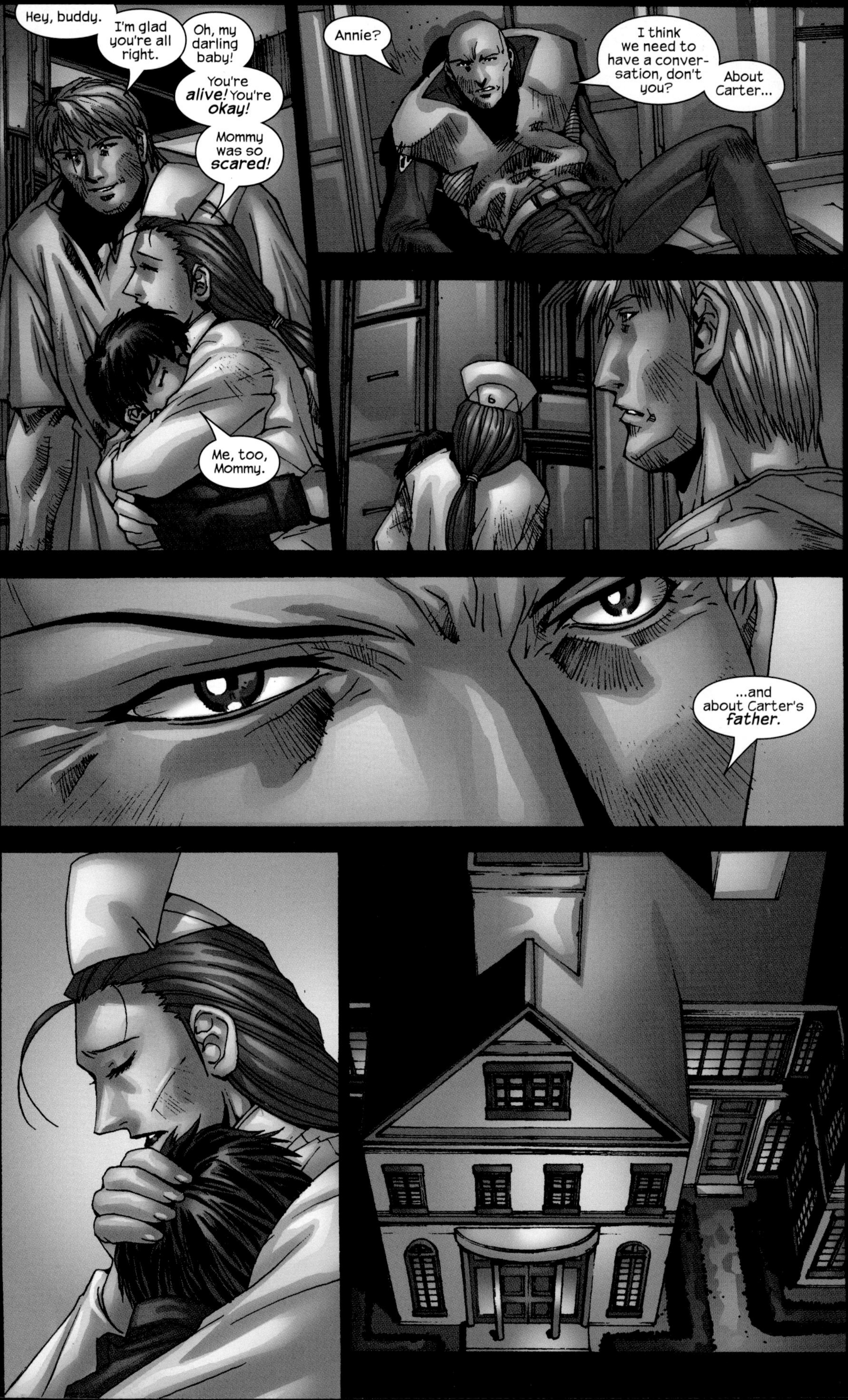
Hey, buddy.
I'm glad you're all right.
Oh, my darling baby!
You're alive! You're okay!
Mommy was so scared!
Me, too, Mommy.
Annie?
I think we need to have a conversation, don't you?
About Carter...
...and about Carter's father.

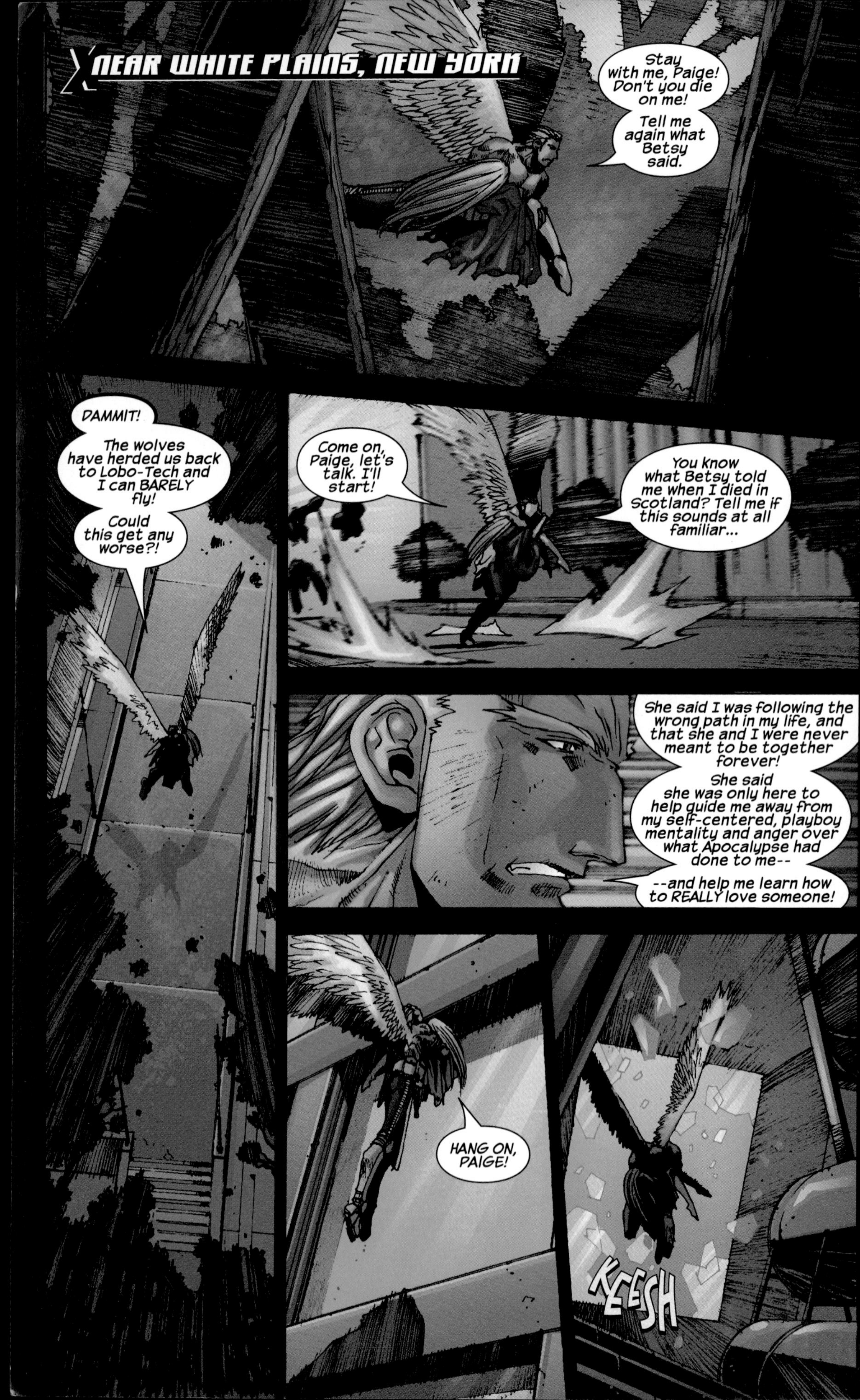
NEAR WHITE PLAINS, NEW YORK
Stay with me, Paige! Don't you die on me!
Tell me again what Betsy said.
DAMMIT!
The wolves have herded us back to Lobo-Tech and I can BARELY fly!
Could this get any worse?!
Come on, Paige, let's talk. I'll start!
You know what Betsy told me when I died in Scotland? Tell me if this sounds at all familiar...
She said I was following the wrong path in my life, and that she and I were never meant to be together forever!
She said she was only here to help guide me away from my self-centered, playboy mentality and anger over what Apocalypse had done to me--
--and help me learn how to REALLY love someone!
HANG ON, PAIGE!
KEESH

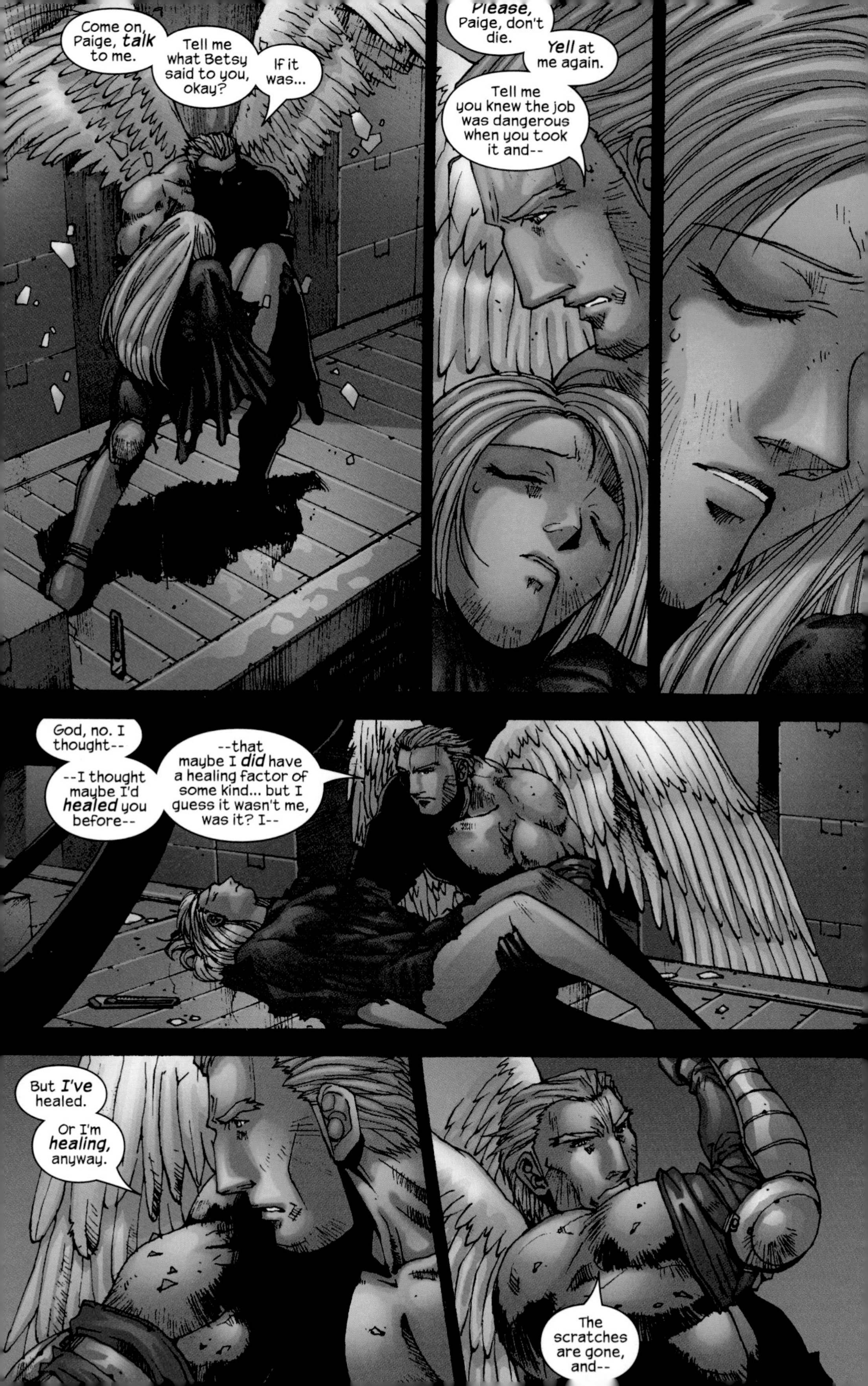
Come on, Paige, talk to me.
Tell me what Betsy said to you, okay?
If it was...
Please, Paige, don't die.
Yell at me again.
Tell me you knew the job was dangerous when you took it and--
God, no. I thought--
--I thought maybe I'd healed you before--
--that maybe I did have a healing factor of some kind... but I guess it wasn't me, was it? I--
But I've healed.
Or I'm healing, anyway.
The scratches are gone, and--

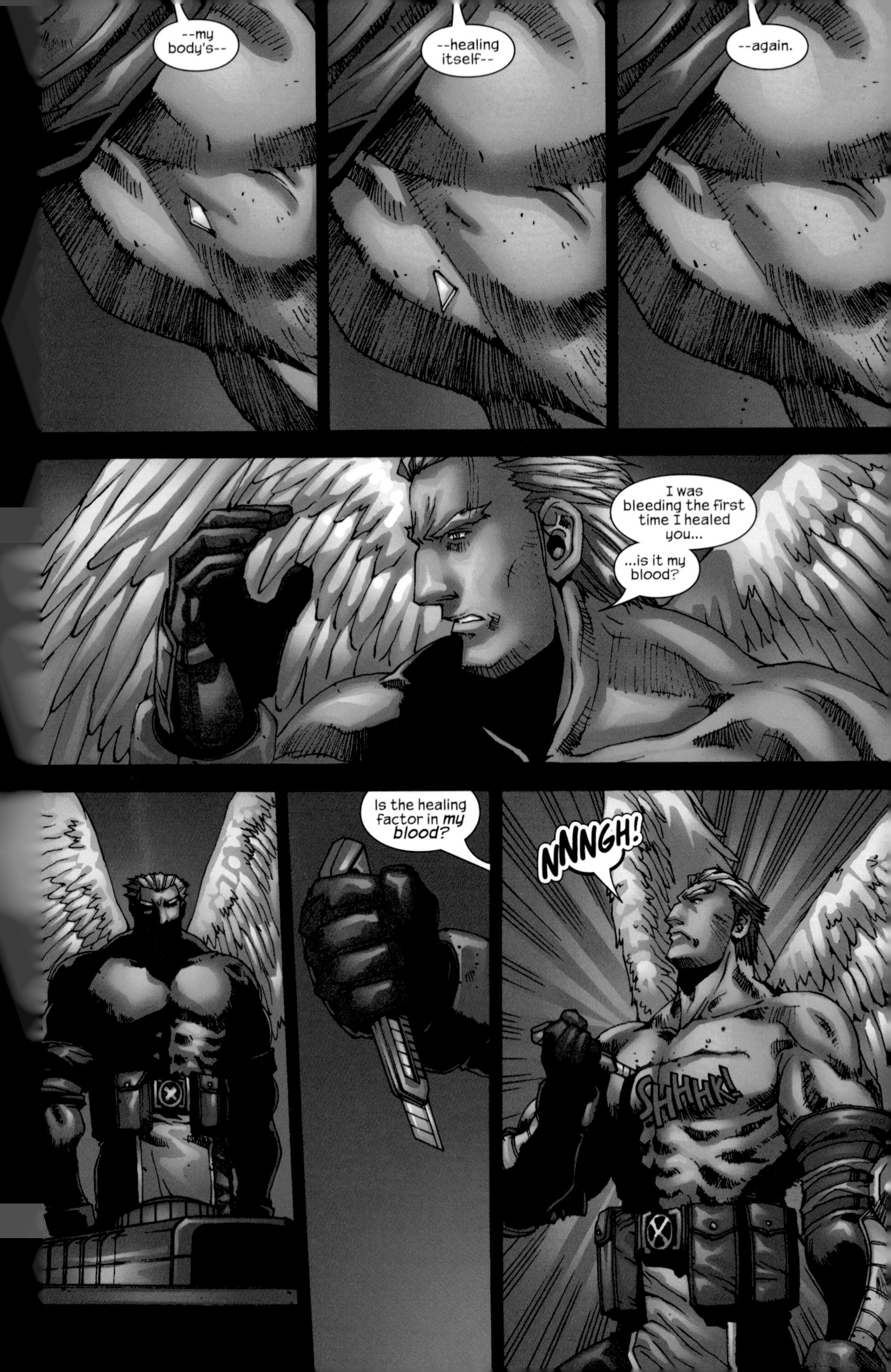
--my body's--
--healing itself--
--again.
I was bleeding the first time I healed you...
...is it my blood?
Is the healing factor in *my blood?*
NNNGH!
SHHHK!

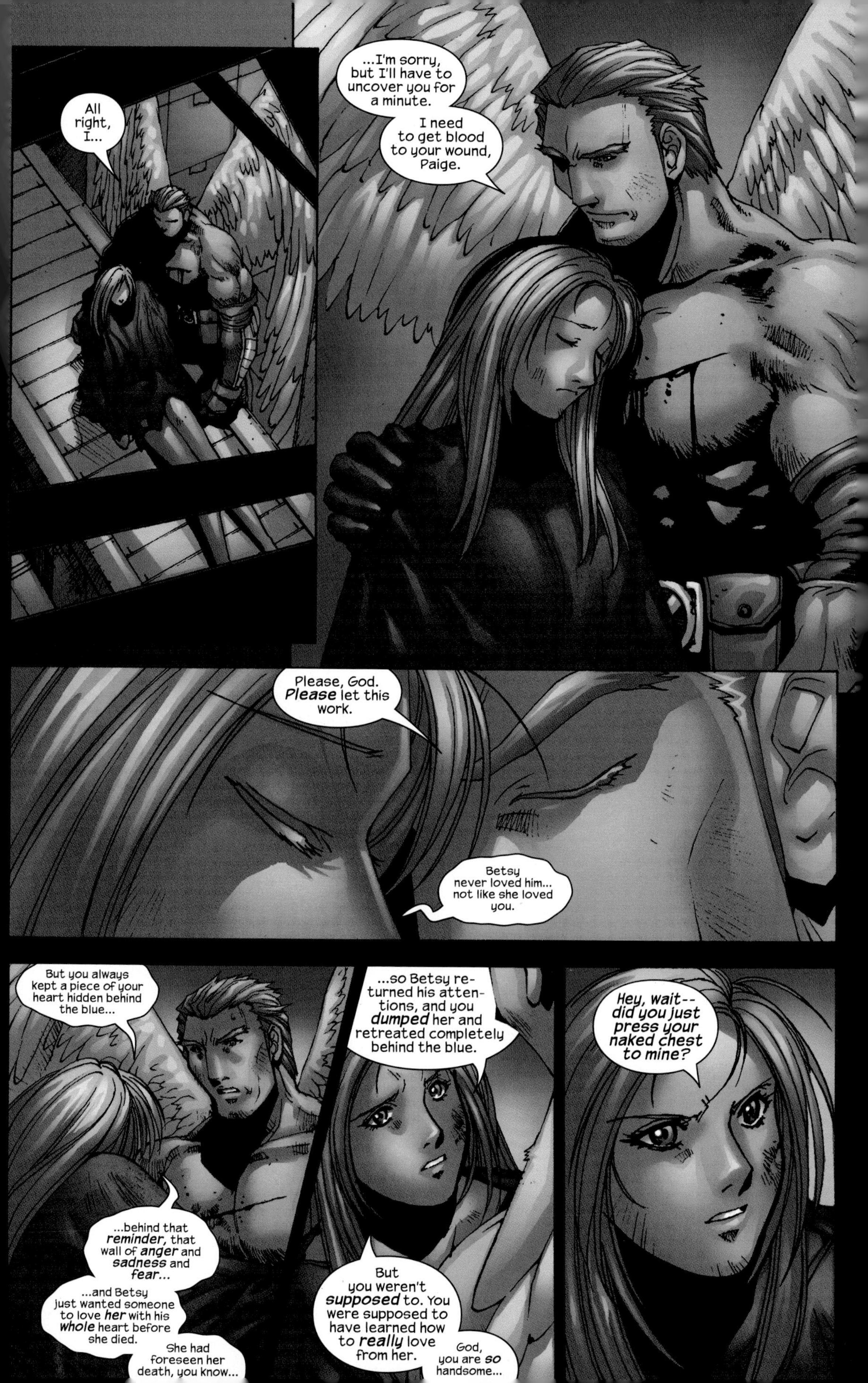
All right, I...
...I'm sorry, but I'll have to uncover you for a minute.
I need to get blood to your wound, Paige.
Please, God. *Please* let this work.
Betsy never loved him... not like she loved you.
But you always kept a piece of your heart hidden behind the blue...
...behind that *reminder*, that wall of *anger* and *sadness* and *fear*...
...and Betsy just wanted someone to love *her* with his *whole* heart before she died.
She had foreseen her death, you know...
...so Betsy returned his attentions, and you *dumped* her and retreated completely behind the blue.
But you weren't *supposed* to. You were supposed to have learned how to *really* love from her.
God, you are *so* handsome...
Hey, wait-- did you just press your naked chest to mine?

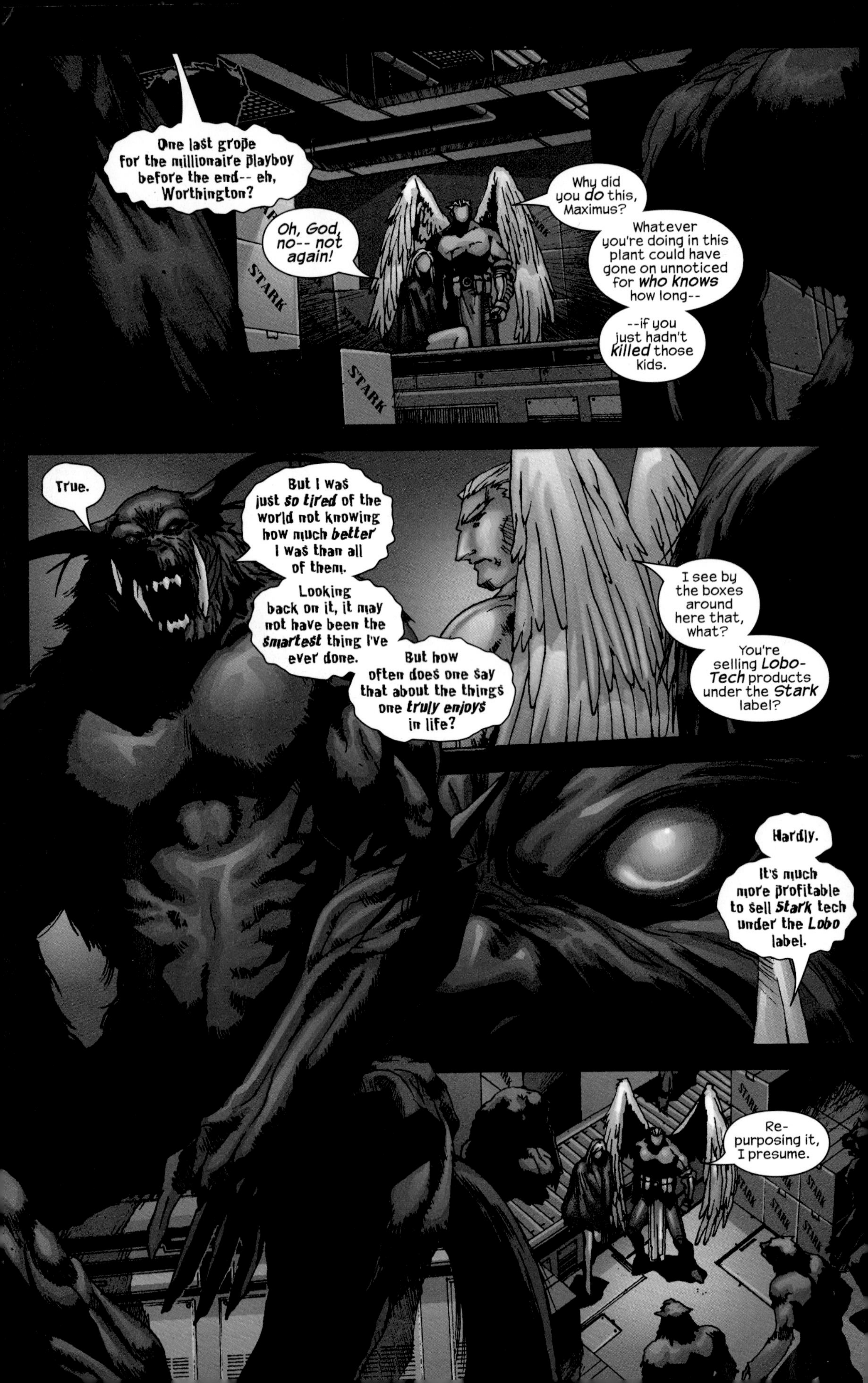
One last grope for the millionaire playboy before the end-- eh, Worthington?
Oh, God, no-- not again!
Why did you do this, Maximus?
Whatever you're doing in this plant could have gone on unnoticed for who knows how long--
--if you just hadn't killed those kids.
True.
But I was just so tired of the world not knowing how much better I was than all of them.
Looking back on it, it may not have been the smartest thing I've ever done.
But how often does one say that about the things one truly enjoys in life?
I see by the boxes around here that, what?
You're selling Lobo-Tech products under the Stark label?
Hardly.
It's much more profitable to sell Stark tech under the Lobo label.
Re-purposing it, I presume.

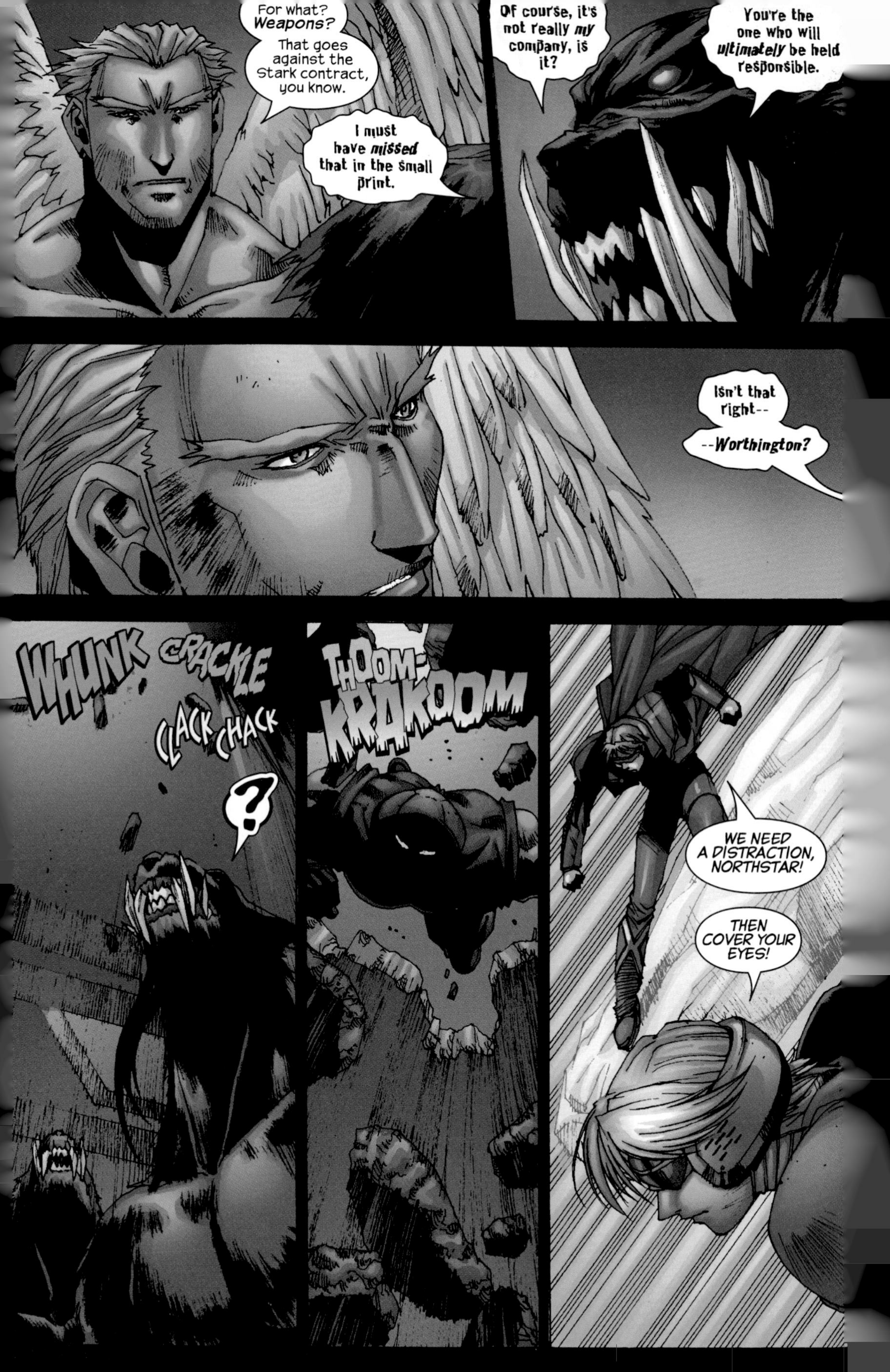

For what? *Weapons?*
That goes against the Stark contract, you know.
I must have *missed* that in the small print.
Of course, it's not really *my* company, is it?
You're the one who will *ultimately* be held responsible.
Isn't that right--
--*Worthington?*
WHUNK CRACKLE
CLACK CHACK
?
THOOM-KRAKOOM
WE NEED A DISTRACTION, NORTHSTAR!
THEN COVER YOUR EYES!

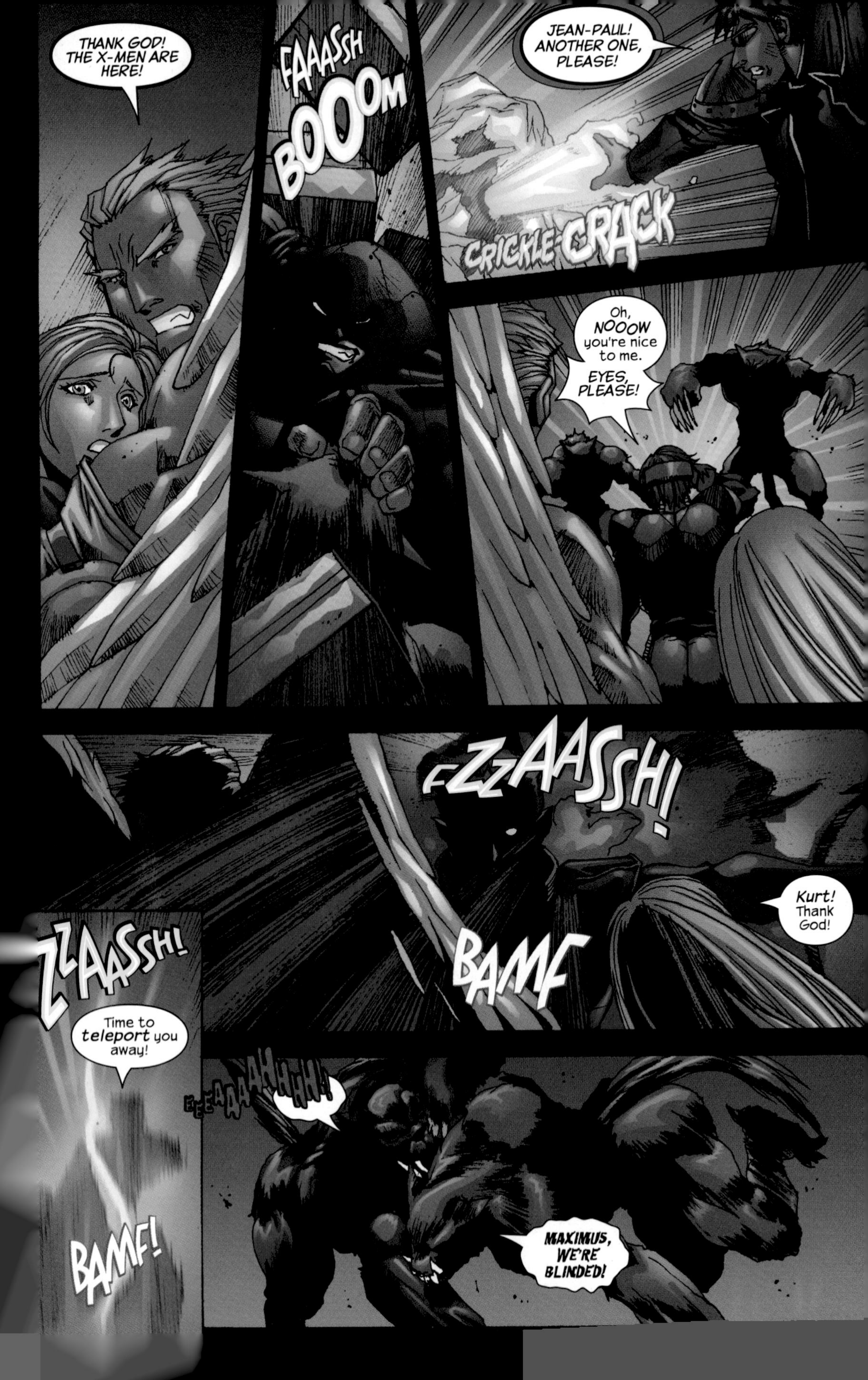
THANK GOD! THE X-MEN ARE HERE!
FAAASSH
BOOOM
JEAN-PAUL! ANOTHER ONE, PLEASE!
CRICKLE-CRACK
Oh, NOOOW you're nice to me. EYES, PLEASE!
FZZAASSH!
Kurt! Thank God!
BAMF
ZZAASSH!
Time to teleport you away!
BAMF!
EEEAAAAHHHH
MAXIMUS, WE'RE BLINDED!

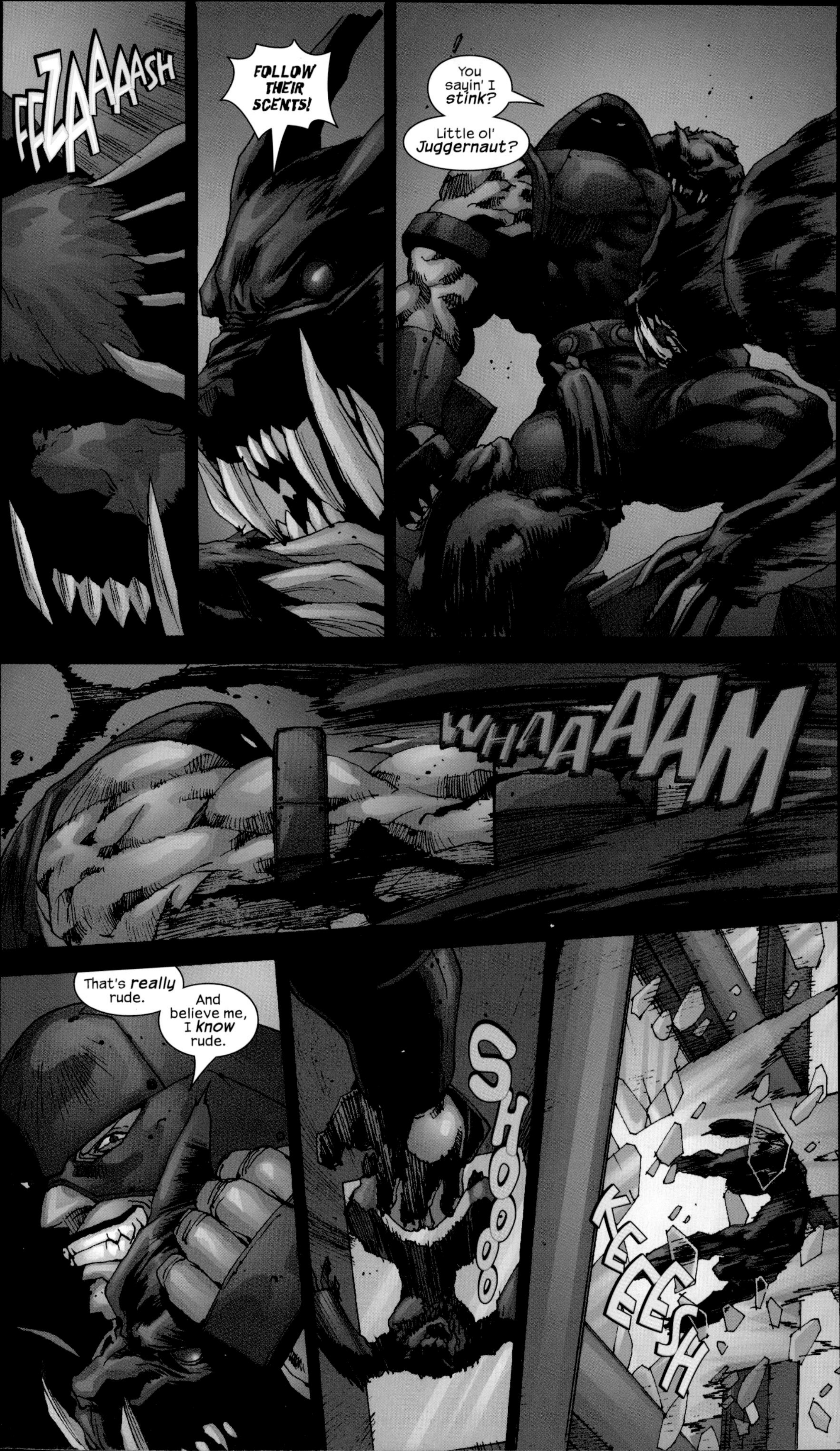
FFZAAAAASH
FOLLOW THEIR SCENTS!
You sayin' I stink?
Little ol' Juggernaut?
WHAAAAAM
That's really rude.
And believe me, I know rude.
SHOOOOO
KKEESH

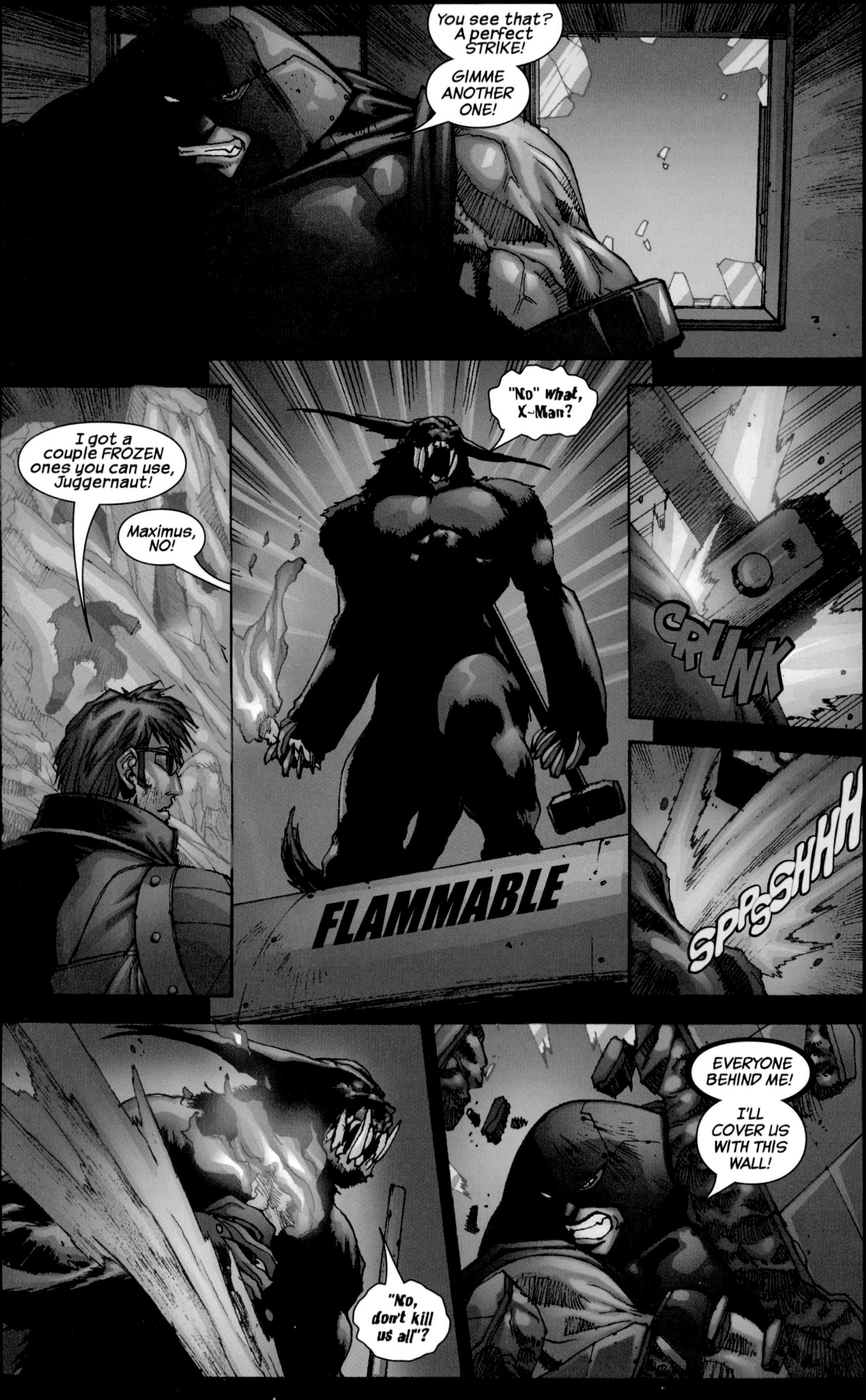
You see that? A perfect STRIKE!
GIMME ANOTHER ONE!
I got a couple FROZEN ones you can use, Juggernaut!
Maximus, NO!
"No" what, X-Man?
FLAMMABLE
CRUNK
SPPSSHHH
"No, don't kill us all"?
EVERYONE BEHIND ME!
I'LL COVER US WITH THIS WALL!

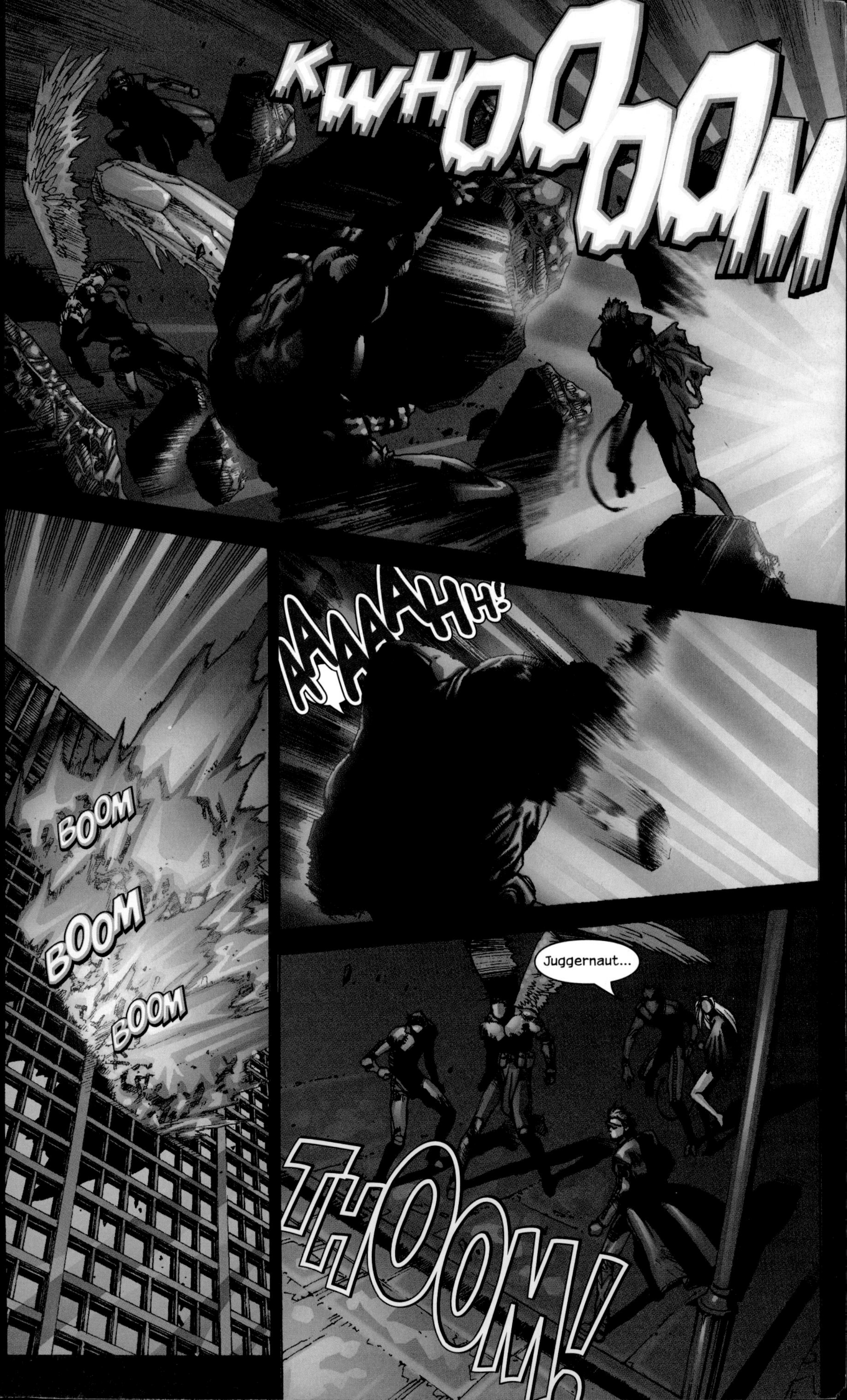
KWHOOOOOM
BOOM
BOOM
BOOM
AAAAHH!
Juggernaut...
THOOOM!

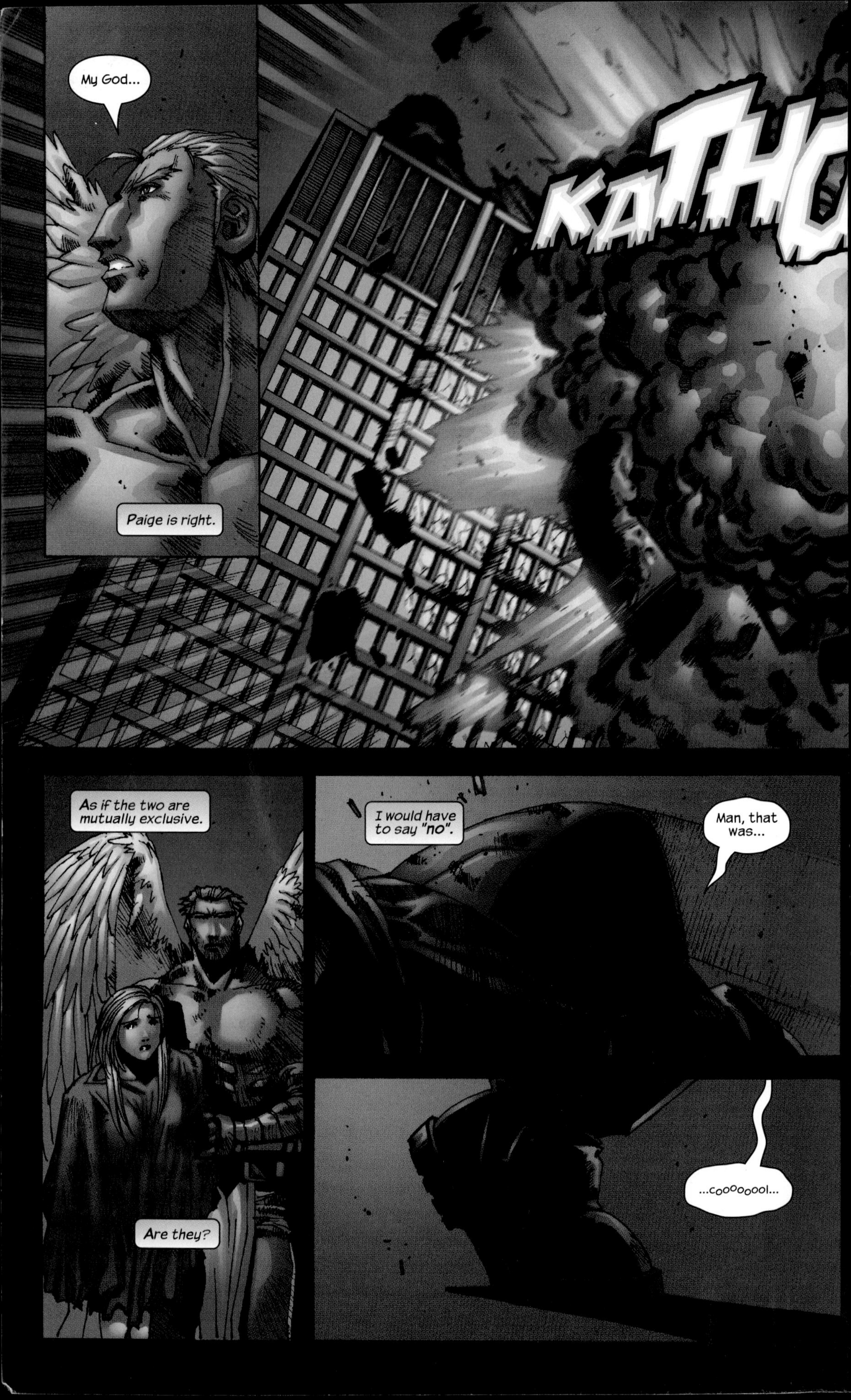
My God...
Paige is right.
KATHO
As if the two are mutually exclusive.
Are they?
I would have to say "no".
Man, that was...
...coooooool...

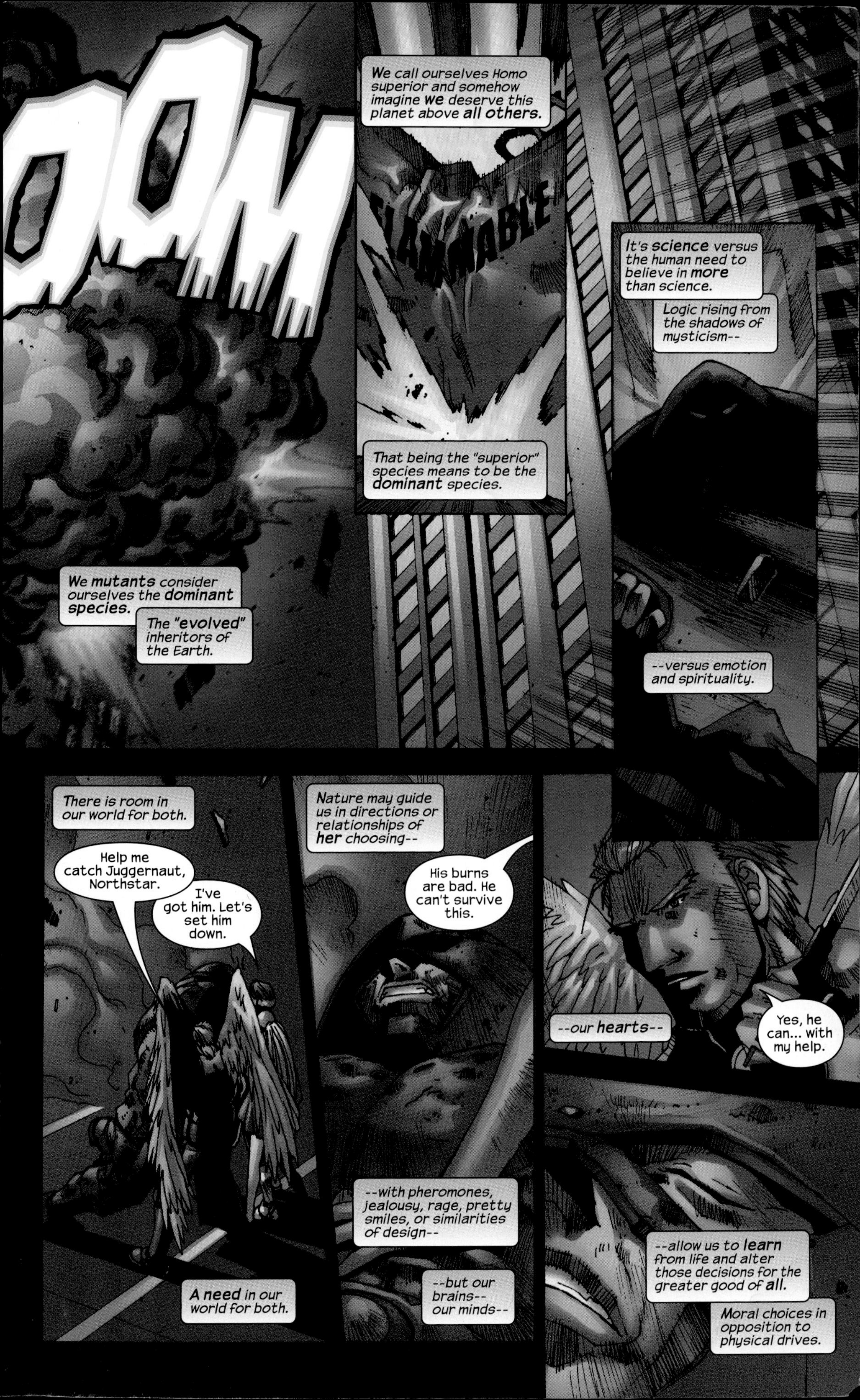

DOOM
We mutants consider ourselves the dominant species.
The "evolved" inheritors of the Earth.
We call ourselves Homo superior and somehow imagine we deserve this planet above all others.
FLAMMABLE
That being the "superior" species means to be the dominant species.
It's science versus the human need to believe in more than science.
Logic rising from the shadows of mysticism--
--versus emotion and spirituality.
There is room in our world for both.
Help me catch Juggernaut, Northstar.
I've got him. Let's set him down.
A need in our world for both.
Nature may guide us in directions or relationships of her choosing--
His burns are bad. He can't survive this.
--with pheromones, jealousy, rage, pretty smiles, or similarities of design--
--but our brains-- our minds--
--our hearts--
Yes, he can... with my help.
--allow us to learn from life and alter those decisions for the greater good of all.
Moral choices in opposition to physical drives.

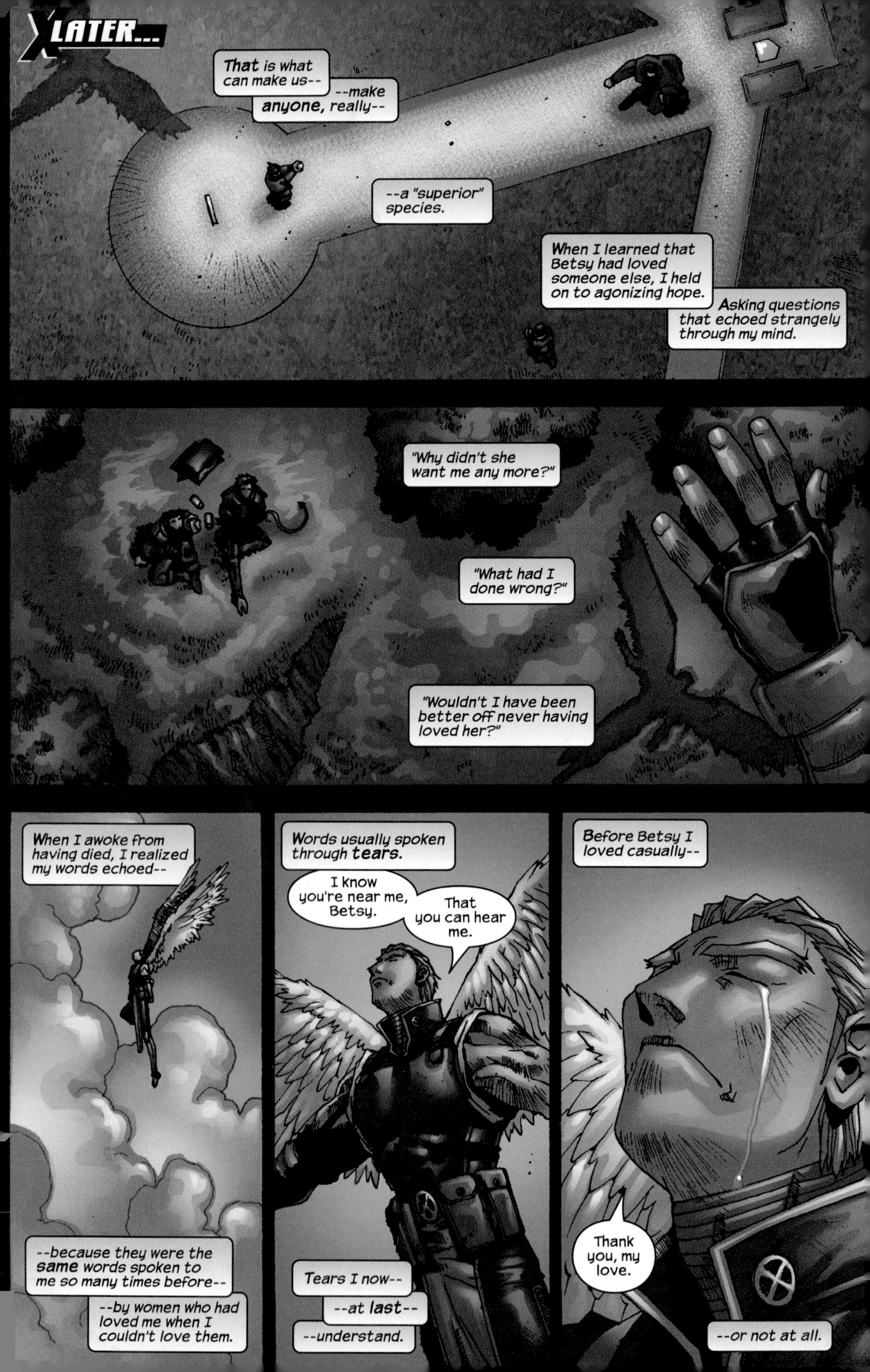
LATER...
That is what can make us--
--make anyone, really--
--a "superior" species.
When I learned that Betsy had loved someone else, I held on to agonizing hope.
Asking questions that echoed strangely through my mind.
"Why didn't she want me any more?"
"What had I done wrong?"
"Wouldn't I have been better off never having loved her?"
When I awoke from having died, I realized my words echoed--
--because they were the same words spoken to me so many times before--
--by women who had loved me when I couldn't love them.
Words usually spoken through tears.
I know you're near me, Betsy.
That you can hear me.
Tears I now--
--at last--
--understand.
Before Betsy I loved casually--
Thank you, my love.
--or not at all.

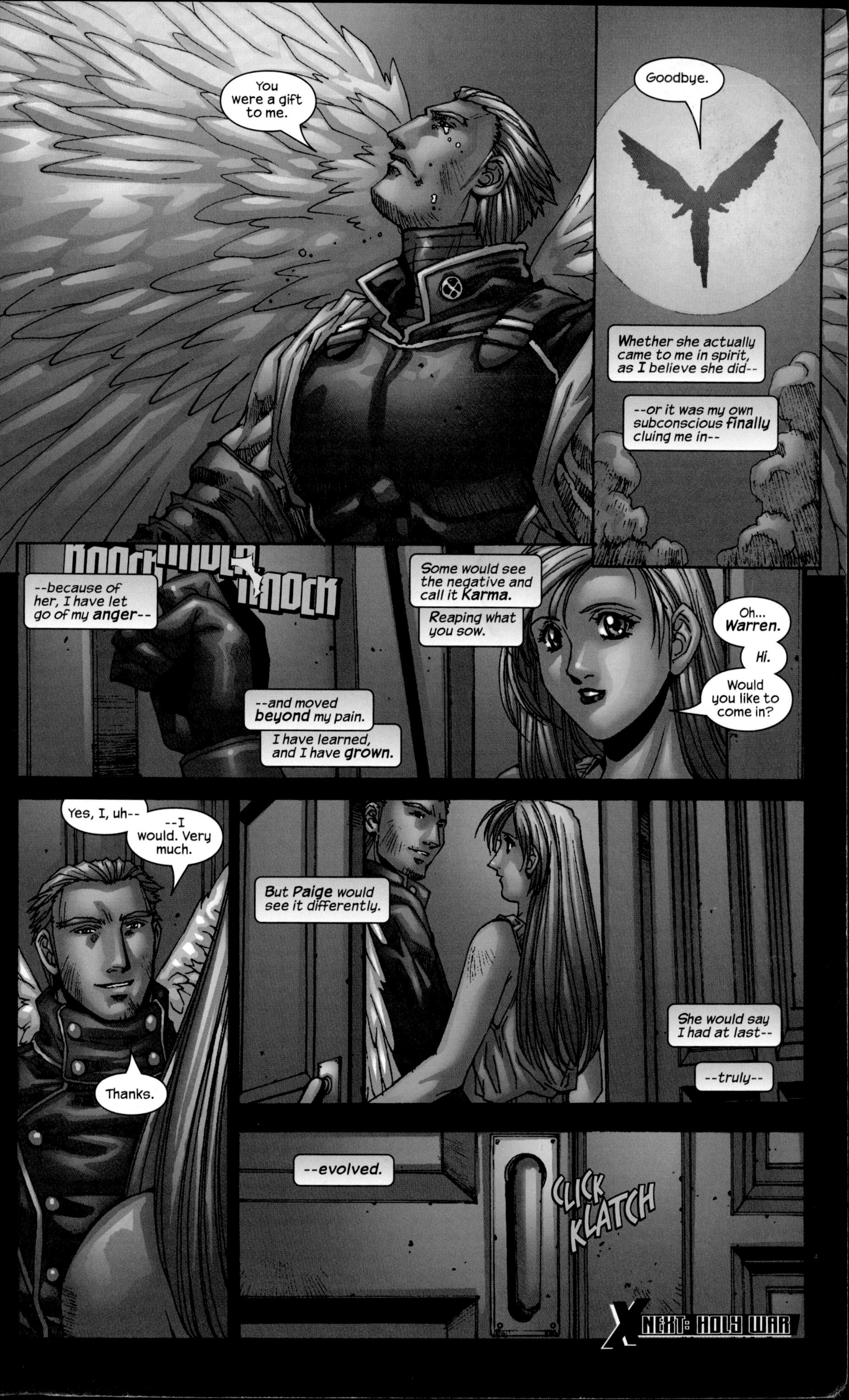
You were a gift to me.
Goodbye.
Whether she actually came to me in spirit, as I believe she did--
--or it was my own subconscious finally cluing me in--
--because of her, I have let go of my anger--
--and moved beyond my pain.
I have learned, and I have grown.
Some would see the negative and call it Karma.
Reaping what you sow.
Oh... Warren.
Hi.
Would you like to come in?
Yes, I, uh--
--I would. Very much.
Thanks.
But Paige would see it differently.
She would say I had at last--
--truly--
--evolved.
CLICK
KLATCH
NEXT: HOLY WAR

MARVELS

10TH ANNIVERSARY EDITION

MARVEL®

CELEBRATE 10 YEARS OF MARVELS!

KURT BUSIEK • ALEX ROSS

TM & © 2003 Marvel Characters, Inc. All rights reserved.

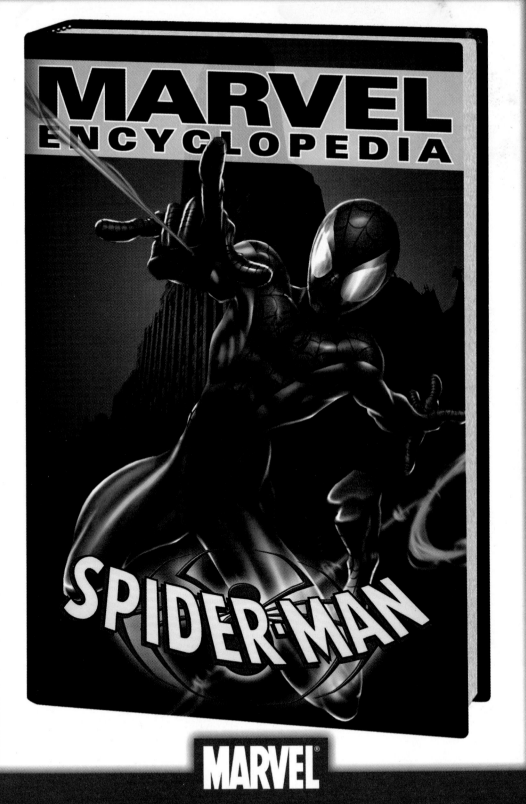

MARVEL ENCYCLOPEDIA
SPIDER-MAN

MARVEL®

EVERYTHING You Ever Wanted to Know About Spider-Man...
And Weren't Afraid to Ask!

TM & © 2003 Marvel Characters, Inc. All rights reserved.

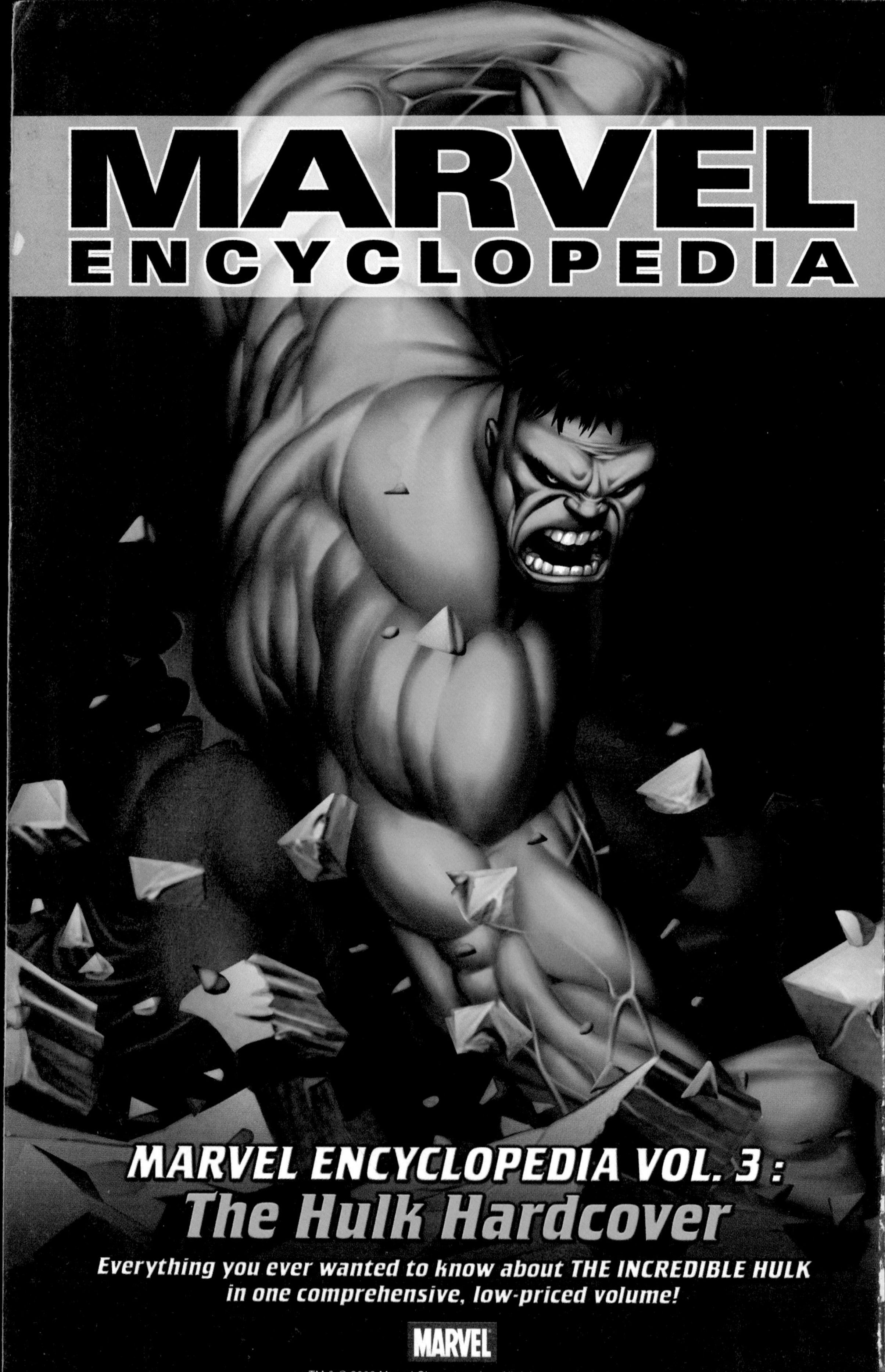
MARVEL
ENCYCLOPEDIA
MARVEL ENCYCLOPEDIA VOL. 3 :
The Hulk Hardcover
Everything you ever wanted to know about THE INCREDIBLE HULK
in one comprehensive, low-priced volume!
MARVEL